The Four Pillars of Retirement Plans

The Four Pillars of Retirement Plans

The Fiduciary Guide to Participant-Directed Retirement Plans

David B. Loeper

WILEY

John Wiley & Sons, Inc.

For general information on our other products and services or for technical support, please contact our Customer Care Department within the United States at (800) 762-2974, outside the United States at (317) 572-3993 or fax (317) 572-4002.

Wiley also publishes its books in a variety of electronic formats. Some content that appears in print may not be available in electronic books. For more information about Wiley products, visit our web site at www.wiley.com.

Library of Congress Cataloging-in-Publication Data:

Loeper, David B.
    The four pillars of retirement plans : the fiduciary guide to participant directed retirement plans/David B. Loeper.
        p.   cm.
    Includes bibliographical references and index.
    ISBN 978-0-470-44999-8 (cloth)
    1. Pension trusts—United States—Management.   2. Pension trusts—Investments—United States.   I. Title.
    HD7105.45.U6L599 2009
    658.3'253—dc22   2009004134

Printed in the United States of America
10   9   8   7   6   5   4   3   2   1

This book is dedicated to the 100 million retirement plan participants that trust the fiduciaries of their plan to act in the interest of plan participants. May each fiduciary reflect upon the profound weight of this responsibility and how their actions, or lack thereof, impact the lives of others.

Contents

Acknowledgments

Acknowledgments, to me, are perhaps the hardest thing to write, because we are a product of all of the people we know. How do you thank everyone who has helped make you who you are? Of course, I need to thank all the people of Financeware, Inc., who have each made a contribution to this book, either directly or indirectly. We have a great team of people that truly care about helping people making the most of their lives, and they do so with unbridled passion. They live as role models for others by consistently acting with unquestioning integrity. George, Jerry, Christopher, Brandy, TJ, Elliott, Joe, Will, Jeremy, Bill, and, of course, my executive committee partners Bob and Karen have all made huge direct contributions to this book. Thank you all for your patience, objectivity, and coaching, and for understanding how to help us to help others.

Of course, I have to thank all of my former associates from my "Wheat First" days who are now, or were, part of Wachovia Securities (soon to be Wells Fargo). These associates had the courage to challenge conventional wisdom and risk being different to serve clients better. I have to credit Dave Monday, Mark Staples, Danny Ludeman, Jim Donley, Marshall Wishnack, and, of course, the late James Wheat, a blind man who had more vision than all of us put together. Respect should be earned, not given, and every one of these people has earned mine. I consider all of them heroes in their own way.

There are a handful of people in the industry I have to thank, because they have truly earned my respect by their actions and courage. People like Len Reinhart, Frank Campanale, Ron Surz, and the late Don Tabone have all contributed greatly to my knowledge, and their willingness to have rational debate on numerous topics has helped me immensely.

I have to thank Donna Wells, who helped to make my normal pontification understandable, is due credit for her enormous contribution.

I have to thank my late father, Kenneth A. Loeper, who said, "Don't let anyone push you around." Without that determination engrained in my brain, I would have never had the courage to face the attacks of the industry groups that hate having their apple cart upset. Also, I thank my mother, Anna, for teaching me that the biggest responsibility we have in raising children is teaching them to be respectable people of integrity who can take care of themselves.

Finally, I want to thank the late Ayn Rand. Whether you like her or not, you have to respect her passion for and vision of a hero or heroine, so often demonstrated in her novels. The abstracts of her concepts, living a moral life and acting with integrity, helped me to understand and express why I am what I am. Who is John Galt?

Introduction

According to the Department of Labor in its 2008 report, there are more than 679,000 private retirement plans covering 117 million participants with assets of more than $5 trillion[1] Retirement plans are *trusts*, and the financial future of most Americans depends on their financial shelter being properly maintained. In short, they count on those who are managing and administering their retirement plans being worthy of the trust they bestow upon them. But, what is holding up the roof of that retirement shelter? *Are they strong pillars of granite, or are they merely pillars made of sand?*

Think about the scale of the responsibility in acting as a steward of this financial shelter for the future of millions of people. We are talking about the impact on how these people can live their lives after a lifetime of labor. We are talking about *trillions* in assets. We are perhaps even talking about the very security of the entire economy of our country. Those who shoulder this burden are known as **fiduciaries,** defined by Congress in 1974 under ERISA (Employee Retirement Income Security Act). ERISA defines all aspects of how fiduciaries should

1

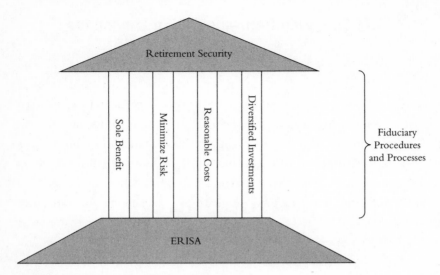

Figure 1 Fiduciary procedures and processes

conduct themselves in managing this multitrillion-dollar responsibility. From the record keeper who keeps track of participant balances, to the custodians who process and hold assets, to the investment managers and consultants who make (or advise on) investment decisions, to the trustees who select each of these vendors of services, the procedures and processes they use in executing their duties form the pillars that hold up the roof of our country's retirement shelter, built on the foundation of ERISA.

The procedures and processes that fiduciaries use form the basis for the decisions they make (see Figure 1). ERISA Fiduciaries are supposedly held to the highest standards of integrity and expertise. But, are these fiduciaries executing their duties in a manner that is consistent with the nature of the plans for which they are *personally* assuming this liability? Were the generally accepted procedures that are still used today born in an era of a different retirement plan landscape? If so, does the changing landscape require fiduciaries to change their procedures and processes to cope with evolving responsibilities? If so, what changes are needed? And, what is the risk to fiduciaries for failing to adapt to the changing landscape in the face of over 100 million potential litigants personally pursuing them for having breached their evolving responsibilities?

The Changing Retirement Plan Landscape

The landscape over the last 30 years in corporate (401(k), profit sharing, etc.), government (457 plans), and nonprofit retirement plans (403b) has shifted toward participant-directed funding (salary deferrals) and participant-directed investment selection. This massive trend has left trustees, administrators, investment managers, consultants and plan sponsors in an awkward position of executing "well-established" fiduciary compliance procedures that were designed for defined benefit plans under ERISA in a bygone era that no longer applies to the current retirement plan landscape. (Defined benefit plans are the traditional pension plans that promise participants a specific retirement income benefit, sheltering participants from any investment risk, while defined contribution plans promise no specific benefit and subject the participant to all of the investment risk.)

Today, more than 92 percent of all retirement plans are defined contribution plans, yet when the standards were developed for defining procedural prudence of fiduciaries, most retirement plans were defined benefit plans. Regardless of whether all of these plans are explicitly subject to ERISA standards, the case law and generally accepted procedures created during the historical dominance of defined benefit plans has also been utilized in defined contribution plans, even though all of the investment risk has been transferred to participants. The shift toward participant-directed funding and investment selection makes many of these procedures at best obsolete, and may, in fact, actually *conflict* with proper procedural prudence for such participant-directed retirement plans under ERISA.

100 Million Potential Lawsuits

In the February 2008 landmark Supreme Court ruling *LaRue v. DeWolff, Boberg & Associates, Inc.*, the Court ruled on the ability for *an individual participant* to sue retirement plan fiduciaries. Justice John Paul Stevens in writing the Court's majority opinion concluded, "*ERISA authorizes recovery for fiduciary breaches that impair the value of plan assets in a participant's individual account.*" This ruling significantly changes the landscape of fiduciary liability and risks for trustees, especially if their processes and procedures for compliance were designed under, and mimic those that have evolved for, defined benefit plans where the sponsor was bearing the cost of both funding the plan and the investment risk. In this particular case, the impairment of assets the Court saw was caused by an administrator failing to execute transactions on a timely basis, which subjected the participant to significant losses. This is a good example of a big difference between a defined benefit plan and a plan offering participant direction of investment assets. Such a case could not even exist in the defined benefit plan world. In many court jurisdictions, until the 2008 ruling by the Supreme Court, winning suits on behalf of an individual participant were rare, as some courts interpreted ERISA fiduciary breaches under a context that required proof that *all* participants in the plan be impaired, not just an individual. In a defined benefit plan, since the participant is not subjected to investment risk because the benefit of the pension plan would be the same regardless of the investment results, it has often been difficult for plan participants to win cases, and proving harm was nearly impossible. (It is also noteworthy there were no dissenting opinions from any of the Supreme Court justices, just a majority opinion and some concurring opinions that differ only on the reasoning in overturning the original Fourth Circuit Court ruling.) The 2008 Supreme Court ruling effectively changes that past defined benefit perspective and ERISA interpretation, and with the Supreme Court's ruling that *any individual* can sue for breaches based solely on the impairment of their *personal plan balances*, a potential floodgate of new lawsuits may have been opened. This has profound implications for exercising new forms of procedural prudence *designed specifically for participant-directed funding* and investment selection.

I predict that a whole new set of case law will be established in the coming decades from suits stemming from fiduciary breaches based on "the impairment" of the balances of individual participants. Many of these suits (and likely large settlements) will come from participants who have sufficient evidence to prove their individual plan balances were impaired, even though the trustees exercised care and diligence that would have otherwise survived a defined benefit plan perspective of the examination of the facts under such now-antiquated and contradictory procedures.

Fiduciaries and trustees of any participant-directed plan must act now to establish some easy-to-accomplish shifts in their procedures to prevent them from becoming one of these future case law examples. As a trustee or adviser fiduciary, the liability you are accepting is *personal*. Taking a few of these steps is akin to spreading salt on the steps of your home after an ice storm so the UPS delivery person doesn't slip when delivering a package. Yet, unlike homeowners insurance that would potentially protect you from such a liability of unintended negligence, fiduciary liability insurance is unlikely to offer you such assurances, because the actions you take as a fiduciary will be measured, not from a perspective of forgetting to salt your steps, but rather, as the equivalent of a homeowner who intentionally pours water over the steps whenever the temperature is below freezing. If you were to act in such a manner, your homeowners insurance would be unlikely to protect you from the liability because you are intentionally creating it. Likewise, if your procedures are viewed as knowingly contributing to the impairment of a least some participants' assets, your fiduciary liability insurance will not protect you from the liability, just as your homeowner's insurance would validly claim you were contributing to the fall by pouring water over the steps. This book can help you easily avoid such contributory negligence breaches.

This book is not intended to rehash many of the well-established (but worn-out) procedural guidelines of prudent fiduciary conduct. In fact, most of what has been "generally accepted" as standards of procedures and processes for retirement plan fiduciaries may actually be contradictory in today's retirement plan landscape. Instead, this book will expose to trustees, investment managers or consultants, plan sponsors, and any other fiduciaries how they need to change key elements of their actions for the retirement plans for which they are entrusted. ERISA has not changed under the Supreme Court ruling. What has changed is the potential for 100 million potential litigants (and their attorneys) to be searching for breaches of ERISA. This book thus serves as a roadmap that all fiduciaries can use to adjust their actions to shelter themselves from the massive liabilities they face. Attorneys representing retirement plan participants can also use this book as the basis for arguing on behalf of their plaintiff clients against fiduciaries that choose to ignore building retirement plan procedures constructed of pillars of granite instead of sand.

Although changing the "pillars" that represent how and why you make the decisions you do on behalf of retirement plan participants is neither costly nor complicated, it nonetheless does require an understanding of how one can be prepared to defend one's fiduciary actions and do so on a strong foundation of ERISA. There are only a few key areas where past guidelines that were established from a defined benefit plan perspective need to change in this new environment where participant direction dominates, and new liability for each participant's individual plan balance has suddenly become your potential responsibility as a fiduciary. This book will walk you through the steps to build your pillars of fiduciary actions in granite, reinforced with steel, to shield you from liability that can be easily avoided if you merely follow these guidelines.

As a fiduciary with nearly 25 years of ERISA experience, the four pillars of retirement plans are my personal fiduciary interpretations of the specific ERISA regulations that require some simple and low-cost procedural adjustments in the context of the future where trustees may be liable for "*fiduciary breaches that impair the value of plan assets in a participant's individual account.*" I am not an attorney, and my opinions on the four pillars of retirement plans do not represent legal advice. Plan trustees and plan sponsors will need to rely on guidance from their own legal counsel specific to those ERISA plans for which they act as a fiduciary.

However, as one "acting in a like capacity as one familiar with such matters," the specific four pillars of ERISA concepts that need simple procedural adjustment by trustees and other fiduciaries are:

1. Assets invested for "the sole benefit of participants."

2. "Avoidance of any investment risk unless it is clearly prudent to do otherwise."

3. Costs are "reasonable for the services being provided."

4. "Investments will be diversified."

In the context of defined benefit plans, violation of these four pillars subject the *plan sponsor* to either a windfall of success that lowers their future contributions or losses that impair the funding level of the trust that the sponsor must make up in an increased cost of future contributions. Participants in such plans are sheltered from either outcome receiving the same benefit regardless, which is why there have been relatively few winning lawsuits by individual participants. Massive amounts of case law exist to prove this notion, particularly for defined benefit plans.[2] Except under extraordinary circumstances, in a defined benefit plan the participants are unaffected by either outcome of such potential fiduciary breaches, and with the odds of proving harm to all participants being the former standard prior to the Supreme Court ruling, few attorneys would take on cases of individuals. Even in extreme cases of poor fiduciary actions, the Pension Benefit Guarantee Corporation (PBGC) provides participants at least a portion of their benefit, and the PBGC pursues the fiduciaries for their cost of making good on the promised benefit.

With a Supreme Court ruling that applies these four pillars of ERISA to the impairment of individual participant balances, the procedural prudence documenting the rationale of what ends up to be a mistake dramatically changes. Past procedural prudence standards that would otherwise protect the fiduciaries from personal liability in a defined benefit context suddenly fall apart like crumbling sand in a world of participant-directed accounts and fiduciary liability being measured for *each participant's personal plan balance.*

If the liability you face is not motivating you to rethink your fiduciary actions, you can choose to ignore your personal risk and just stick with the antiquated procedures you have used in the past. But, personally, I would change my perspective and look at the faces of plan participants differently in the future.

Perhaps you are a trustee of a small private retirement plan in addition to being the controller of your company. The next time you see a crowd at the water cooler discussing football scores, imagine them as litigants testifying against you in a lawsuit based on your actions as a fiduciary that impaired their retirement plan assets. At the company holiday party, imagine your employees' spouses crying on a witness stand for the sacrifice they are now forced to make in their retirement lifestyle because of your actions (or inactions) in complying with the four pillars of retirement plans.

Maybe you are an investment adviser or consultant who holds enrollment meetings and educational sessions for several retirement plans. The next time you are flipping through your slide show in front of that audience, imagine the audience suing you and using your slides as Exhibit A in the case of how you advised them to impair their retirement.

You might be an investment manager who has a solid, long-term track record of superior market relative results, but the next time you look at the balances of the accounts you are managing, imagine the people that own that money in the retirement plan and the weight of the responsibility you have in managing those assets. Then, think about the gamble you are taking in attempting to outperform the markets that also subjects every participant to a risk of underperforming the markets, and how that risk can be avoided with near certainty by indexing. Then, page through your marketing material and think about whether there is anything misleading in the content from *this* perspective of the lives you are impacting.

This book does the following:

- It highlights how to interpret these four pillars of retirement plans in the context of simple procedural processes that can be implemented to protect fiduciaries (whether plan sponsor or adviser) from needless liability for breaches that would otherwise occur under antiquated defined benefit perspectives.

- It will also contrast how existing defined benefit plan fiduciary processes contradict and may actually act to impair individual participant balances. Additionally, it will expose how such processes, normally considered as a means of protection for fiduciaries, may actually be increasing the likelihood of future liability.
- It will reveal to all fiduciaries (like investment advisers outside the context of ERISA) how they must rethink the nature of the services they offer to both retirement plans and individuals, as the interpretation of prudent fiduciary standards is sometimes referenced in case law involving ERISA as exemplary for acting with fiduciary care and procedural prudence.

As a fiduciary, the liability you face is *personal*. Imagine the cost *to your life* if just one of the numerous retirement plan participants that may have a claim against you wins a lawsuit. Are you complacently unconcerned about this, or do you care enough about your own interests, not to mention the responsibility you have for others in your role as a fiduciary, to take the actions needed to build on the foundation of ERISA with strong pillars that protect *both* you and the participants you are serving? Whether you are seeking to protect your own interests or benevolently care enough about the participants you serve to adjust your actions, it is your duty to read on to understand how the four pillars of retirement plans need to change.

Part One

PILLARS MADE OF SAND?

In Part One, we examine each of the four pillars of retirement plans from a perspective of the changing landscape toward participant-directed retirement plans, the generally accepted procedures of the past that have become outdated, the actions all fiduciaries need to take to adjust to this landscape, and, perhaps more importantly, the rationale behind such changes.

Be prepared to have *an active mind* when reading Part One. Many sacred cows will be sacrificed on the altars of past procedural prudence guidelines, but their sacrifice will not be in vain if you adopt the needed changes to protect you and your actions from future liabilities. Perhaps even more importantly, the premises and rationale will also enable you to protect the future of the participants in the retirement plan(s) you serve.

I ask you to have an active mind, not an open mind, because there is a massive difference between the two. An open mind implies that one is open to accepting the words on the pages, merely because they are written. For you to really benefit, you need to have an active mind that is willing to question the challenges posed and objectively consider the rationale that is provided. In your role as a fiduciary, over time you will be faced with numerous decisions based on premises outlined throughout this book. No book could outline every potential situation, so it is critical that you actively understand not only the specific actions you need to take, but also the rationale behind each of them to serve you as guardrails in all of the future decisions you bear.

Chapter 1

The Four Pillars of Fiduciary Conduct

The role of a fiduciary under ERISA has long been measured under what is known as the **prudent expert rule.** It is often confused with the *prudent man* rule, but there is a significant difference. Under ERISA, the specific language of the regulations states that a fiduciary will act:

> with the care, skill, prudence, and diligence, under the circumstances then prevailing, that a prudent man acting in a like capacity and familiar with such matters would use in the conduct of an enterprise of a like character and with like aims.[1]

This language expands the standard to which fiduciaries are measured beyond merely being a prudent man exercising, care, skill, prudence, and diligence, to a more sophisticated and higher standard of a person who is also "familiar with such matters." The benchmark for being an ERISA fiduciary is thus not measured relative to your average Joe or Jane. It is a benchmark that measures each fiduciary relative to experts (i.e., those who are familiar with such matters).

In my opinion, the main premise of ERISA is to interject ethics into corporate retirement plans by both regulation (as a carrot by granting tax incentives for those who comply) and the exposure of personal liability and denial of tax-favored status (as a stick for those who do not comply). When I served on the $30 billion Virginia Retirement System, the trustees adopted a policy that all fiduciaries would be held to the standards of ERISA, even though government plans are exempt from ERISA. This is not uncommon for well-managed government plans.

The Four Pillars of Retirement Plans outlines some of this regulatory-induced behavior. For example, the whole notion of the assets of the trust being used for "the sole benefit of beneficiaries" establishes the regulatory framework to examine both clearly unethical actions, as well as potential conflicts of interest that may be a bit less clear.

Pillar #1: Assets Are Invested for the Sole Benefit of Participants

Pretend for a moment that you work for Joe's Cabinet Shop with 25 other employees. Joe owns the company, is the CEO and chief cabinet maker. He, along with his daughter Alison, who does bookkeeping for the company, are the trustees of your pension or profit sharing plan.

Now, let's say Joe's daughter wants to go back to school to get her degree in accounting. The cost for schooling will be $50,000 over the next four years. Joe and Alison look into student loans, and with their excellent credit rating they qualify for an education loan to be paid back over the next 10 years at a very favorable interest rate of 4.5 percent.

One day, while they are reviewing competing proposals from various lenders for Alison's education loan, they also receive a statement on the company's pension plan. It showed that the $1,000,000 trust had $50,000 in cash balances that were earning only 3.5 percent. If Joe and Alison, with kind-hearted intentions of improving the return on your retirement assets, borrowed the money from the trust and paid the same 4.5 percent rate the competing lenders were offering them on a loan, how would you perceive that action?

After all, they did not receive any economic benefit. They paid the same prevailing rate offered by other lenders. And, they improved the return on the cash within the pension by 1 percent!

This is a good way for trustees to end up in jail, and the penalties are so severe for this kind of obvious prohibited transaction that it rarely happens. It is a clear violation of the notion of sole benefit, because part of that concept also contains rules about such prohibited transactions and self-dealing.

These ERISA concepts are designed to go beyond just having a good heart and trying to improve the return of the retirement trust. They also seek to regulate *potential* conflicts of interest and, in essence, ethics.

This means your CEO is also unlikely to be able to get away with investing the assets of your retirement plan in some raw land he just happens to own. It means he can't use the assets of the trust to buy a condo in Vegas that is rented out and produces income to the trust, if he also is one of the renters of that condo. The rules for such obvious self-dealing (and prohibited transaction) situations are clear, and the penalties severe.

But what if things weren't quite as clear as using the trust assets to buy an education for the CEO's daughter, unload some raw land a trustee owns, or give the trustee a fun place to stay when visiting Vegas? (These are all egregious violations of the rules.)

What if, for example, Joe, the CEO and chief cabinet maker, is looking for brokers to execute trades in the trust? He seeks bids from three different major firms. All of these firms can provide best execution and are financially sound, with excellent references. They all quote a price of five cents a share, so there is no price difference. However, one of the brokers happens to be an old classmate of Joe's. He tells Joe that he can get Joe in as a member guest at least once a month at the local country club if Joe awards the business to his firm.

Although this is clearly a violation, considering how Joe is personally using the assets of the trust (in the form of trading commissions) to avoid paying greens fees by awarding the brokerage business to his former classmate, in theory the trust is not harmed since all of the brokers were charging the same price and could provide best execution. However, this would still be a violation of ERISA. Instances such as these happen every day because they are so difficult to identify. If Joe were not completely objective, ethical, and clear on what constitutes sole benefit of participants' rules, it would be easy for him to justify awarding the business to his former classmate.

In pension plans, the commissions paid for transactions are known as "soft dollars," and even they must be used for the benefit of plan participants and their beneficiaries. Registered investment advisers are required under SEC rules to have soft-dollar policies and examine the quality of execution from the selected brokers. Trustees who direct specific brokers to be used are responsible for justifying the costs incurred. There are even commission recapture programs that recoup excessive commissions and return the money to the trust. Unfortunately, in the case of participant-directed plans, the massively overpriced commissions built into the pooled investment products have escaped this level of scrutiny. But that will not last under the 2008 Supreme Court ruling.

A similar type of conflicted situation has been known to occur with many banks. Banks, of course, are in the business of lending money. Many provide lines of credit to businesses. Although it would be illegal and a clear violation for a trustee to award custody, trust, administration or investment services for a retirement trust to a bank so that the business can obtain a line of credit or other loan (perhaps at favorable terms), I have witnessed it being sold by banks numerous times. This is clearly unethical, but it still occurs with a wink or a nod.

There are many other potential conflicts that might occur.

Might your payroll vendor be able to lower (or even include "for free") your payroll processing costs if you award it your company's 401(k) plan (that happens to use overpriced funds the plan participants pay from their investments, and the payroll vendor receives some of those excess fees in the form of 12b-1 fees)?

Might your insurance agent be able to negotiate better director's liability insurance rates for the company if the insurance agency's expensive (to the participant) 401(k) platform is used?

Might your personal investment adviser be willing to discount his advisory fees for your personal investment portfolio if he is also managing your company's retirement plan?

These are all obviously unethical acts (at least to me) where either the trustee or the sponsoring company is receiving benefits of vendor selection for the retirement trust that are not related to the sole benefit of participants.

The notion of the first pillar, then, is conceptually simple:

- Do not self-deal or stick your hands into the trust.
- Do not mix personal assets with trust assets.
- Do not do business personally with the trust.
- Do not give even the appearance of a potential conflict.
- Do not receive personal benefit in any form for decisions you make as a fiduciary.
- Be careful of doing business with friends or businesses that also service your company in areas unrelated to the retirement trust.
- Examine potential conflicts of interest and avoid them whenever possible.

Chapter 2 will go through how to build a strong pillar by ensuring your actions are for the sole benefit of participants. It will help you to avoid the conflicts of which you may not even be aware.

Pillar #2: Minimize Risk of Large Losses

The actual language of ERISA requires fiduciaries to:

> diversify plan investments so as to minimize the risk of large losses, unless under the circumstances it is *clearly prudent* [emphasis added] not to do so.[2]

Since this language will be revisited in Chapter 5, the point that we want to focus on here is the notion of what might constitute "large losses" and what standards might have to be met to determine that an action is "clearly prudent" under the previously introduced perspective of an expert applicable to retirement plan fiduciaries. Like the difference between a *prudent man* and *prudent expert*, one must consider the difference between being prudent under the expert standards of ERISA versus "*clearly* prudent" under those same expert standards.

With the retirement plan prudence standards already established as being measured relative to experts, why did the drafters of ERISA go to the extra step of inserting the word "clearly" in front of "prudent" when it comes to bets against diversification as a measure of investment risk? If you think about this in context of the entire set of regulations, in essence ERISA is saying that experts who would by definition recognize uncertainty of bets against diversification, would have to have compelling proof (i.e., be clearly prudent) to make a bet with retirement plan assets that introduces a risk of large losses that could be otherwise be avoided (through diversification).

In the case of defined benefit plans, the sponsor reaps the rewards of winning such bets, and usually ends up paying the price of losing such bets. But, as case law has shown, as long as the trust is adequately funded, there is little recourse for participants even if there is a 100 percent loss on $20 million in assets, per the 3M case.[3] In this case, a class action lawsuit by participants was brought against trustees of the 3M plan for failing to monitor an investment in a hedge fund (Granite) that ended up filing bankruptcy resulting in a loss of the entire $20 million investment.

Is a 100 percent loss on an investment considered a "large" loss, as in the 3M case? Is a $20 million loss considered large? Apparently not, according to the case law as it applies to an overfunded defined benefit plan. And in fact, with the spirit of ERISA as it applies to such a defined benefit plan, it is hard for participants to show any harm. The plan is well funded. The company made excess contributions that more than exceeded the loss. *No harm, no foul* has been a frequent historical perspective for defined benefit trusts.

But, as a trustee or fiduciary adviser, one now has to think about this issue under the context of the 2008 Supreme Court ruling. If the same hedge fund that blew up for 3M were instead an alternative investment option for participants in a defined contribution plan and the materials given to participants showed a great historical record for the doomed hedge fund (an enticing means of misleading the participants about the risks), and the participants lost all of their retirement money for the portion (participants are not expected to be experts) in such an investment, might the fiduciaries be at risk? I would argue a strong case could be made.

What constitutes large losses, from an expert perspective, is also worthy of considering. Clearly, if losses under these regulations simply were to be examined only from the perspective of absolute dollar loss, the clearly prudent thing to do would be to put all of the money in Treasury bills or even just cash in a vault. Neither would have nominal declines in the dollar value. The authors of ERISA recognized that the spending power would erode if that action were taken, that it would be just as imprudent to be excessively safe with the investments because of the long-term nature of such trusts and *the opportunity* for a higher return that would be lost. *In essence, a large loss might be measured over a long time period not relative necessarily to a decline in balance, but instead just a significantly inferior return.* If this were not the case, all trustees would merely invest all of the assets in T-bills. The ERISA authors and the later interpretations (particularly under 404(c) safe harbor provisions) must have considered diversification across asset classes and the uncertainty of making a bet on any one asset class or subsegment thereof. They must have grasped the notion of real returns, relative returns, and *relatively inferior returns* relative to something that is more diversified.

If the ERISA drafters were determined to hold fiduciaries to the standard of an expert, if they were expecting such experts to understand the uncertainties introduced by making bets on specific asset classes, and if they considered the risk of large losses relative to higher returns in mandating diversification, then there are some interesting perspectives to consider in terms of what constitutes a large loss in terms of a participant-directed plan.

Is opportunity cost a large loss? On a relative basis, one could consider that to be the case. It is likely the drafters of ERISA didn't intend for retirement trusts to be invested in cash stuffed into a secure mattress because of the erosion of spending power and lost opportunity for higher returns. Some of the ERISA language even references the context of risk relative to returns. It is possible they were also sophisticated enough to understand *the risk of underperforming an asset class* and thus inserted the notion that accepting such risk requires *extraordinary evidence* (i.e., it must be "clearly" prudent).

For many, this concept may be considered a leap of faith, or too literal of an interpretation of the ERISA language. But it is really no different than the cash–in–a–mattress comparison. Odds are fairly low of a nondiversified T–bill–only portfolio producing a return materially higher than zero on a real (inflation adjusted) basis. Although a balanced portfolio (of just domestic stocks and bonds) introduces some risk of a "large" loss (historically a 23 percent chance of a negative return in any one year, versus essentially zero for T–bills for the period of 1926 to 2007), retirement plans are supposed to have a longer time horizon than one year. Over five years, the risk of a diversified balanced portfolio producing a negative return drops to about a 6 percent chance in all historical periods back to 1926. Extend this to 10–year historical periods, and the balanced-portfolio lowest return was a positive 2.74 percent compounded for the 10 years starting in the Crash of 1929 through the Great Depression until 1938 (T–bills only produced 1.02 percent over this period). The next worst 10–year period was 3.12 percent starting the year before in 1928, where T–bills produced 1.37 percent. Even with the devastating markets of 2008 our balanced portfolio returned 3.43 percent for the 10 years ending 12/31/2008.

In fact, although retirement plans should be evaluated from a much longer time horizon, even looking at just 10–year periods, T–bills produced a return of less than 2 percent in about one third of all historical 10–year periods. The balanced portfolio never produced such a low return in any 10–year period. Thus, diversify.

The *opportunity cost* to the upside must have been a consideration in what constitutes large losses with ERISA under clearly prudent standards.

In Table 1.1 we see that less than 3 percent of the historical 10-year periods for the balanced portfolio produced returns less than 4 percent, while the majority of the 10-year periods for T-bills produced less than 4 percent. Think about these odds. Relative to the absolute safety of T-bills, it would be fairly easy to argue that it is "clearly prudent" to take the risk of losses in some years with a balanced portfolio, to avoid the 51 percent risk of producing less than a 4 percent return in T-bills.

These are clearly some compelling odds as long as there isn't a significant immediate cash need (like withdrawing all of the trust's money within five years). In fact, it would be fairly easy for a fiduciary to argue that T-bills are very risky, having a 51 percent historical chance of returning less than 4 percent over 10 years, while the balanced allocation had only a 3 percent chance, despite the balanced portfolio risks of negative returns in any one year, or the small chance of a negative return over five years. Even returns of less than 2 percent appear far safer in the balanced portfolio (no historical 10-year period produced less than 2 percent) versus more than a third of all 10-year periods for T-bills. It appears, therefore, that ERISA contemplated a relative measure of choices when it comes to diversification, and may in fact have considered such compelling (i.e., clearly prudent) evidence.

Table 1.1　Historical Observations of a Diversified Balanced Portfolio versus 90-Day Treasury Bills

Actual History 1926 to 2007	Balanced Portfolio	T-bills
% of years with negative return	23%	0%
% of 5-year periods with negative return	6%	0%
% of 10-year periods with return <2%	0%	34%
% of 10-year periods with return <4%	3%	51%
% of 10-year periods with return <9.9%	50%	100%
% of 10-year periods with return > 8%	82%	12%

Based on our FWC Balanced Model and Center for Research in Securities Prices asset class data. Portfolio allocation is 40% large cap stocks, 20% small cap stocks, 37% government bonds, and 3% cash.

At this point, it is helpful to define some measures of risk especially in the context of diversification as stated within ERISA. Systematic risk, also known as market risk, is the risk of the asset class in its entirety. This is non-diversifiable risk, because it cannot be diversified away. Systematic risk recognizes that the market is influenced by events outside its control, such as war, government action, and natural disasters or overall economic malaise or euphoria. Introducing risk that can be diversified away, known as nonsystematic risk is not a prudent fiduciary decision. Nonsystematic risk is introduced by not being as diversified as the asset class. If your benchmark is a market cap weighted portfolio of 3,000 stocks, like the Russell 3000 index, any portfolio that does not own all 3,000 stocks weighted by market cap will introduce some amount of non-systematic risk. For example, any 100 stock portfolio introduces a risk of underperforming the 3,000 stock benchmark, a risk that could be avoided by owning all 3,000 stocks in the same proportion as the benchmark. It also could outperform the benchmark, but it is subjecting you to nonsystematic risk that could be diversified away nonetheless. It is important to note that basic math demonstrates that nonsystematic risk is not rewarded on average which is why diversification is so important and why it is a fundamental requirement of ERISA.

By definition, in participant-directed plans, it is possible for participants to design an imprudent investment selection. It is their choice. Many participants do the equivalent of investing in 100 percent T-bills via a money market or stable-value investment option. The question then becomes, does the act of the participant making such a decision relieve plan fiduciaries from *all* responsibility for diversification? Section 404(c) provided a DOL-endorsed safe harbor provision that protected fiduciaries from such participant actions. Will such safe harbors survive under the perspective of the 2008 Supreme Court ruling regarding individual plan balances? A compelling case could be made under ERISA that the selections they offer, while complying with 404(c), still must meet basic fiduciary provisions. Recently proposed regulations by the DOL actually explicitly state this to be the case, so that safe harbor may not be so safe. In fact, there never was any really valid reason to think

404(c) "safe harbors" suddenly exempted other ERISA standards when it comes to prudence. We will explore more on this topic in Chapter 3, along with how the normal safe harbor provisions may no longer be all that safe for fiduciaries in this context.

The key thing to remember about this pillar, though, is that accepting an investment risk that could otherwise be avoided by diversification not only is held to the standards of experts, but also must have extraordinary evidence to justify accepting the risk in order to meet the standard of being "clearly" prudent. This reality means that there must be exceptional evidence in order to accept nonsystematic risk that could otherwise be diversified away.

Pillar #3: Costs Are Reasonable for the Services Being Provided

This is the time bomb that is about to explode on trustees, product vendors, *and advisers* in defined contribution plans. The media attention about fees (not to mention my book *Stop the Retirement Rip-off*, 2009) in 401(k), 403(b), and 457 plans has been extensive.[4] No less than three bills about fee disclosures and conflicts of interest are currently pending in House and the Senate.[5]

Early in 2008, the Labor Department received comments on proposals to make fee disclosures clearer to trustees and is now working on proposals for participant disclosures. As of this writing, the comment period for better participant disclosures has ended and it appears the proposed rules will not go into effect. The GAO (Government Accountability Office) and AARP[6] have both produced studies that show few plan participants know what they are paying. This is only a matter of time. The 2008 Supreme Court ruling will grease the skids and accelerate the inevitable.

In the case of fees, the old standards of procedural prudence and soft dollar policies used in defined benefit plans are going to be applied to participant-directed plans. It has been a long time since a broker could get away with charging outrageous retail commissions far higher than institutional rates in a reasonably managed defined benefit plan. The product vendors to date have been able to escape having their packaged product commissions and expenses evaluated on the same basis. It will not last.

If the DOL convulses over a $50 million defined benefit plan paying 12 cents a share for brokerage executions and expects documentation as to why the cost is so much higher than the prevailing rate, and what all those excess soft dollars are "buying" for participants, then the extra 1.00 percent many insurance companies charge or the huge 12b-1 fees or retail share classes of mutual funds being used in defined contribution plans is going to come to an end.

Frankly, I think part of the popularity of defined contribution plans is due to the fact that they are so much more profitable than defined benefit plans for the product vendors. Such plans have been able to escape providing institutional pricing by using retail products (with retail fees) for institutional accounts. When you are a product vendor and can get away with charging retail pricing for institutional relationships, you have a money-making machine. This is what the product vendors have sold and will defend to their death to keep the gravy train rolling. But, all of the conflicts of interest, revenue-sharing kickbacks, side deals, bundling of services, and sales commissions paid to nonfiduciaries will not survive the lawsuits looming from 100 million potential plaintiffs.

Trustees and advisers to date generally have escaped scrutiny of these excessive costs for defined contribution plans, but Chapter 4 will expose how trustees can protect themselves for even small plans and achieve institutional pricing levels that will be expected going forward, just as they have been doing for defined benefit plans for years.[7]

Regardless, in the context of the impairment of any individual's plan balance, making sure that the expenses borne by participants are reasonable relative to the services they are receiving is a critical pillar of ERISA and your actions as a fiduciary. The standards will be changing in the future, and the cover-up that product vendors have used in merely comparing themselves to average retail expenses will not survive the scrutiny of millions of litigants and trial lawyers. The main thing that trustees need to do is make sure that expenses are indeed reasonable and that the services that are bundled into these expenses are actually being utilized if everyone in the plan is paying for them.

Pillar #4: Diversification Applied to Participant Direction

In Pillar #2, minimizing the risk of large losses, we examined a few points about ERISA in terms of the need for plans to diversify to avoid large losses, discussed what might constitute a large loss under ERISA, and analyzed why the notion of "clearly" prudent was inserted into the regulations when the standard for fiduciary conduct was already established to be at the level of an expert. We also noted how in defined benefit plans, the real issue was harm to the overall plan and that if the plan was adequately funded, little liability has been awarded in lawsuits to individual participants.

In the case of a participant-directed plan, could fiduciaries be held accountable for diversification when the participant is in control? After all, the selection of investments is left to participants (*subject to the choices being made available by trustees*). In the world of defined benefit plans, many bets against diversification are made every day. Like the gamble made by a blackjack player, a little more than half of the time these bets end up performing less than what was otherwise achievable by avoiding the bet. To the sponsor of a defined benefit plan, the opportunity for such bets paying off with a significant win against indexing is sometimes worth the risk of also potentially underperforming. When the sponsor is making this bet in a defined benefit plan, the sponsor reaps the reward (lower future contributions) or pays the price (higher contributions), and even relatively material deviations from their "procedurally prudent investment policy statement benchmarks" do not really affect participants.

However, under the landscape of liability of potential suits from individual participants' personal plan balances, what would be completely defendable under a defined benefit plan suddenly becomes a massive risk.

In the defined benefit plan, bets against the ERISA standard of diversification that don't pay off are shared *against all* participants and end up creating an additional liability that is funded by the plan sponsor in larger future contributions, or a greater plan liability. You do not see many winning cases against trustees of defined benefit plans for having selected, for example, the Legg Mason Value Trust (LMVTX).

Trustees can defend themselves for making that gamble very easily. Three years ago the fund had an incredible 17-year track record. It was a five-star fund. The fact that LMVTX is now a one-star fund and has compounded at more than 10 percent a year under the S&P 500 might merely mean that the overall defined benefit plan might now be 87 percent funded instead of 100 percent funded, and the sponsor might have to increase contributions in future years. So what! No lawsuit here. All that happens is the sponsor increases its contributions in future years to make up for the losing gamble it made, and actuaries attest that the increase in those contributions bring the plan up to an adequate funding level.

But, defined contribution plans uniquely affect *each person's personal plan balance* by this same choice of such a gamble against being fully diversified. For example, if the trustees of a defined contribution plan used the Legg Mason Value Trust as their large-cap investment option, there would be some young people who would be unhappy, but unlikely to have a valid suit. The reason a suit would be hard to prove for such participants is that a potentially defendable case might be made for what the vendors selling this product advertise. They simply would say "that it will turn around" or offer the alternative of switching to a "better fund" (as opposed to the "better fund" that fell apart on them). In essence, the case of young plan participants is unlikely to become a valid claim for a lawsuit because there exists a hope that in the future they can recover a portion of the losing bet in some lucky or skillful gambles in the investment alternatives in the future.

But, what if three years ago, you hired a senior executive who rolled over $2,000,000 from his prior employer into your plan? Having come to you after selling out of his previous company, he planned to retire in three years. Although he was still in his early fifties, he took a conservative approach, allocating half his portfolio to large-cap stocks and the other half to bonds, contemplating the safety needed for his coming retirement. So far, so good—except as trustee or an adviser to the trust, you picked the Legg Mason Value Trust as the alternative for large-cap stocks in your 401(k) plan. (At least, that's how it would have looked with the track record three years ago.) In fact, all of your funds back then beat the S&P 500, so you didn't even bother to offer an index fund.

What was *his personal impairment* of *your* fund selection? If he had a fully diversified index fund alternative, his large-cap portion of the portfolio would have grown to $1,247,000 even with excessively expensive index fund fees of 0.50 percent. Instead, it is now worth $937,000. Could *you* be on the hook for the $310,000 difference? A reasonable case for it could be made. The problem you have as a fiduciary in this case is that you didn't offer him a choice that avoided the risk of materially underperforming and, in essence, forced him to expose one of his major asset classes to a material risk of underperforming that could have been otherwise avoided by a more diversified alternative. This limitation materially impaired his plan balance by $310,000, due solely to your decision as a fiduciary.

Let us review ERISA and the Supreme Court ruling together to examine whether there might be a legitimate case here. Was the fund diversified (a requirement of ERISA)? The only answer to that could be no. The fund was known to make large bets, and even the fund manager (Bill Miller) was publicly quoted as saying his portfolio shouldn't be compared to the S&P 500 (www.fundgrades.com shows what the grade for diversification would have been three years ago: D+, along with an F for risk as of this writing). It was a risky fund as evidenced *because* it outperformed so much. You cannot make big wins without making big bets. *If the portfolio were more diversified, the excess returns in the track record **could not** have occurred.*

Chapter 5 will examine the risks that you might be taking when you are relying on product vendors and salespeople as a source of supposed advice, yet do not acknowledge fiduciary responsibility within their contracts. Such vendors also should reacquaint themselves with the notion of being a *fiduciary by implication*,[8] something that will be dusted off when trustees are being sued by participants. The trustees will point to how they relied on your advice (even though it was "incidental" to your product selling services[9]) and you received compensation, and the appeal of your firm's deeper pockets will drag you and your firm into such suits despite the contracts in use to try to evade that responsibility.

The essence of this pillar, then, is related to the notion of avoiding needless investment risk, but is explicit in ERISA and expanded now beyond the notion of merely labeling asset classes for diversification purposes but also including the risks of any product selection accepting a risk that could be diversified away.

The Pillars that Hold the Roof of Our Nation's Retirement Security

These four pillars of retirement plans, their context from what has been established in the past as procedural prudence, and how they might be interpreted in the future under the 2008 Supreme Court ruling are all in question, with potentially 100 million plaintiffs waiting in the wings.

If you are a trustee, an officer of a company sponsoring a plan, an investment adviser, or a product seller to qualified ERISA-governed plans, you must act now to adjust what you are doing to mitigate the massive risks that lay before you.

Even if you are not involved in ERISA plans, if you are merely a fiduciary or even a product seller who might be at risk of being accused of acting in a fiduciary capacity, you need to rethink your actions.

In either case, whether these fiduciary risks appear in the future or not, I appeal to you to consider the ethics of your actions and responsibilities.

Chapter 2

Pillar #1: Assets Are Invested for the Sole Benefit of Participants

A s was briefly discussed in Chapter 1, historically there have been few cases in defined benefit plans where participants could win suits for how retirement funds were handled unless there was an egregious violation of prohibited transaction rules since the employer was on the hook for the cost of mistakes. The recent Supreme Court ruling dramatically changes this landscape, since such mistakes or conflicts of interest now potentially apply to the retirement fund balance of each individual participant as a potential litigant.

From this "impairment of individual account balance" perspective of the 2008 Supreme Court ruling, we will now delve deeper into how common practices in participant-directed plans, borne from procedures designed for defined benefit plans, may actually be creating a fiduciary breach in the future. We will also explore how such procedures put plan sponsors, product vendors, and advisers at risk, often legitimately at the harm of individual participants (in my opinion).

My Plan, My Benefit, My Life, YOUR Liability

My book targeting 401(k), 403(b) and 457 retirement plan participants (*Stop the Retirement Rip-off*), where the price to the participant of excessive needless costs was the focus, exposed a mountain of fiduciary breaches in many participant-directed plans. At least, there will be many cases proven based on the 2008 Supreme Court ruling.

For example, there are a large number of participant-directed plans where the trustees have contracted with an insurance company and now use a group annuity contract, with various mutual funds as investments bundled under pooled separate accounts (known as PSAs) as the sole investment options. There is no reason to package the mutual funds under a PSA since mutual funds can be purchased directly by the plan trust, other than that the PSA packaging enables the insurance company to skim additional fees and avoid some disclosure rules. Also, the additional M&E fees (mortality and expense charges, which are sometimes 1 percent or more on assets) for the annuity features in such plans have been defendable from the previous perspective of having to prove impairment of all participants together. After all, some of the extra fees the insurance company is charging is for the risks they are taking (often for guaranteeing a participant nothing more than they will at least get their money back at a 0 percent return) if they were to die, instead of having heirs subject to market losses that might occur with an untimely death.

It is interesting to me that the securities-selling industry has been fined for numerous violations for inappropriately using these products, particularly in IRA rollovers, many of which come from participant-directed retirement accounts.

In a speech given on September 13, 2006, Commissioner Annette L. Nazareth of the U.S. Securities and Exchange Commission stated:[1]

> . . . we have seen variable annuities used to fund retirement accounts that are already tax deferred. Indeed, the tax benefits of variable annuities are largely negated when an annuity is

held in a qualified plan because all of the growth within those plans is already tax deferred.

And Kimberly Lankford of *Kiplinger Personal Finance* stated in January 2007:[2]

But even a good deferred annuity isn't suitable for most people.

Yet, many smaller companies use these products as *the only* option for their participants. The future ERISA standard, though, under the context of evaluating a fiduciary breach (for the impairment of an individual's personal plan balance), is not going to be perceived from the notion that *some* dead participants had their heirs benefit from the cost associated with the annuity features. It will come from the long list of participants who did not need, or value, the features and services associated with the costs they were forced to incur in such annuity products.

This notion of **choice** is critical for trustees and other fiduciaries to consider. In the past, "choice" was simple to comply with under section 404(c) safe-harbor provisions. All that was needed was to offer all participants the ability to materially control the risk and return characteristics of their plan balances by offering a sufficient number of investment alternatives with differing characteristics and providing some documentation about "education" being offered. Under that landscape, prior to the recent Supreme Court ruling, even if many participants were harmed by the needless expenses of the insurance add-on cost or other excessive fees, trustees falsely felt comfortable that they fell under the safe harbor because it was difficult to prove harm *to all* participants.

Imagine, however, that you are the trustee selecting, or the adviser recommending, such a variable annuity product as the sole alternative for a small company, *now* based on the liability of any *one* participant's balance.

Assume the product has M&E costs of 0.75 percent a year, and unlike many of the variable annuities being sold, it even offers some index funds as investment options (although at expense ratios of 0.50 percent a year due to 12b-1 fees).

Those M&E expenses and/or the 12b-1 fees are used to pay a commission of 0.50 percent a year on all the assets of the trust to the financial adviser. The adviser earns this commission for doing semiannual participant "education" meetings and providing personal advice to all participants, *regardless of whether or not the participant uses such services.*

We roll forward 30 years, and the participant files a suit against the trustees individually, the plan sponsor, and the adviser. How would you respond to the accusations of the counsel for the plaintiff on the following?

Your honor, the plaintiff is suing the named fiduciaries and the financial adviser as a fiduciary by action (and for compensation) for breach of their fiduciary duties under ERISA for impairment of my client's individual plan balance under the 2008 Supreme Court ruling regarding the impairment of individual plan balances. My client has been employed by the plan sponsor for the last 30 years and has diligently elected to defer $15,000 of his income into the sponsor's 401(k) plan. Over this time, my client has been forced to incur what I will prove to be needless expenses paid to the adviser of $148,257 in the form of commissions for services that were not used. Additionally, my client was forced to pay for an insurance feature he did not need or want totaling an additional $134,079. We seek reimbursement of my client's impaired individual balances for breach of fiduciary duty under the following premises:

1. The plan sponsor and trustees did not exercise care and prudence in evaluating the costs borne by my client and other participants as being reasonable for the services provided as required under ERISA. In fact, we intend to show that 30 years ago, all it would have taken was a simple Internet search to expose that there were equivalent index options to what my client used in his portfolio for at least 0.25 percent less in investment fees, without the needless M&E and sales

commission costs of 0.75 percent. These excess needless expenses were brought to the attention of the trustees and even the adviser that earned the excess commissions on this trust, and despite the standard under ERISA that fiduciaries act with the care, skill, and diligence as one familiar with such matters, they did not act on this disclosure. Because the expert standard of ERISA does not exempt fiduciaries from liability for lack of knowledge and actually requires them to exercise procedural prudence in regularly evaluating the reasonableness of costs (which was not done in this plan) and because the plaintiff directly pointed out to all parties the expenses were excessive, we seek total damages for the impairment of my client's personal plan balances in the amount of $282,336 for contributory negligence in intentionally violating their fiduciary obligations.

2. These damages are reasonable and we seek no punitive damages. My client incurred fees of 1.25 percent a year for 30 years in investment alternatives that were commonly available in the marketplace for 0.25 percent a year and often available for far less than that. These lower cost alternatives were identical in all material aspects as the alternatives offered to my client, except for the expenses. All we are seeking is reimbursement of the excess needed costs incurred. The $282,336 we seek in damages represents only the 1 percent in excessive fees based on the fiduciary breaches of procedural prudence in examining the costs as being reasonable for the services being provided to my client.

Prior to the 2008 Supreme Court ruling, such a case would be hard to win. First, in some jurisdictions, you would have to be able to prove that *every* participant was harmed, and the insurance vendor could easily defend that merely by showing just one participant benefited from the advice costs or expensive insurance features. They could probably even defend it based on the example that a different company had a participant who received a benefit, since it is unknown whether any one participant will die, or seek the advice in the future.

But when the context of fiduciary liability and breaches thereof switch to the impairment of any one participant's balance, the notion of the sole benefit of participants becomes an individual issue and makes it much more difficult to defend the harm caused to an *individual participant* by evidence based on the benefit to *another participant*. **THIS is how the landscape has changed.**

It has massive implications for how plans and services are provided. It will, in my opinion, force an unbundling of services and their associated costs. Insurance companies will ultimately be forced—either through the courts or by informed trustees—to offer pure mutual fund investment options without the burden of the costs of the insurance and PSA wrapper or needless commissions.

Advisers will likely be unable to justify their asset-based fees and commissions for participant education and individual advice charged against all plan assets regardless of whether the individual participant uses such services. This is common practice currently by advisers. They might charge 0.50 to 1.00 percent on all of the plan assets for providing semiannual participant education meetings and offering individual consultation to participants. The problem is going to come from an evaluation of how many participants are paying for this service relative to how many actually use it. Although some amount of cost for advising the trustees under a fiduciary advisory agreement charged against all assets may be defendable as reasonable even if bundled with "education," the pricing needs to be institutionally based. Under the context of ERISA applied to the individual participant, if even *one* participant is not using the advice, but *his* assets are materially impaired so that *all other participants* can use the service, that lone participant is justified in the perspective that he was personally paying for everyone else's advice. Unfortunately, it is more likely that fewer than 10 to 20 percent of the participants take advantage of receiving the personal advice for the advice fee they are paying, which means often 80 to 90 percent are paying a fee for something they do not use.

Imagine that you are the adviser to a 401(k), with $10 million in total balances and you earn a 0.75 percent commission or fee for your advice to plan participants and trustees. Your commission is $75,000 a year. Now, put yourself in the shoes of an individual participant with $1 million in the plan. A participant with $1 million is paying $7,500 of this cost. Is this reasonable to you the participant if you are not using the service? The adviser earning this compensation will need to have some proof of the value she is providing by skimming $7,500 in fees from the participant's account. If the adviser's main proof of her value is the one-hour presentation done once or twice a year, she had better be able to document that she is worth speaking fees of $75,000 or have had people pay $7,500 to attend a one-hour seminar.

Now, I know many advisers will say that the fee or commissions are not "just" for speaking at annual meetings. They justify their expenses by "superior fund selection and research," monitoring the performance, writing and amending an investment policy statement as needed, providing individual consultations with participants and enabling access to a web site for the 401(k) plan. The investment consulting industry has managed to package these services together as a standard for procedural prudence based on its roots in the defined benefit plan market and old-fashioned nonparticipant-directed money purchase pension and profit sharing plans. This is not going to continue with participant-directed accounts. As we will explore in Chapter 5 discussing Pillar #4 on diversification, this suite of consulting services is actually going to cause both advisers and trustees a mountain of future lawsuits.

Also, disclosure of fees and conflicts are going to become a litigation nightmare for trustees and product providers. Currently, the Department of Labor (DOL) has not expended any perceivable effort in evaluating the nature of the content in "education" meetings with participants, a common practice to help comply with safe harbor education provisions of section 404(c).

But, when such "education seminars" become Exhibit 1 in the cases brought from individual participants, the content of such sessions in many cases will not survive the scrutiny of an ERISA perspective of a breach of fiduciary duty to the individual participant. Historically, these education seminars have often amounted to nothing more than a company-endorsed generic sales pitch to participants where little if any personal advice occurs and the commissioned sales person gets to spin why participants should select overpriced or risky products (that generate more commissions or justify advisory fees). With the DOL's historical main concern not being the content, but just that "education" is being provided, it is unlikely that the content of many of these seminars will change in the near future. But as more and more participants trot these presentations out before a judge or jury, the price of misleading content and lack of any individual advice will be recognized.

Action Steps to Prevent Needless Liability from Pillar #1 for Trustees, Sponsors, Advisers, and Product Vendors

The action steps that fiduciaries should take to avoid needless liabilities from the first pillar (ensuring assets are used for the sole benefit of participants) are as follows:

- **Disclose fees.** At least annually, trustees should seek competitive pricing bids, document that they have done so, and require any bids to be submitted in the DOL-suggested format.[3] Existing vendors should also be required to complete this fee disclosure document, and if the higher-cost alternative is used, the trustees need to document the specific rationale as to why the higher-cost alternative is beneficial for *every* participant.[4]
- **Offer flexibility for participants to avoid needless costs.** Trustees need to make sure that participants have *the option* to avoid any needless *retail-priced* advice costs (whether billed as an advisory fee or bundled in product expenses). Although it might be appropriate for the trustees to contract with an adviser that admits fiduciary responsibility for investment selection alternatives and to levy that fee across all participant balances, such contracts should not bundle

excessive retail costs for educational sessions or individual participant advice, and such fees should be reasonable for the services being offered based on institutional pricing levels. Trustees electing to use such services should do so consciously and have the option of avoiding them if they have the experience and knowledge to operate the plan without such services.

- **Explain education and associated costs.** Educational sessions should not be charged for on a percentage of assets basis at retail pricing levels. Retail expenses charged against all participants will ultimately be converted to what each participant is personally paying for such sessions based on his or her plan balance. The educational content should explicitly expose how participants can avoid any applicable individual advisory fees, commissions, or insurance contract expenses.

- **Disclose costs for individualized advice.** Fees for individual advice should be fully disclosed to the participant and apply only to those participants who use such services. They should not be assessed based on overall plan assets or total number of participants. Retail-level pricing for asset-based, hourly, or per-participant fees for individual advice should be charged only to the individual's plan balance so that those who are not using the service are not paying for those who are. Institutional-level pricing should be applicable to any other nonindividualized service. The DOL will need to change the current regulations regarding "level fees" that the product vendors have lobbied as a benefit to protect participants from conflicts of interest yet result in every participant paying advice fees even though most do not use the advice they are forced to pay for in such level fee arrangements.

- **Offer flexible, diversified, and low-cost investment options.** Investment alternatives offered to participants should accommodate a broad array of needs and personal choices. There should be alternatives so that annuity contract expenses can be avoided (in fact, there is nothing in ERISA or the 2008 Supreme Court ruling that would require annuities to be offered at all). There should also be low-cost passive alternatives, as well as the ability for any participant to access a broad selection of active alternatives. Under the new landscape of being judged for each individual participant's plan balance, it is critical that trustees offer very broad and flexible options. A self-directed brokerage account is now available in many plans at no additional administrative cost and enables trustees to offer a short list of appropriate investment alternatives to the majority of participants, while accommodating anyone's preference through the brokerage account where only those who elect such an option pay the additional commission costs in the self-directed brokerage account. Plans that offer self-directed brokerage accounts (at a reasonable cost and unrestricted in amount allocated to the account) will make it very difficult for individuals to pursue fiduciary breaches for the lack of choice, or even for the pricing of the default investment alternatives.

- **Avoid explicit or implicit benefits to the business.** Trustees and product vendors need to make sure that there is no benefit to the business (i.e., line of credit to the business, reduced payroll processing costs, favorable business insurance rates, and so on— think of our example of Joe in Chapter 1) in the selection of a vendor to the trust. In the context of the impairment of individual participant balances, such business benefits for vendor selection will ultimately be judged in many individual cases as prohibited transactions.

- **Avoid personal benefits obtainable by your role as a fiduciary.** Incidental benefits to trustees (reduced personal advising fees for assets held outside of the trust, entertainment, etc.) should be avoided. Crony relationships should be closely evaluated and avoided unless there is clear documentation of the benefit to participants.

None of these actions is difficult for trustees or product/advice vendors to execute, and all of these types of alternatives are widely available in the marketplace at very low costs, even for very small (less than $1 million in assets) plans.

The trustees who ignore action on these basic steps are subjecting themselves to personal liability from each and every plan participant.

Advisers assessing retail-level advisory fees across all assets, regardless if none or all of the participants use or can be proven to benefit from such services, are at risk of each participant who does not use or benefit from such service becoming a future plaintiff seeking suit against the adviser.

Product vendors and commissioned salespeople who sell plans on costly limited product offerings will be forced through the courts to reimburse their short-term greed and biases to a litany of individual suits that will be difficult to defend. If you are such a vendor, you have two choices. You can hope to keep trying to get away with it (not recommended), or you can proactively prevent future suits by acting on these common-sense steps before too much liability accrues.

Chapter 3

Pillar #2: Minimize Risk of Large Losses

n Chapter 1, we highlighted some key premises of the difference between participant-directed plans and defined benefit plans under the context of the massive shift of the liability trustees and advisers face under the 2008 Supreme Court ruling.

We discussed three main issues in this regard:

1. Risk taking must be clearly prudent under ERISA from the perspective of an expert (i.e., one familiar with such matters).
2. ERISA must have contemplated the notion of risk relative to the return and not just the avoidance of short-term nominal losses (i.e., losses might be measured over a longer time horizon of the trust relative to lost return opportunity).
3. The price of losing risk-taking bets in defined benefit plans did not normally impair participants as a whole and merely subjected the sponsor to increased future contributions to maintain or achieve sufficient liability funding.

Under the context of potential liability at the individual participant level, this historical context for the procedures used by defined benefit plans will do nothing to prevent a large number of participants from having valid lawsuits under the context of how investment risk affects the impairment of each individual's balance.

It is common today and generally accepted procedural prudence for trustees or their consultants to draft and adopt a written investment policy statement that outlines selection criteria for investment managers, establishes benchmarks to measure and monitor the managers against, and establishes a time horizon and risk tolerance for each selected investment management alternative. These documentation efforts and monitoring reports will not work in your defense when you are a fiduciary adviser or trustee at risk for litigation from each individual participant.

How could such past "proven" procedural prudence fall apart on you in a participant-directed plan? Here again, the tipping point is the difference between documenting your actions as applied to all participants together (past law, but current procedural prudence standards) versus how decisions affect each individual participant (current law based on the 2008 Supreme Court ruling, but lacking any procedural prudence standards that are defensible from individual participant perspectives).

In Chapter 1, we discussed an example of the Legg Mason Value Trust. From the perspective of "plan as a whole and all participants" standards in prior law, it would merely be unfortunate timing if an executive joined the company and utilized this fund for his investment, during which it underperformed the index by 10 percent a year for three years. The executive would have been unlikely to win a lawsuit trying to recover lost investment dollars. Yet, under the new standards, the trustees could legitimately be on the hook for $310,000 of potential liability from just one participant, the cost of underperforming the benchmark in the investment policy by 10 percent a year over three years with a $1 million allocation to the fund.

Past law and procedures would have had the trustees documenting the long superior track record of their bet made with this fund against diversification, monitoring the recent underperformance, and seeking advice from their consultant. The severe underperformance probably would not have immediately triggered (say the first year) switching to

42

another alternative. After all, the investment policy might have stated that performance relative to benchmarks would be measured over the last 3, 5, and 10 years or *a full market cycle*—however one might define that. Is one year of bad performance something that would trigger a change when the same manager has been in place and has a 17-year record of *prior* superior results?

In all likelihood, the first year of material underperformance would have been brushed off as an anomaly by the consultant and the trustees. The consultant invariably would have highlighted that there was no change in the discipline or management team (the consultant's supposed value-add) and noted that the superior long-term record (something the trust never enjoyed based on when it chose the fund) was indeed still superior.

A year later, with another terrible year, the consultant may have suggested that the manager be placed on the "watch list" and the consultant would closely monitor the performance.

By the time three years passed, and the fund had underperformed the passive benchmark by 10 percent a year compounded, something is going to change. Mind you, this three-year period is when the *individual plan participants* actually OWNED and EXPERIENCED the poor performance, thus creating the liability for the sponsor, trustees and consultant. After three terrible years, the consultant would have probably considered seeking a replacement due to poor performance ensuring that participants lock in those poor results and start the process with another fund that, you guessed it . . . has a great track record. And so, the cycle continues until the new smarter fund becomes dumb.

Personally (as a fiduciary), this common series of events for numerous investment selections made by ERISA plans seems like a breach of ERISA under the notion of accepting only those risks that are *clearly prudent*. Still, the actions that the trustees and their adviser consultant have taken make it practically impossible to prove that *all* participants were harmed, and thus there have been few cases in which the trustees or the consulting adviser would be liable under the circumstances outlined, at least in the past.

Under old procedures, ignoring the effect to individual participants of their investment choices, the trustees have pretty good documentation. The trust has a long-term horizon (individual participants may not). It reviewed a long-term track record (of past results individual participants did not enjoy). It established benchmarks and was aware of the deteriorating results (something an individual participant will actually use as evidence in their case against trustees if advantageous in a lawsuit relative to their personal plan balance). These common procedural prudence actions will not fly for such investment selections when the measurement of a fiduciary breach is moved from the plan as a whole (all participants) to the impairment of an individual's balance. Chapter 6 will examine in detail the impact of uncertainty of *when* superior or inferior results will occur, not only from a perspective of ERISA trustees or advisers, but also from the perspective of any fiduciary who represents his or her services as that of a wealth management adviser under an advisory contract. The fallacy that returns are tied to dollars of wealth will be exposed in depth in Part Two. But remember, the liabilities fiduciaries face will be based on *dollars of wealth* and not based on returns. This issue of *when* superior (or inferior) results occur is critical in a dollar-based wealth measurement.

As a simple example, say you are saving $10,000 a year for two years and that you know that you will average 10 percent over that two years. That average of 10 percent will come in the form of a 0 percent return in one of the two years, and a 20 percent return in the other; we just do not know *when* either will occur. Since you don't know *when* (or which) of the two years will receive the 0 or 20 percent return, but regardless of the order in which they occur it will not affect the average return, the compound return (9.54 percent in this case) or the standard deviation, does it make any difference? YOU BET IT DOES!

If the 20 percent return occurred the first year when you only had made your first $10,000 contribution, that would result in $2,000 of additional wealth in the form of return. Adding another $10,000 the second year and earning a 0 percent return in year two would have your account balance at $22,000 for a total profit of $2,000 over two years. If the returns occurred in the opposite order (0 percent the first year and 20 percent the second) you would have accumulated $24,000 for a $4,000 profit, DOUBLE the dollars of profit. Of course, if you were spending money out of the account instead of saving, the reverse order would be preferable. This is the reality of measuring dollars of wealth instead of returns. Part Two starting with Chapter 6 will expose this return versus dollars fantasy that will fall apart for fiduciaries when liabilities are measured based on an individual's personal plan balance (note the Supreme Court didn't say return . . . it said PLAN BALANCE . . . that means DOLLARS).

For now, though, we will focus on some simple actions both trustees and advisers need to take to protect themselves from liability from individual participants based on their unique circumstances. These steps are based on an assumption that there will be a reversal, or at least an amendment, of previous DOL safe harbors and changes to accepted procedural prudence will emerge under the context of the Supreme Court ruling.

In Chapter 1, we examined a comparison of how it might be clearly prudent to own a balanced investment portfolio that subjects a plan to a loss in any one year, or even five years, relative to the short-term safety of T-bills. When pension assets were pooled for the benefit of all participants and the fiduciary standard was measuring impairment as all participants together, the case for clear prudence in taking the risk of a balanced portfolio was fairly easy to defend (see Table 1.1 in Chapter 1). But we are no longer there, and this is a dramatic change.

Documenting Risks as Clearly Prudent for *Every* Participant Instead of *All* Participants— The New Landscape

In the past, trustees and advisers had little to really worry about when it came to taking investment risks that might underperform the passive benchmarks established in their investment policy statements. This is because of the long-term time horizon of the trust, the track records and research used to select investments, the monitoring of perform-ance, and the forever unknowable future of whether past losers might be made up by future winners in this approach. When measurements for accepting investment risk move from the long-term unified trust overall to an endless number of individual time horizons, the landscape of what constitutes "clearly" prudent dramatically changes.

This notion is not meant to convey that the future of fiduciary prudence for risk taking is going to require that all investments are short term or indexed because a lone participant has a short-term horizon. It does, however, require that trustees have alternatives avail-able for short-term horizons that participants can select, and do not take risks for material underperformance that would not meet prov-able new standards of what might constitute *clearly prudent* in this context.

Likewise, in nearly every plan, there are (or could be) participants who have a very-long-term time horizon. The investment selections available to such participants need to accommodate the long-term horizon they have, and documentation must be crafted for choices that are made in this context as well.

Of course there will be a myriad of participants in between these extremes who may blend their portfolio in various proportions, but in a participant-directed plan, the individual investment option alterna-tives offered will need to consider the extreme perspectives and all of those in between.

The wording of ERISA has not changed under the Supreme Court ruling, nor have the standards of being a prudent expert and only tak-ing investment risks that are clearly prudent. What has changed is the case that can be made by an individual participant against trustees and other named fiduciaries, and this will dramatically affect the future case law in interpreting this standard of ERISA.

As an example, let's look at some theoretical odds for risk intro-duced by trustees or their advisers for the same balanced portfolio from Table 1.1. However, instead of looking at it from a perspective relative to T-bills, short-term chances of losses, and absolute returns, we will look at it from a perspective of *relative returns* to the benchmark in the investment policy.

One look at Table 3.1 shows us it is difficult to defend *clear prudence* of the risk being taken relative to the benchmark in the investment policy. These are just theoretical odds, are not real, and are generously gifting a statistical advantage from what the real statistics would probably be in reality. The odds were tilted assuming superior selection—a very risky assumption, and something that we will later expose as less than likely in Chapter 5.

But, if one is to meet the standard of clear prudence for accepting investment risk that could otherwise be diversified away, is this as defendable as the case that was made for the balanced allocation relative to T-bills based on 80 years of actual data instead of theoretically favorable odds in Table 3.1?

For the one participant in the plan that is five years away from retirement, having safely accumulated enough resources in a balanced portfolio to plan on retiring after a lifetime of labor, is it clearly prudent to take his balanced allocation and subject him to a 25 percent chance of underperforming for the next five years by 0.5 percent for a 20 percent the chance of outperforming by 1 percent or a 60 percent chance of outperforming by any amount? It might squeak by as being clearly prudent if these theoretical odds are provable, since there is an obvious statistical advantage of making the bet.

Table 3.1 Theoretical Odds of Investment Selection for a Balanced Portfolio Benchmark in Measuring Clearly Prudent Standards

Returns Relative to Policy Benchmark % of:	Benchmark Indexed Alternative	Portfolio Selection Risk
Years with return > 1% under benchmark	0%	35%?
5-year periods with returns >0.5% under benchmark	0%	30%?
10-year periods with return >0.5% under benchmark	0%	25%?
10-year periods with return >1% under benchmark	0%	10%?
10-year periods with return > benchmark	0%	60%?
10-year periods with return > 1% over benchmark	0%	20%?

But, as we already established earlier in the T-bill versus balanced portfolio comparison, on a relative basis of the risk, clear prudence of an expert would dictate the consideration that the risk of underperforming in a material way can have complete certainty of being avoided by merely owning the fully diversified index. Thus, it will be difficult to defend the notion that subjecting various participants with varying time horizons to *any* significant risk of material underperformance was *clearly prudent* relative to the certainty of *no chance* of it.

You might ask yourself, what about the notion of liability introduced by merely investing in the benchmark while there were other alternatives that outperformed? The standards of ERISA appear to be relative on both a risk and return basis, and so if I merely offer the benchmark of my investment policy as an indexed investment option, am I as a fiduciary not at risk for being compared to the other alternatives that did better? Indeed you are. This is why the self-directed brokerage account option is so critical in what you are offering participants in your plan.

It would appear that as a trustee or adviser, from a context of individual participant balances, all with unique time frames, you are in a catch-22. If you offer only active selections in an attempt to outperform, you will be accused by some participants of taking a needless risk that could have been avoided and you will have difficulty of defending any choice that materially underperforms your investment policy benchmark when you had the clearly prudent choice of avoiding that risk. Yet, if the only selections you offer are passive alternatives, participants will come up with an endless revolving list of many skillful or lucky alternatives that would have produced a higher return based on their unique time horizon. Again, this is why you need to offer a self-directed brokerage account option.

But, in reality a case for benchmark-indexed alternatives is easy to defend as default or primary investment options, *as long as* you have a means (the option and flexibility) for participants to select from a broad array of any of the alternatives that may outperform the benchmark in the future. The risk to you as a trustee or adviser in a plan structured in this manner is very low. ERISA requires diversification and the avoidance of investment risks unless it is clearly prudent to do otherwise. The benchmark-indexed portfolio is defendable both as being diversified and as avoiding the risk of materially underperforming. It would be difficult to argue that trustees should be taking a risk of unfortunate timing of material underperformance when they are expected to be responsible for each individual's plan balance and the timing of returns impacts each individual differently. The effect of this timing of under- and overperformance impact to individuals will be covered extensively in Chapter 6.

Even in the absence of a self-directed brokerage account option, it would be difficult to expose or prove odds in a case against fiduciaries for underperforming some superior investment alternatives. This is especially true when such active options would also introduce the risk of underperformance and, by definition, is a bet against diversification. It will always be difficult to prove an active, less-diversified investment selection as being a clearly prudent selection. This is especially true when there is complete uncertainty of the timing of when outperformance and underperformance might occur and how that might impact any individual participant. Finally, with the costs of index funds available being 0.07 to 0.25 percent, trustees and advisers have an additional defense that would be unavailable with higher expense active funds. That additional defense is that of defraying needless expenses to comply with the obligation to make sure costs are reasonable. If you are an investment manager, you need to think about this risk.

Say you manage an asset allocation fund as an alternative for a 401(k) plan that is benchmarked relative to the same balanced portfolio we used in Table 1.1. Your investment fees are 0.50 percent in the fund, about five times the fees that would otherwise easily be available in equivalent passive alternatives. Clearly, you are likely to have some environment where you will underperform. And, as a manager held to the standard of the benchmark and a named fiduciary, the environment where you underperformed might trigger some suits. *In the past you really didn't have to worry about this. But now you do.* You might be forced to rebate your management fees because it will be argued that you needlessly impaired the participant's balance. You had the choice to diversify and match your benchmark; consequently, the least you could do is rebate the revenues you received for taking a risk that was not clearly prudent and could have been avoided. This may sound like a stretch to you, but don't be surprised if such cases are made in the future. There are a lot of attorneys out there and a myriad of judges and juries who might hear such cases.

So, the self-directed brokerage account that permits participants to make such bets to achieve better than benchmark results by *their own choice* does remove any material risk to fiduciaries that offer passive alternatives as the standard default investment options, at least from the perspective of the unlikely case against them for not picking investments that outperform. Avoiding the risk of underperforming is probably a winning case in the first place. The self-directed brokerage account alternative merely adds suspenders to the belt holding up your fiduciary pants. But, many fiduciaries are concerned that offering a self-directed brokerage account option introduces additional risks to them as trustees. What if participants day trade individual stocks? What if they pick poor investments? What if they do not know what they are doing? What if they trade away all of their assets? Aren't I at risk for enabling this?

You could be at risk for the actions participants take in a self-directed brokerage account, if you encouraged, promoted, or touted in educational sessions the use of the self-directed brokerage account. To mitigate this risk, all that is needed are proper disclosures and comments in educational content and enrollment materials. The provider of the brokerage account already incorporates significant disclosures, too, which help you in limiting your exposure to liability. As long as your default or primary investment alternatives are not overly expensive (if they are, it would encourage use of the brokerage account), as long as all of your standard investment options meet the clear prudence standard of avoiding the risk of material underperformance (introducing one variant on this might be deemed as endorsing taking such risks), and as long as you constantly communicate that the brokerage account is risky, you will have little risk from participants who elect the brokerage option, and in my experience very few do.

Action Steps to Prevent Needless Liability from Pillar #2 for Trustees, Sponsors, Advisers, and Product Vendors

The action steps that fiduciaries should take to avoid needless liabilities from the second pillar (avoid risk of large losses to prevent fiduciaries from exposing themselves to a liability they can easily avoid) are as follows:

- **Make sure your Investment Policy Statement acknowledges your recognition of the risk of underperforming.** Amend your investment policy to recognize the risk of material underperformance any individual participant may be subjected to in the attempt to outperform benchmarks.
- **Offer a self-directed brokerage account to document flexibility.** Add a self-directed brokerage account option for up to 100 percent of any participant's balance, and make sure disclosure is adequate.
- **Review any and all educational materials provided to participants.** Make sure educational materials and other information are balanced in content and do not artificially overweight past performance relative to the future uncertainty. Make sure they clearly disclose that attempting to outperform any benchmark introduces a risk of material underperformance that could otherwise be avoided.
- **Use low-cost passive alternatives for investment options.** For passive alternatives that are offered, make sure the expenses are competitive for what is available in the market and do not have needless 12b-1 or administrative expenses.

- **Accommodate everyone's needs, but protect yourself in default selections.** Through flexibility and choice, accommodate the perspective of what any one participant might desire, yet avoid responsibility for making bets on specific investments you might otherwise be responsible for making from the perspective of clear prudence standards.

As a fiduciary, if you are balanced and objective in your actions, you can avoid introducing risks for personal preferences or philosophies. Accommodating broad choices, while avoiding needless risks, is the safest way to protect your actions from the new perspective of fiduciary standards that will emerge from the impairment of individual plan balances.

Chapter 4

Pillar #3: Costs Are Reasonable for the Services Being Provided

Participant-directed plans like 401(k) plans and profit-sharing plans have escaped the scrutiny of costs that defined benefit plans have for the use of soft dollars. According to a Government Accountability Office (GAO) report commissioned by Congressman George Miller (D–CA),[1] the Department of Labor received only *10* complaints about fees in 2005. At the time, with *47 million participants*, you would think that maybe a few more complaints would have been triggered.

Boston College also provided a study that stated, "*The bottom line is that over the period of 1988–2004, defined benefit plans outperformed 401(k) plans by one percentage point.*"[2]

With no less than three bills pending in the House and the Senate, and the DOL working on proposals for better participant level disclosure; this will not go on forever. Even though the DOL attempt at new regulations in 2008 appears to be dying on the vine in 2009, one day it is likely that better participant disclosure will occur.

Should 401(k) Plans Cost More?

When you think about it, it is rather ironic that defined benefit plans have better control over costs than 401(k) plans. After all, defined benefit plans require costly actuarial certifications and calculations that 401(k) and other defined contribution plans do not need. The impact to the participant in a defined benefit plan of excessive costs is negligible because excessive costs increase the funding by the plan sponsor and have no effect on the participant's ultimate benefit. So it appears as though the regulatory enforcement for defined benefit plans has lowered employer costs and provided essentially zero benefit for participants.

In defined contribution and participant-directed retirement plans, though, where the participant bears the burden of excessive costs and there is no impact on the employer, costs for mutual funds in 401(k) plans have not kept pace with the decline in costs for mutual funds overall. According to a report by the Investment Company Institute (ICI),[3] in the case of money market funds, in 1996, 401(k) money market funds averaged 0.09 percent less expenses than money market funds overall, but by 2005, they actually exceeded the costs of money market funds overall! How could the cost of what was supposed to be an institutional buyer in the form of a 401(k) trust end up costing more than the generic retail product in the overall marketplace? Over this same period, fund expenses for equity funds overall declined by 0.11 percent (from 1.02 to 0.91 percent), while for 401(k) plans, the fees only declined by 0.08 percent (from 0.84 to 0.76 percent). These are not simple averages; these are dollar-weighted averages, so billion-dollar trusts with massive negotiating leverage count in these figures 1,000 times more than those of million-dollar trusts. Imagine what the expenses must be for the typical 401(k) plan of the 600,000 that exist, mostly with lower balances than a billion!

While the DOL, House, and Senate work to expose some of the hidden costs to sponsors and participants, as a trustee, fiduciary, or product vendor, you would be prudent to act sooner.

54

Pillar #3: Costs Are Reasonable for the Services Being Provided

The ERISA language on fees was not all that strong. ERISA was drafted with the notion that fiduciaries are experts and thus wouldn't waste money in the trust. It was probably also written in the context of defined benefit plans where sponsors had a big incentive for saving costs. Essentially, all ERISA required was that costs be reasonable in relation to the services provided. In fact, what is happening with retirement plans is not too dissimilar to what happened in the 2008 financial crisis. Wall Street, banks, insurance companies, and financial consultants all profited from the short-term opportunity of exploiting unethical activities, some at the encouragement of the government in the name of social engineering, others from a blatant disregard for rules and regulations. But in almost all cases there existed a complete lack of ethics and integrity. It wasn't just mortgages and real estate deals that swindled investors. Sophisticated asset allocation models that were supposedly super diversified with "non correlating" assets suddenly had much more risk than a simple 60/40 blend of stocks when all of the invented asset classes correlated quite well in a market meltdown . . . the very thing the expensive asset classes were supposed to protect you from. Auction rate notes were hustled as being the same as cash with an extra 1 percent return, until they became illiquid. Madoff's $50 billion Ponzi scheme based on a track record of what is now known to be completely fictitious added fuel to the hedge fund popularity and all the safety of those hedges have left investors with huge losses. Every week we hear of another hedge fund that was really just another Ponzi scheme. Participants in retirement plans have become victims too when fiduciaries succumb to the smooth-talking polish of the product wholesaler, well dressed consultant, or friendly smiling insurance agent. ERISA was meant to prevent this, but until now, it has not been very effective. It isn't that the regulations are insufficient, the intent is there in ERISA. There are two causes. One is a fundamental lack of ethics and integrity while focusing on short term profits and commissions throughout the financial services industry. If 2008 hasn't awakened trustees to caveat emptor principals then nothing will. The other reason these slimy financial creatures can creep into participants' wallets is that the regulations that are currently in existence are not effectively enforced.

To date, this weak language in ERISA has prevented many potential lawsuits. What's reasonable? How do you evaluate the level of services? If there are *some* other plans paying more, does that make my expensive plan "reasonable"? The DOL has been pondering how to provide clarity on this but little has resulted in concrete rules or regulations. In one fell swoop, though, a Supreme Court ruling created the potential for 100 million or more litigants, and that will force a solution to this problem, regardless of whether the DOL or Congress acts.

In Chapter 2, we discussed what steps must be taken to protect yourself from needless fiduciary liability under Pillar #1 regarding sole benefit. We examined how sweeping changes are required to survive the assault of an army of litigants by unbundling and exposing fees. We looked at how to avoid subjecting participants to expenses for services they are not using and documenting prudence in both regular evaluation of costs and the rationale as to why higher costs might be justified if selected.

Keep in mind that the language of ERISA does not require the lowest cost. It *does* require that costs be reasonable for the services being provided. Here is where each individual participant as a potential plaintiff will dramatically change the landscape.

In the past, fiduciaries have successfully defended against lawsuits based on costs by demonstrating that the costs are in line with the industry. ERISA doesn't require lowest costs, just reasonable costs, and with the source of the higher costs being active bets against policy benchmarks, it was hard to prove the impairment to all participants combined. Yet under the 2008 Supreme Court ruling, a mountain of individual cases (brought to a plethora of different judges) will start to expose and create new case law that adds some meat to the reasonableness standard.

You will still not be required to have the lowest-cost plan under this perspective of ruling. But, if you haven't evaluated your costs in a couple of years, if your index funds are 5 to 10 times the expense of what is available in the marketplace, if your administration fees are bundled within product expenses and are costing participants $10,000 a year where essentially the same services are available for $2,000 to

$3,000 a year, and if all participants are bearing advice costs for services regardless of whether or not they use them, be prepared to become a defendant in a suit.

Action Steps to Prevent Needless Liability from Pillar #3 for Trustees, Sponsors, Advisers, and Product Vendors

Many of the actions to prevent needless liabilities from product selections have already been outlined throughout the first three chapters. PAY ATTENTION TO THEM! But, when it comes specifically to the third pillar of retirement plans (making sure your expenses are reasonable under the context of potentially new guidelines of the impairment of individual plan balances), fiduciaries should make sure they execute the following steps:

- **Put your plan up for bid annually.** There is no need for you to meet with salespeople pitching their wares and investment mysticism. Many vendors are happy to provide quotes to you with very basic information, often over the Internet. Trustees should do this regularly and maintain documents of the actions. It is not imperative that the lowest-cost vendor is used, but it is important that if a higher-cost vendor is used, documentation should explain the rationale of the trustees for using a higher-cost vendor. If sound rationale cannot be created (saying the insurance agent is a nice guy won't cut it), then perhaps it would be prudent to switch to a lower-cost vendor.
- **Go to www.retirementripoff.com/plansponsors.htm.** My company offers a free fee research tool over the Internet for plan sponsors. We search the marketplace for the lowest-cost alternatives and provide a custom competitive marketplace quote for your plan by simply completing an easy form over the Internet. At a minimum, this will expose to you what some of the lowest-cost

vendors are offering and can be used as negotiating leverage with your current vendor(s). The pricing estimate is provided to you in the standard DOL-suggested full-fee-disclosure format.

- **Require all vendors to submit standard DOL fee disclosures annually.** As a matter of policy, you should require all vendors to complete the fee disclosure forms suggested by the DOL. Any vendor unwilling to do so has obviously got something to hide. Part of the free fee compliance kit on www.retirementripoff.com is a form letter you can use with existing vendors, along with a blank DOL-suggested format fee disclosure form for them to complete.

- **Require vendors to fully and conspicuously disclose their costs to participants.** Although legislation and proposed DOL rules may make some of these disclosures a mandate, from an ethical perspective it is up to you as a trustee (or a vendor of products) to act with the ethics and integrity expected of you as a fiduciary. All participants should be fully and easily aware of their expenses. It is your obligation to provide it. Hiding costs in fine print in documents that are difficult or impossible for participants to acquire will not survive the scrutiny forthcoming from trial lawyers waiting to pounce on you.

Although fees are not the only thing to consider, they are certainly one of the four pillars in the foundation of ERISA that explicitly require fees to be reasonable for the services being provided. It is easy to comply with best practices and lowest costs, as well as to document your prudent actions to help strengthen this key pillar holding the future of your participants' financial shelter.

Even if future guidelines from new regulations come from Congress or the Senate, or if the DOL revises their previously proposed rules and finally ends up adopting them, and presuming your vendors comply, since the participants in your plan bear the burden of expenses, in most cases the ethical actions (regardless of legal obligation or liability) would require you to act with the care and diligence of one familiar with these matters.

Chapter 5

Pillar #4: Diversification Rule Applied to Participant Direction

Diversification has long been a key tenant of ERISA. Most investment policy statements dictate that "the assets will be diversified so as to minimize the risk of large losses," effectively copying the language right out of the ERISA regulation. Some investment policy statements go even further and include language stating, "unless it is clearly prudent to do otherwise."

But as we covered earlier, measuring what constitutes a large loss is not necessarily simply a matter of charting decline in absolute value; otherwise, pensions would be invested 100 percent in T-bills. It might also be measured on a relative basis, consider the time horizon, and even assess the odds of superior or inferior results. Also, interpreting what might be *clearly* prudent is an even higher standard than the already prudent expert perspective of ERISA fiduciaries, and it requires bets against diversification to be highly defensible (*clearly* prudent).

We have also seen that many of the procedures, processes, and case law from a defined benefit perspective have not really held all that much liability for trustees, because with past law it was difficult to prove harm for all participants, and the sponsor paid the price of losing bets against diversification (or reaped the rewards of winning bets) in the form of higher contributions to maintain adequate funding levels. *All of these* dramatically change when it is a participant-directed plan, with participants having widely varying time horizons; and evolving ERISA standards become something that will be measured based on the impairment of an individual's balance.

Of course, participant-directed plans with their differing time horizons for each participant have been around for a long time. Unfortunately, the services financial advisers or consultants offer in such plans are often just minor tweaks of the standards established in the early defined benefit days. Frankly, they should have changed years ago, but there was no catalyst to do so under the liability shelter of needing the proof of a fiduciary breach to negatively affect *all* participants. This, of course, changed in February 2008, and trustees, advisers, and product vendors need to act now if they wish to avoid exposure to needless liability.

In participant-directed plans, some of the typical services consultants sell to pooled plans really are not applicable. For example, for a money purchase pension, defined benefit plan, or nonparticipant-directed profit sharing plan where retirement assets for all participants are pooled into one giant trust with one investment objective, the consultant's first step is to determine the asset allocation for the trust. Trustees are often interviewed to determine an average **risk tolerance** across the trustees. The adviser determines an overall asset allocation based on this (I'm not saying this is rational or prudent, but it is a very common practice) and then conducts manager searches for each slice of the asset allocation pie. The consultant may tactically tweak the allocation based on some sort of theoretically predictive model (over- and underweight pie slices) relative to the policy allocation and may establish how big of a bet can be made against the allocation target weights by setting up specific ranges right in the investment policy statement.

As a sample case study, say the average of the trustees' risk tolerances points to a portfolio that is 60 percent equity and 40 percent fixed. The investment policy statement may establish allocation ranges like a maximum of 75 percent and a minimum of 45 percent equity. This movement and bet against the baseline target asset allocation policy creates an opportunity for consultants to justify their fees. Someone has to create recommendations for shifts to the allocation and someone has to monitor it. Consultants using this approach are helping to justify their existence by "assisting" in the creation of an investment policy statement that creates monitoring work for them. Of course, the whole notion of conducting manager searches and due diligence on managers based on the preferences of the trustees just adds to this perception of the value of the consultant.

In a participant-directed plan though, most of these choices are in the hands of participants, not the trustees or consultant. In some cases, the consultant to a participant-directed plan might offer some generic allocation models for participants to select and even tweak the tactical allocation based on some forecast, prediction, or Ouija board for that matter. But often in participant-directed plans, consultants sell their value in the selection of the funds offered to participants, the benchmarks trustees should use to measure the selections, and monitoring the performance of the funds relative to these benchmarks.

These consulting services are going to create individual participant lawsuits under the *diversification* and *clearly prudent* tenants of ERISA and the new standards that will be based on the 2008 Supreme Court ruling.

How Many Hairs Make a Mustache?

The historical context of ERISA as it applies to diversification has thus escaped any real teeth, despite the higher "clearly" prudent standard required.

How "diversified" is diversified? Some say all you need is about 32 stocks in a portfolio to accomplish 95 percent[1] diversification, and by the time you have 60 stocks you are effectively completely diversified. This is based on some old, arcane research that did not even really measure diversification, it measured standard deviation. In fact, many in the industry have just accepted this old study as fact (it works for what they are selling), despite other papers demonstrating how misleading this study was.

For example, in a paper by Ron Surz and Mitchell Price published in the Winter 2000 edition of the *Journal of Investing*,[2] it was clearly proved that even a 60-stock portfolio leaves 12 percent of nonsystematic (diversifiable) risk on the table when one measures it by true diversification statistics like *R*-squared or tracking error. Even the original 1970 study's measure of *average* standard deviation was exposed in the Surz paper as a 60-stock portfolio having equal odds (5 percent chance) of producing standard deviations ranging from +2.7 percent relative to the entire market to −0.9 percent. According to the paper, a 60-stock portfolio has a 75 percent chance of having more volatility than the more-diversified index and 50 percent chance of producing 0.7 percent more standard deviation.

Is a 60-stock portfolio a "clearly prudent" bet? Is a 25 percent chance at less volatility worth a 75 percent chance of more?

This commonsense result has escaped being measured or pointed out in past suits against fiduciaries because of the past standards requiring proof that all participants were harmed. *Some* chance, of *some* hope, for superior results in risk or return, for *some* participants, always exists in such gambles; but was probably not the intent of ERISA. However, when the standard of proving breach was proof that *all* participants were harmed, not just some or even the majority, the breach of clear prudence was defensible. Frankly, to me, it is questionable as to how nonparticipant-directed defined contribution plans have by and large escaped the clear prudence requirement of diversification. In the face of impairment of asset values at the individual participant level, *that will no longer be the case.*

Remember in Table 1.1 (see Chapter 1) how we examined a defendable "clearly prudent" case for the short-term risk of losses in a balanced portfolio relative to the certain safety of T-bills? It illustrated that while the balanced portfolio had some chance of losses, the relative risk (odds) of producing an inferior return to T-bills dropped significantly over time, and at 10 years, T-bills appeared to have a high risk of "large losses" if measured relative to returns in the balanced portfolio (e.g., 34 percent of historical 10-year periods of producing less than 2 percent return with T-bills versus no historical 10-year period back to 1926 for the balanced portfolio).

When bets against diversification and relative returns are measured against each individual's plan balance for his or her unique time horizon, instead of the long-term life of a trust overall, the lack of any definitive evidence that it was a "clearly prudent" gamble to make will result in suits that trustees and advisers have never imagined.

Under the 2008 Supreme Court ruling, it is possible that participants will bring suits against trustees and advisers for merely having their investment materially underperform its benchmark.

As already stated, in the past, there was little risk of this because of the yardstick that was required (harm to all participants) and the eternal hope that better bets will be made in the future. But, when a fiduciary can avoid the risk of material underperformance by indexing, bets against indexing (full diversification for the asset class benchmark) can now become a liability merely because such bets introduce a risk to the impairment of any one participant's balance based on *when* underperformance occurs.

Betting Assets against the Market House

To consider the potential change in the way courts might interpret bets made by fiduciaries against diversification under the 2008 Supreme Court ruling, let us consider the same type of relative odds analysis that justified a balanced portfolio as being "clearly" prudent relative to T-bills, despite the risk of losses. To measure this in the case of bets made against diversification for selecting particular funds, we clearly will not have the 81-year history that we had for broad asset classes in the balanced versus T-bill comparison of Table 1.1. Also, we can no longer rely on the assumption of the long-term time horizon of the trust overall since each participant has his or her own time horizon, and that is our new standard for measuring our clearly prudent choices.

As potential defendants in such a fiduciary case, we could speculate on the premise of such a case brought by an individual participant for materially underperforming the benchmark. What evidence might the participant's counsel assemble? As fiduciaries making selections for investment options that might be perceived as making a bet against diversification, shouldn't we be prepared to defend our choices as clearly prudent for every participant?

For experts, clear prudence, by definition, would require that bets made against diversification would not be made if the odds were massively stacked against you. Were they?

Do you think a judge or jury would perceive the statistics in Table 5.1, brought by the counsel of a plaintiff against the fiduciaries, as a clearly prudent expert bet against the diversification of the index?

Lawsuits against fiduciaries are unlikely to come from participants where the investment alternatives performed near the benchmark. Thus, the measurement in Table 5.1 of *material* deviations in superior or

Table 5.1 Percentage of Total Domestic Equity Funds that Materially Outperformed or Underperformed the Benchmark*

		Grade >C	Grade <C	Grade = C
# Funds	Time Period	Materially Outperformed	Materially Underperformed	Within +/– 10% SD
1076	Last three years	19.80%	43.48%	36.52%
765	Prior three years	16.73%	31.37%	51.90%
799	Last six years	26.53%	53.32%	20.03%

* Based on the www.fundgrades.com database for the period ending 3/31/2008. Material underperformance or outperformance is measured as those funds whose highest correlation coefficient was the Russell 3000 (relative to 31 asset classes and greater than 0.82 or an R-squared greater than 0.67), with holdings that matched macro asset class minimums and maximums, and materiality of under- or outperformance measured by +/–10% of the standard deviation of the benchmark. For example, if the standard deviation of the benchmark was 15%, for a fund to be counted as material underperformance (grade < C), it would have to underperform the index benchmark of the Russell 3000 by 1.5% annualized, and for it to be measured as outperforming (grade > C), it would have to outperform by 1.5% annualized. A grade of C would apply if returns were within +/–1.5%. Fundgrades.com is a free web service designed for ERISA level evaluation of mutual funds and ETFs.

inferior performance being defined as returns that are +/–10 percent of the volatility of the benchmark.

As a fiduciary, if you by chance select one of the 53 percent of the alternatives that materially underperformed over the last six years, how would you defend that selection in this basic case? Does taking a 53 percent chance of underperforming justify the less than 27 percent chance of outperforming by the same amount? These odds are worse than blackjack! Would the bet being made against the full diversification of the benchmark be justifiable from the clearly prudent standard? Maybe you could defend it from the perspective of you and your adviser's research and due diligence in an attempt at risk control. You could try that, but you will likely lose.

If you and your consultant attempt to defend the case against you for imprudence (by accepting twice the odds of materially underperforming compared to outperforming per Table 5.1) on the notion that you were not seeking higher returns but instead were attempting to control risk, be prepared to defend yourself based on plaintiff's exhibit, Table 5.2. Your counsel will advise you that your defense should be based on a concern over investment risk, which is what you were attempting to control in your investment selection. As a fiduciary, you will be advised to say, controlling risk is a good thing, and the bets you made against the benchmark (which could have been easily avoided with an index fund) were meant for controlling risk, not higher returns—that is your story, and you are sticking to it! This sounds plausible; what do those odds look like, and do they make the case for the bet being a clearly prudent thing to do?

Table 5.2 Distribution of 1,076 Total Domestic Equity Funds Evaluation of Risk, Return, and Both Combined (Three Years Ending 3/31/08)[3]

Criteria	% of Funds
Return greater than material underperformance (>C–):	56.3%
Risk less than material additional volatility (>C–):	57.8%
Both risk and return greater than C– combined:	34.3%

Now what is your defense? The odds were stacked against you for superior returns. The odds of controlling risk without materially paying for it in the form of a reduction of return is a losing bet nearly two thirds of the time. Is this a clearly prudent bet against diversification?

In a last-ditch hope to defend yourself, you go back to the old standard of the long-term track record of the investment you selected (even though those results were not enjoyed by your plaintiff plan participant). This has worked as a defense in the past. But, when you are a fiduciary to a trust and the measurement of a fiduciary breach is the impairment of an individual's balance, the past track record that applied to other people's money (not the participant's balance) will be (or should be) inadmissible. The track record you used to select that fund as an offering to your participants had ZERO money from your participants in it during the track record period. What happened to a fund before you made it available is thus not germane, is not an indication of future results, and thus should be inadmissible. If you start offering a fund to your participants on January 1, 2009 based on its ten-year record as of December 31, 2008, what happened prior to January 1, 2009 had zero effect to your participants. All that matters for their balances is what happens *after* you make it available.

Besides, the choice you have, and obligation you are to deliver in your role, is to **not make bets against diversification unless they are clearly prudent**, and now that is measured by each individual participant's balance.

The plaintiff's counsel trots out the last evidence you will have to defend in your choice that cost just one participant either excessive risk or a return under your investment policy's benchmark, as shown in Table 5.3.

Unless you are an adviser who sells your value as trying to pick winners to justify your costs, you might as well just throw yourself on the mercy of the court and pull out your checkbook. A short-term large loss, relative to the benchmark, is now a valid suit under this evidence. An active fund selection that materially underperforms for two, three, or six years is now a valid suit for any one participant whose account balance is impaired during his or her tenure. How could anyone justify a bet

Table 5.3 Distribution of 1,076 Total Domestic Equity Funds Evaluation of Risk, Return, and Both Combined Relative to Low Cost Index Funds (Three Years Ending 3/31/08)*

Criteria	% of All Funds	Index Funds
Return greater than material underperformance (>C–):	56.3%	100%
Risk less than material additional volatility (>C–):	57.8%	100%
Both risk and return greater than C– combined	34.3%	100%

* An index fund matched to the investment policy benchmark (if low cost without the burden of excessive 12b-1 fees) has an effective 100% certainty of producing a return greater than materially underperforming; it also cannot produce materially more risk than the benchmark. Being completely diversified, the index has complete certainty of avoiding the risk of material underperformance or additional volatility. Grades are based on www.fundgrades.com.

against diversification with these kinds of odds and the choice to avoid all of these risks as clearly prudent from an expert fiduciary standard?

If you add to this equation the additional management, trading, monitoring, research, and consulting costs of active management, you are just asking for trouble. When you examine the standard of *clearly prudent* for any active bets against the fully diversified index and then layer on a potential additional case for the liability of not making sure the costs were reasonable in the context of the value of the services being provided, you are going to eventually become a defendant from nearly every participant in your plan. It is just a matter of time as various funds underperform at different times impacting different participants.

Just Put Me in Handcuffs, I'm Guilty!

Why, as a trustee, would you subject yourself to this risk? Forget your personal investment philosophy or your consultant's spin about how he has skill and can make up these odds that are stacked against him.

YOU are the one with *personal liability* for making these gambles. Do you get enough credit for picking winners with the aid of your skillful consultant to justify the risk you are assuming when any one participant loses money relative to the benchmark (or underperforms for some period of time)?

Of course, the consultants who say they are more skillful and can make up these odds with their skill need to say this to justify their existence (and fees).

Some consultants will indeed pick winners. It could be luck or they might be skilled, just like some people win at blackjack by luck or by skill (as in card counting). The odds against unskilled players in blackjack are nowhere near as bad as the odds against those fiduciaries who gamble against the fully diversified benchmark. In blackjack, play based on basic strategy has the house advantage at usually less than 1 percent. Skilled card counters can flip these odds to a 0.25 to 2 percent advantage over the casino. But, all it takes for the casino to fend off the advantage skilled players have over them (with these narrow odds) is to change the rules on a single deck game to pay out 6:5 on a black-jack instead of the more common 1.5:1. Doing so completely elimi-nates the advantage for the skillful player. Think about how skillful you would have to be to make up the odds in betting against diversification. Is it worth the risk? Is it clearly prudent?

Adviser consultants taking this gamble are going to be co-defendants in the suits brought against trustees. You will bring them in to help share in the blame, but just wait until you hear what they say in the court room. That adviser that claimed to be a fiduciary will show as an exhibit in their defense a contract the trustees signed that they were only a fiduci-ary in name and were not responsible for the final selection. They will testify they offered numerous choices and the poor performing one the trustees selected, and agreed in the contract was their ultimate respon-sibility for selecting, was one of many potential funds the consultant offered trustees for consideration. But, even if the advisory contract was with a section 402(a) independent fiduciary accepting full responsibility for the selection of alternatives (few do) as an adviser consultant, why would *you* take this risk of underperforming with active management? Are you trying to protect and justify excessive fees? If so, you better set aside a large legal reserve fund for the future, because those excess fees will one day be returned to the 100 million potential litigants with the army of lawyers just waiting in the wings for *any* of your picks to under-perform the investment policy benchmark.

Advisers who wish to prevent their apple cart from being upset by the 2008 Supreme Court ruling may attempt to convince their trustee clients that the evidence presented so far in this chapter on the risk of underperforming is offset by the risk that trustees may also be accepting in utilizing the fully diversified index benchmarks that have no chance of producing superior results. They will argue that while it is true that attempting to outperform introduces risks that participants may bring suits for the times the performance is below the benchmark, and such action can be avoided by indexing; there is also a risk that suits could be brought for not outperforming or not avoiding market-level risks (since there always will be some investment alternatives that do exactly that over any number of time periods). Although this may be presented to trustees in a way that infers equal odds of the choices (which is not even close to accurate), it also evades the ERISA obligation of it being a *clearly prudent decision against diversification.*

The language in ERISA regarding diversification does not require prudent fiduciaries to make bets against being fully diversified in an attempt to produce a higher return, or less risk, than the fully diversified benchmark. It requires trustees to be able to prove that if they make bets against diversification, they need to meet the criteria of an expert making a clearly prudent decision. Thus, the standard isn't that a bet against diversification is OK because it has *a chance* of being beneficial. Instead, the standard is that if you are making a bet against diversification, you need to have exceptionally compelling evidence that it is more prudent than diversifying (i.e., clearly prudent).

Could a participant win a case based on her personal plan balance being impaired because it subjected her to the risk of the benchmark and only produced a slightly (due to small expenses) inferior return to the benchmark? Let's examine that.

The participant might make the case that 20 to 35 percent of all other investment options in the universe of alternatives for the asset class performed better than the index that the trustee could have selected, but did not. If he had, the participant may have benefited. The participant might say that the trustees, by not attempting to select such better performing investments as options, and merely settling for alternatives that mirrored the benchmarks caused her personal plan balance to be impaired. She might accurately state that those other options, regularly available in the marketplace, materially improved risk, return, or both for the asset class options available to her. She would be completely correct on all these points, **but this would be a very difficult case for her to win.** As an adviser, if you are insistent on ignoring the implications of the 2008 Supreme Court ruling, and to justify your fees you emphasize the risk of not attempting to outperform and keep playing the active management game, you should be careful about overselling this sort of risk to your trustee clients lest you become the primary defendant instead of a co-defendant based on your representations to the trustees. The active management risk of underperforming is a far easier case for a participant to win against you and is clearly an easier case to win than a participant that claims you should have been able to outperform.

The same evidence used by the plaintiff's counsel for proving the impairment of an individual participant's balance for making bets against diversification could also validly be used as the defense by any fiduciary who offered (low-cost) index funds as the primary alternatives for each asset class available to participants.

If a plaintiff tried to sue on the basis that the retirement fund underperformed some active funds because it cautiously offered only index funds, your counsel's defense for such a suit would sound something like this:

ERISA requires investments to be diversified. All of our investment alternatives were completely diversified. ERISA requires any decision made by fiduciaries to be nondiversified to be a clearly prudent decision. We could not, in our policy committee meetings, draw the conclusion that even a 60 percent or 70 percent chance of materially outperforming the asset class benchmark would meet the ERISA definition of clearly prudent when doing so would also subject each individual beneficiary to a substantial risk of materially underperforming, as well, and such risk was easily avoided. We determined this in the full context of ERISA requiring us to be fully diversified unless it was clearly prudent to do otherwise. In such consideration of our obligation as fiduciaries, when we could avoid any risk of material underperformance or any risk of material additional investment risk by being completely diversified and offering low-cost index investment options that matched our investment policy benchmarks, we could not possibly deem it clearly prudent to accept any amount of such risks of either underperforming or exposing participants to additional investment risk when we could have near certainty of avoiding these risks to participants. The fact that the plaintiff would have preferred that we ignore our obligation to make such decisions that would not meet a standard of being clearly prudent, and the fact that the odds of materially better results are actually less than 30 percent per Table 5.3 in our evidence, clearly proves that we were indeed clearly prudent in our choice to comply with full diversification and avoiding the risk of large losses on behalf of each and every participant.

The case your counsel makes above for being diversified and avoiding risk is far more defensible then the case a participant might bring for material underperformance when you had an easy way to avoid material underperformance and you are required to prove that the bet against diversification that resulted in the participant's underperformance was clearly prudent.

Fooled by Labels

In participant-directed plans it is common to have investment options grouped by asset class. The selections you offer as a fiduciary cannot have your asset classification rely on merely a label offered by a consultant or even Morningstar if you are being held to the standard of an expert. The asset classifications cannot be individually analyzed against only the benchmark you are selecting for the fund. The selections you make need to be viewed in combination with portfolios, as 404(c) educated participants would use the funds. Since well educated participants would be expected to assemble diversified portfolios from the available selections, your individual selections for each asset class alternative not only need to be evaluated relative to the asset class each fund is being selected for, but also according to how the investment options might be used by a prudent participant in combination. As a fiduciary, while you still might be tempted to introduce the risk of underperformance or additional volatility, the new standard of measuring the impairment of each individual participant's balance requires that you examine the investment options you select to make sure they are truly diversified both individually *and* in combination. For example, say that for domestic equities you offered options for both small-cap and large-cap stocks in both growth and value styles. You base your selection on "proven records" and track records of at least four stars, as rated by a "reputable" rating service like Morningstar.

Let us presume for a moment that the education you provide to participants discloses the risks of not being diversified, and one of your participants diligently pays attention to this disclosure of the risk of betting on any one segment of this simple four-by-four set of style box choices.

What is popular and common is based on marketing and public relations. The advent of technology that exposes massive amounts of information also is simplified to make them consumable. These simplifications create the *fooled by labeling* problem and lead trustees to erroneous conclusions. The nature of the assets you select must be the basis of your decisions. Perhaps this is best summed up in this quote:

> For a successful technology, reality must take precedence over public relations, for Nature cannot be fooled.
>
> —RICHARD FEYNMAN, NOBEL LAUREATE

Unfortunately, this quote isn't very true when it comes to fund ratings, as public relations tend to trump *nature*. My company released FUNDGRA+DES as a free service to fiduciaries in October 2007. The system simply exposes what any prudent fiduciary would want to know before choosing a fund that he would be accountable for selecting. We used this methodology in our advisory business and then thought, "Why not publish it, since we are going through the effort of analyzing the data anyway?"

The system is designed to evaluate mutual funds and exchange-traded funds (ETFs) from an objective, market-relative benchmark perspective of an ERISA fiduciary. It measures each fund on five key criteria (an extra "pillar," if you will) that, when used in combination, show there are pluses and minuses to every fund and there is no such thing as a fund that is universally good. When it comes to being a fiduciary, you should raise the bar a bit, since an expert should be able to cope with something a bit beyond a pass or fail grade.

When we released it, and particularly after the *Wall Street Journal* mentioned the web site (www.fundgrades.com) in a cover story of Section C, I received many phone calls from financial advisers who said they "hated it," or "the grades suck." Their preference was obviously to keep the price of choices and risks hidden from their clients. Exposing those choices on the Internet, showing the public that there is always a trade-off in one form or another, was disruptive to their sales efforts. As of December 31, 2008, there were over 22,300 funds in the database and only ONE received an honor roll grade (B or better) for ALL the criteria for the last three years. The prior three years had a couple of D grades though, exposed through the system. The biggest complaint advisers gave me was comparing funds to benchmarks instead of peer groups because the grades don't look very good if you compare many funds to their passive alternative. The other thing they complained about is the topic of this chapter, diversification. How dare we expose a grade for diversification relative to the user-selected benchmark! Understand that each individual grade criterion is fairly generous, and about a third of all funds get a grade of B– or better for this grading criterion. We could ignore this measure if we wish; it is just a correlation coefficient. (When did this become an evil measure?) As we have already exposed in this chapter, for the risks fiduciaries are taking in the selection of investment options relative to individual asset class benchmarks, we will now further examine diversification from a portfolio perspective of all of those individual investment options *in combination*. If you are a participant modeling an asset allocation, a trustee evaluating the options you are offering to participants, or an adviser making recommendations to trustees or even wealth management clients, diversification is an important measure. ERISA more or less requires you to pay attention to it as well.

To examine how germane this diversification grade might be, let us examine a simple example of domestic equities. Domestic equities would include large-, mid-, and small-cap stocks in both value and growth styles. This could be just the domestic piece of an overall balanced global allocation that includes fixed income, foreign securities, and even alternative investments. To simplify it, though, we will analyze just domestic equities—the math carrying forward in any overall allocation model, too, and even moreso with assets that have less covariance than segments of domestic equities.

Of course, one could make bets on style or market cap by over-weighting such segments with a bit of a tweak here or there. If the participant was informed about the risk of making such bets in the education provided, the trustees and fiduciaries would be protected relatively well from the participant's investment elections. Asset allocation is one of the main decisions in a participant's investment election, so when it comes time to select securities to fulfill the allocation model you desire, **do you merely look at labels or do you pay attention to *the nature* of your selections** (i.e., how they actually behave relative to the asset class you are selecting for such securities)? As a fiduciary, if an educated participant chose a diversified allocation, did you consider whether the selections you offer in combination actually provide the diversification implied by the asset class labels? After all, if asset allocation is so important and is the main thing I need to consider, am I really getting any value out of my allocation modeling effort if the funds do not *behave* like the asset classes I modeled? Or, is it just the label that is important?

Imagine that a consultant tells you that you do not need to offer small-cap, large-cap, growth, or value alternatives. She suggests that if participants want domestic equity exposure, all they need is to allocate their entire domestic equity portion of their portfolio in a mid-cap blend index fund. How would you perceive this obvious contradiction to ERISA's requirement of diversification?

Might you suggest that the consultant's recommendation for all of your participants' domestic equity allocation is making a big bet and not very diversified? Would you suggest that small- and large-cap value and growth stocks should be part of the equation? Would *you* recommend in your educational content that 100 percent of the domestic equity allocation should be in mid-cap stocks? Before you answer that, make sure that you are not being *fooled by labels*.

What's wrong with a domestic equity portfolio excluding large- and small-cap stocks? Is that a risky thing to do? All one needs to do to see the effect of making such a bet is to look at a mid-cap index ETF (IJH) on www.fundgrades.com to expose the risk relative to total domestic equities, as shown in Figure 5.1.

Fund Report Card

IJH❶ - iShares S&P Mid-Cap 400 Index Fund

Selected: Total Domestic Equity

	Fund Grades					
	Overall	Diversification	Expense	Relative Risk	Return	Risk of Material Underperformance
Last 3 Years	C−	D+	A+	F	C+	C−
Prior 3 Years	B−	D+	A+	C	B	C+
Last 6 Years	C+	D+	A+	D+	B−	C

Figure 5.1   Mid-cap ETF (IJH) grades relative to total domestic equities

Here we see the impact of how investors (and many advisers) are fooled everyday by ignoring the diversification grade. **Three years ago**, that consultant touting the nondiversified (relative to total domestic equities) mid-cap ETF would have seen an honor roll grade of B for return, with only market risk of C (see "Prior 3 Years" in Figure 5.1). If all I paid attention to were the risk and return statistics (as many of those advisers might suggest), it would be easy for someone to label this fund as "total market active winner" *if* we didn't pay attention to the name of the fund or its misbehavior evidenced in the diversification grade. Surely it would be a four- or five-star total domestic equity fund! Since the correlation is irrelevant (according to those who hate having their top fund picks exposed as having some price to what is otherwise marketed as a free risk and return ride), a mid-cap index fund would receive top scores relative to total domestic equity (just as total market index funds are four-star funds relative to large-cap blends today).

As a fiduciary, you are supposed to be smarter than that. You know that there is a big bet being made by putting 100 percent of all participants' domestic equity allocation elections into a mid-cap index fund. It is easy to see that, merely by the name of the fund; we know it is 100 percent mid-cap and not very diversified. But, what if the name of the fund and its holdings do not expose this? Would a D+ diversification grade for a fund regarding which we were ignorant about such details be otherwise OK? Does the mismatch and risk only apply to ETFs?

So, as a prudent fiduciary, you proceed to design an allocation model that is more diversified relative to domestic equities. You equally weight growth and value to avoid style bets. You design an allocation that considers market cap. You make sure this is exposed in your educational content. The portfolio you model for those participants seeking diversified domestic equity exposure falls on the efficient frontier and exposes the risk of a 100 percent mid-cap allocation (see Figure 5.2).

The 100 percent mid-cap portfolio is clearly taking a lot more risk than a more diversified domestic equity portfolio.

Now that you have a model for how participants might assemble investment options into a diversified domestic equity portfolio, it is

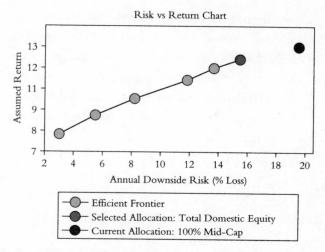

Figure 5.2 Portfolio weighted 35 percent each to large value and growth and 15 percent each to small value and growth relative to 100 percent mid-cap based on Financeware Capital Market Assumptions

time to pick investment options for our "more diversified" and "less risky" allocation, relative to that foolish consultant who suggested just using the mid-cap ETF. You pick four funds, all currently rated four stars based on Morningstar's asset classification.

With equal weights of growth and value thus equaling a market-style weighted blend, there is supposedly no style bet. Market capitalization (again, based on the label, thus ignoring the fund's correlation relative to the asset class I'm using it for) is weighted 70 percent large versus 30 percent small, so there is a bit of a small-cap tilt, but not meaningful enough to move it off the efficient frontier as we saw earlier. So, how does this portfolio of four-star winners grade relative to the asset allocation I'm educating participants to use if they are to be diversified in their domestic equity exposure? Do my combined selections lower the risk relative to that nutty consultant who suggested using just the mid-cap ETF? (See Figure 5.3.)

OUCH! I was supposed to be lowering the risk relative to that wacky consultant advising to bet 100 percent of domestic equities on mid-caps, but my portfolio grade for this blend of "four-star winners" *based on their labels* and my designed allocation ended up with a standard deviation of more than 115 percent of the asset allocation I modeled (F grade for risk), with only a touch more return (C+) for the last three years (see Figure 5.3). Isn't that what we saw on the risk versus return chart for a 100 percent mid-cap stock portfolio—a lot more risk with only a bit more return?

My 401(k) Report Card

	Portfolio Grades					
	Overall	Diversification	Expense	Relative Risk	Return	Risk of Material Underperformance
Last 3 Years	C	C+	B−	F	C+	B−
Prior 3 Years	C	C	B−	C	C	C
Last 6 Years	C	C	B−	D+	C	C+

Figure 5.3 Portfolio grades relative to the portfolio asset allocation for the asset classes for which each fund is used

In fact, if I graded the portfolio versus total domestic equities as we show in Figure 5.4 (and shown in Figure 5.1 for the mid-cap ETF), I see this supposedly more diversified and less risky portfolio had the same or higher risk in all periods and a lower return grade in all periods, versus that nutty consultant's 100 percent mid-cap allocation relative to domestic equities!

What this shows is that *neither* the portfolio you created *nor* the mid-cap ETF is behaving like the more-diversified domestic equity portfolio you modeled and educated participants about in your educational materials on asset allocation. The superior return grades for the mid-cap ETF (see Figure 5.1) *are not* representing that the mid-cap ETF is a "better" alternative for a domestic equity portfolio, *because* of the lack of diversification (D+ in all periods as shown in Figure 5.1). **Therefore, the reverse is true as well.** (Well, in reality it is true, but probably not if you are just acting as a salesperson coming up with

My 401(k) Report Card

	Portfolio Grades					
	Overall	Diversification	Expense	Relative Risk	Return	Risk of Material Underperformance
Last 3 Years	C−	C	B−	F	C+	C+
Prior 3 Years	C−	D	B−	D+	C	C+
Last 6 Years	C−	D+	B−	D−	C	C+

Figure 5.4 Portfolio grades based on the fund weightings relative to total domestic equities

misleading information to distribute the funds you are selling.) Just because a fund, or portfolio of funds, has better risk and return grades *does not* mean that it is a good selection to fulfill the asset allocation you are modeling. It might be as bad, as imprudent, as undiversified as putting 100 percent in mid-cap!

What good is your or your consultant's attempt to offer different asset classes to assemble diversified portfolios if you are using labels to give participants the appearance of diversification while in reality you are essentially putting participants who want to diversify 100 percent in mid-caps?

You may wonder how this portfolio of funds, that by labeling standards has no mid-cap stocks, ends up looking an awful lot like 100 percent mid-cap stocks. Here again, the diversification grade exposes this issue, *which is why it is important and should not be ignored.*

None of these funds in this example had a high correlation to their label as seen in Figure 5.5 (and we also see the problem with peer rankings with the DFA fund getting four stars with only market level returns and a lot more risk).

In Figure 5.5, we see that the *diversification grade* for three out of four of these funds relative to their "labeled" asset class are the same or worse than the diversification grade for a mid-cap stock ETF relative to total domestic equities (D+, which is also an obviously bad fit). *This exposes the reality* that they are not behaving like their label. In

Note: The following grades are based on the last three years of data.

				Fund Grades					
Ticker	Description	Asset Class	Overall	Divers.	Expense	Relative Risk	Return	Underper. Risk
⬤ MALHX	BlackRock Large Cap Growth Inst	Large-Cap Growth	D+	D	C+	F	C+	C+
⬤ DFUVX	DFA U.S Large Cap Value III	Large-Cap Value	C−	D	A+	F	C	C+
⬤ FVFRX	Franklin Small Cap Value R	Small-Cap Value	C	C−	C−	B−	C	C
⬤ NBMVX	Neuberger Berman SmallCap Gr A...	Small-Cap Growth	C	D+	C	C	B−	B

Figure 5.5   Individual fund grades relative to their "label"

Note: The following grades are based on the last three years of data.

				Fund Grades					
Ticker	Description	Asset Class	Overall	Divers.	Expense	Relative Risk	Return	Underper. Risk
⬤ MALHX	BlackRock Large Cap Growth Inst	Mid-Cap Growth	D+	C−	B−	D+	D+	D+
⬤ DFUVX	DFA U.S Large Cap Value III	Mid-Cap Value	C+	D+	A+	B	C	C−
⬤ FVFRX	Franklin Small Cap Value R	Mid-Cap Value	D	C−	C−	D−	C−	D+
⬤ NBMVX	Neuberger Berman SmallCap Gr A...	Mid-Cap Growth	D+	C−	C−	F	C+	C+

Figure 5.6   Individual fund grades relative to their best-fit diversification (correlation coefficient) grade

fact, most of them behave more like their mid–cap style counterparts, as shown in Figure 5.6.

The diversification grade exposes that three out of four of these funds behaved more like their mid-cap style counterparts than their asset class label. Blending them together and grading them versus the blend of their mid-cap style counterparts shows how much this portfolio of supposedly only small- and large-cap funds behaves like mid-cap stocks (Figure 5.7).

If my allocation is modeled around having a diversified domestic equity portfolio, but the funds combine into behavior that is more similar to a 100 percent mid-cap portfolio, how would I know this without looking at the correlation? The labels certainly do not expose this! *None* of them is identified as mid–cap! In fact, the labels of these funds are, at best, off track, and at the worst, are downright misleading and

My 401(k) Report Card

	Portfolio Grades					
	Overall	Diversification	Expense	Relative Risk	Return	Risk of Material Underperformance
Last 3 Years	C	B	B−	C−	C	D+
Prior 3 Years	C−	B−	B−	C−	D+	D+
Last 6 Years	C−	B−	B−	C−	D+	D+

Figure 5.7 Portfolio grades for our portfolio of large- and small-cap funds relative to their best fitting mid-cap counterparts

wrong! If you are a fiduciary, shouldn't you check out this sort of situation before you select funds? As an adviser to trustees, do you really want a participant lawsuit for neglecting this basic level of due diligence? Or, should I just feel OK about it because the labels say otherwise and **a chunk of the fund's actual holdings are not mid-cap, but a significant piece of the portfolio really is in mid-cap?** Should my enrollment and educational materials mislead participants and tell them they are diversified by style and market cap because of labels when the portfolio selections I use to implement that allocation basically have the portfolio's *nature* behaving like 100 percent mid-cap?

I understand how fund sellers do not like having their sales pitch disrupted by exposing the price of the choices that are being made. But we are advisers, not sellers. Milton Friedman said, "There are no free lunches." *We* don't wish to hide uncertainties and instead prefer to expose and disclose them.

Of course, it is easier *to sell* a fund, or portfolio of funds, if we ignore the risks and uncertainties we are introducing. Unfortunately, that is the net result of the advice many trustees receive and proceed to endorse in participant education.

Alternatively, one could expose that there are no free lunches and pay attention to the real (as opposed to labeled) asset allocation behavior and how it affects the investor's goals.

Part Two

RETURNS AND WEALTH DO NOT NECESSARILY GO HAND IN HAND—EMERGING FIDUCIARY STANDARDS

Whether you are a plan sponsor, investment manager, plan consultant, or a fiduciary in any form to a retirement plan, the steps you need to take in amending your procedures and processes are outlined in Part One to protect yourself from future liability based on the landmark Supreme Court ruling in 2008. Part Two examines the reason the Court's ruling will change the landscape in measuring your responsibilities and liabilities in years to come.

The Supreme Court's ruling explicitly stated that fiduciaries can be sued by participants for breaches by fiduciaries that caused an impairment of the participant's personal plan balances. Observe that the Supreme Court's ruling stated participant plan *balances* (measured in dollars), not *returns* (which are measured in percentages).

The wording in the ruling has profound implications because it means that in the future, breaches of fiduciaries' responsibility will be measured in wealth, not investment returns. Intuitively, and what is generally assumed, is that a higher return will produce more dollars of wealth in participants' plan balances. Yet, this oversimplified assumption ignores the dollar wealth effect (the new standard of the Supreme Court "participant balances" measure) of *when* different returns occur over a participant's life.

It may be counterintuitive that one could average a higher return but end up with less wealth, but that is a mathematically provable reality that is now the standard for measuring your liability as a fiduciary. To help you unravel the misconception of how returns and wealth are or are not connected, Part Two will peel this onion of misunderstanding in five chapters.

Chapter 6 will expose the basic wealth management contradiction in the form of easy-to-follow mathematical realities that will show you why your liability of dollars (i.e., individual participant balances) will be different than the past standards measured by investment returns.

Chapter 7 outlines the misalignment of the approach generally used today by sponsors, investment consultants, and investment managers, and contrasts the current common approaches to what will be the new standards when one is measuring wealth—the individual's plan balances.

Chapter 8 uncovers how some of the most sophisticated mathematical tools that measure probabilities of outcomes are actually working against the reality of each participant's wealth, creating false expectations and misleading information and advice. The reality that the markets will misbehave relative to the best-laid plans will highlight the need for a continually evolving plan instead of a long-term plan cast in stone.

Chapter 9 will provide you with the detailed evidence of the realities outlined in Part Two with 80 years of supporting data.

Finally, having exposed where erroneous assumptions about risk and return occur, Chapter 10 guides you to see contradictions in basic premises that will result in numerous future fiduciary breaches under the standard of each participant's personal plan balance.

If you are an adviser, trustee, or sponsor who is responsible for the wealth of the beneficiaries you serve, you need to understand your sources of liability. This part of the book will teach you how that is changing. If you are an adviser that delivers wealth management services to those outside ERISA plans, yet you still act as a fiduciary, you will need to reconsider not only how you advise ERISA plans but how to adapt your services relative to the emerging standards exposed in this book.

Wealth management is (or at least should be) much more personalized than the trust level advice and procedures advisers deliver to qualified plans. Unfortunately, the reliance on many of the practices established for defined benefit plans, now out of date, nonetheless have often carried forward even to individuals outside of the purview of an ERISA plan. I predict that both will converge in the future now that dollars of wealth (and not investment returns) have become the new ERISA standard.

Chapter 6

Exposing the Wealth Management Contradiction

There's none so blind as those who will not see.

—JUSTIN HAYWARD

I f you asked a meteorologist what the current temperature was outside and she responded, "Eight and a half inches," you would likely be more than a bit perplexed. You might think to yourself, why is she measuring temperature with a ruler? Clearly this meteorologist is an expert, certified as such with impressive credentials, so what seems to be a nonsense response must make sense somehow, at least to the expert. Or, perhaps, you might think she didn't clearly understand your question, and you repeat it, only to get a more detailed response of, "I understood your question to be the current temperature outside, and as I said before, it is eight and a half inches."

Since the dawn of the investment consulting industry, plan sponsors, money managers, mutual fund managers, and investment consultants have measured, advertised, researched, and reported investment returns.

To be specific, it has been an industry focused on *time-weighted* returns. This is the ruler the industry has been using to measure the temperature of your wealth. Why would the professionals do this? The notion is simple. According to these wealth meteorologists, *dollar-weighted* returns (i.e., a thermometer to measure the dollar temperature) are not determined by the "skill" of advisers or trustees and are "not a fair" measure of their service. Dollar-weighted returns are, according to such advisers, "outside their control," since they are determined *by clients' choices;* consequently, advisers emphatically state these returns should *not* be how THEY are measured. But, the wealth reality is that dollar-weighted returns are determined by BOTH the *client's choice* of when to make contributions (savings) or withdrawals (spending) as well as the returns. (Hmmm . . . does that sound like wealth management goals to you?)

These advisers are right that the client-specific goal choices influence wealth (dollar-weighted returns) more than the time-weighted returns they choose to use as their measurement of "effectiveness," and this is a very simple mathematical fact. But, with all the promises about achieving your dreams, about "connecting" to your goals, and providing "comprehensive" wealth management services, shouldn't "wealth managers" be taking responsibility for these choices about your goals? Instead, many financial advisers play a bait and switch game that can leave you exceeding "your" (their) return goal for your investments (or *benchmark,* as they measure it with a ruler), yet nonetheless broke, sleeping under a bridge in a cardboard box . . . next to smelly people . . . licking your meals from the remnants of discarded cat food cans.

The Bait and Switch of Market-Relative or Absolute-Return Managers

The reality is that the math behind this bait and switch return game (as a naive proxy for wealth) is quite simple to understand. As an easy example, take the **wealth result** (i.e., actual dollars one could spend) for someone saving $2,000 a year. In the first year, the market does 5 percent and your *ruler-based wealth manager* produces a hot 15 percent return on your portfolio and tells you that your wealth temperature is quite cozy, as evidenced by beating "your benchmark" by 10 percent. Your account after the first year is worth $2,300, so you proceed to add another $2,000 *as you had planned, and a comprehensive wealth adviser would know,* bringing your starting value for the second year to $4,300. That next year, the market is a bit warmer and happens to produce a 10 percent return, and your adviser underperformed the market by 8 percent, with a 2 percent return. This leaves your account at $4,386.

The "good news" is that over the two years, YOU BEAT THE MARKET! Hurray! Maybe you should break out the champagne! It is hard to beat the market, and your adviser did it!

Your adviser flaunts his (time-weighted ruler-based) brilliance to you in a colorful performance report, demonstrating that your return beat your market benchmark and even exceeded your "goal-based absolute return" of 8 percent, as shown in Table 6.1. The dollar values of these "better" results are shown in Table 6.2.

Clearly you hired the right adviser! Or did you? Should you consider breaking out the Champagne of Beers®[1] instead of the real thing? *Isn't your "wealth manager" supposed to be managing your wealth?* Did this superior return result in more wealth? If not, what are you paying the wealth manager to do? Try going to a grocery store and spending a time-weighted return. Let's examine *how much wealth* this simple example has after two years by looking at Table 6.2.

Simple question to you: **Would you prefer to have more money** yet only equal (the time-weighted) return of the market, or **would you rather have less money** but be able to boast to fools

Table 6.1 Sample Performance Report Since Inception Returns

Market benchmark return	7.47%
Absolute return goal	8.00%
Your account	8.30%

Table 6.2 Simple Difference between Wealth Result and Returns

	Your Account	"Your Benchmark"	Absolute 8% Return
Starting value	$2,000	$2,000	$2,000
% return year 1	15%	5%	8%
Year 1 return in $	$300	$100	$160
Year 1 ending value	$2,300	$2,100	$2,160
Year 2 contribution	$2,000	$2,000	$2,000
Year 2 starting value	$4,300	$4,100	$4,160
% return year 2	2%	10%	8%
Year 2 return in $	$86	$410	$332
Year 2 Ending Value	*$4,386*	*$4,510*	*$4,492*
Average return	8.50%	7.50%	8.00%
Compound return	**8.30%**	**7.47%**	**8.00%**
Growth of $100	**$117.30**	**$115.50**	**$116.64**

who do not understand basic math that you beat your adviser's market benchmark (which he keeps insisting is "your" benchmark)?

Be careful who you show this example to, because there is a high likelihood that a ruler-based wealth manager will be defensive about how this simple mathematical fact is "flawed" because it doesn't consider the risk (even though the compound return really does consider risk, as evidenced by the growth of $100 that has opposite wealth results versus *this particular investor's* wealth plan, and the higher-returning *zero-risk* 8 percent absolute return produced less wealth, too.) This simple example is what happened after only two years, but does this mathematical fact of the impact of dollar-weighted returns on actual wealth hold true over longer time periods?

Let's take an 80-year track record of lower returns and higher risk and see where the wealth ends up, to give you some ammunition if your wealth temperature ruler manager tries to play this game.

Here is the case. A 21-year-old begins with a $2,000 contribution to her investments in 1926. Each year, she adjusts the contribution for 3 percent inflation. At age 65, she retires and begins withdrawing a $90,000 annual inflation-adjusted income from the accumulated wealth. Her blood pressure runs out at the ripe age of 100. Based on her risk tolerance, a portfolio asset allocation target of 75 percent stocks and 25 percent bonds is selected and rebalanced annually. Which portfolio would you choose, if you had these actual 80-year records to look at **in advance?** See Table 6.3.

Many advisers will sell you on how they are controlling risk. Notionally, in the (time-weighted) market-relative return world of ruler-wielding wealth managers, reducing the risk improves the compound return, as is demonstrated by the "odd manager" in Table 6.3. Since such advisers evade taking responsibility for your wealth and choose to judge themselves by the meaningless return and risk numbers, they tell you this higher-compound return is a good thing and attempt to convince you that it is the way they should be measured. But what if in *your* wealth plan, achieving this "improvement" actually *reduces* your wealth? Would you care? Or, would you still congratulate him (and perhaps yourself for picking him), despite having less money?

By the way, many advisers, in an attempt to at least theoretically accomplish such microscopic and imperceptible improvements in your risk, will sell you all sorts of expensive and illiquid investments (generally known as *alternative investments*) that introduce a lot of uncertainty and happen to pay your adviser very well, too. That's not the reason they say they suggest them, though—it is purely in your risk-reduction interests. Regardless, you will observe that there is a benefit of the slightly lower risk (as measured by standard deviation) and a slightly higher compound return, and thus a bit more growth of an assumed $100 investment. **But a $100 one-time investment isn't what our sample investor is doing.** That probably isn't what you or any of your retirement plan participants are doing, either!

Table 6.3 Two Return Scenarios

	Odd Manager	Even Manager
Average return	11.35%	11.35%
Risk (standard dev.)	15.31%	15.56%
Compound return	10.24%	10.22%
Growth of $100	$243,488	$241,037

Like most people, she is saving toward retirement and then spending during retirement. She isn't just doling out $100 in the beginning and forgetting about it for 80 years. She has goals like a retirement income, and a savings plan that enables that income.

The Reality

The odd and even managers are nothing more than the actual 80-year record of a 75 percent stock and 25 percent bond blended portfolio, rebalanced annually, that outperforms this benchmark by 0.75 percent over the entire time period. The managers just do it in different years. The odd portfolio outperforms by 3 percent in odd years, and underperforms by 1.5 percent in even years. The reverse is true for the even portfolio. Both have the same average return. The compound return, and thus the growth of $100 for the odd manager, happens to be a bit better than the even manager because of the slightly lower risk, the value so many of ruler-wielding return managers seek and claim is their supposed value in their sales pitches to investors.

But, since this 21-year-old had specific goals, and since her wealth manager was supposedly advising about her specific goals, and since he had clairvoyant knowledge of what would happen for the next 80 years with this portfolio, **could he make the most of her WEALTH?**

The slightly "better" odd manager had this poor woman broke the last year of her life. Imagine being elderly and bankrupt. The "worse" manager with the slightly higher risk and lower compound return met her cash needs throughout her life and left an estate of $214,885 to boot. **Which do you think she would prefer? Which would you prefer?**

Now, many advisers will say they cannot control and manage "when" (e.g., odd or even years) their superior results will occur. That is exactly the point I am attempting to convey. If the *timing* of returns matters to actual wealth and the timing is uncontrollable, then why focus on achieving something that doesn't create wealth? Yet, they chant, "We are long-term investors," and, "It is critical you stick with your long-term plan." **If THAT is what your adviser says, he is admitting that he is not managing your portfolio to produce superior wealth, but is instead attempting to produce returns that may *cost you* wealth, but may be *defendable* as superior.**

Now, what if your wealth manager really managed your wealth instead of potentially meaningless return numbers? Is that possible, or is managing your wealth something that is outside of the adviser's control, as so many have posited in the past? If your adviser holds himself out as a wealth manager, should he take responsibility for actually doing so? This *is not* impossible if your adviser takes responsibility for really managing wealth and crafts advice about the best wealth (as opposed to return) decisions for you. Chapter 7 will expose you to the millions of dollars of potential benefit that may come from managing wealth, as opposed to returns.

Table 6.4 Supporting Data for Odd and Even Managers

INPUTS:

Starting Value:	$2,000
Savings to Age 65:	2000
Retirement Income:	$(90,000)
Inflation Adjustment:	3.0%
"75/25 Alpha	0.75%

		Average Equity Exposure:	75%	75%		
		Portfolio:	Odd$	Even$	Odd %	Even %
Contribution (Withdrawal)	Age	Starting Value:	$2,000	$2,000		
$2,000	21		$4,261	$4,171	13.06%	8.56%
$2,060	22		$7,504	$7,576	27.75%	32.25%
$2,122	23		$12,322	$12,080	35.94%	31.44%
$2,185	24		$13,730	$14,047	−6.31%	−1.81%
$2,251	25		$14,060	$13,700	−13.99%	−18.49%
$2,319	26		$11,516	$11,897	−34.58%	−30.08%
$2,388	27		$13,796	$13,638	−0.94%	−5.44%
$2,460	28		$21,698	$22,092	39.45%	43.95%
$2,534	29		$25,136	$24,552	4.17%	−0.33%
$2,610	30		$36,795	$37,105	36.00%	40.50%
$2,688	31		$50,228	$48,960	29.21%	24.71%
$2,768	32		$39,244	$40,526	−27.38%	−22.88%
$2,852	33		$53,044	$52,861	27.90%	23.40%
$2,937	34		$55,622	$57,818	−0.68%	3.82%
$3,025	35		$56,646	$56,162	−3.60%	−8.10%
$3,116	36		$54,058	$56,149	−10.07%	−5.57%
$3,209	37		$67,397	$67,354	18.74%	14.24%
$3,306	38		$83,257	$86,237	18.63%	23.13%
$3,405	39		$101,868	$101,510	18.26%	13.76%
$3,507	40		$132,249	$136,366	26.38%	30.88%

41	$3,612	$132,155	$130,020	-2.80%	-7.30%
42	$3,721	$139,852	$143,503	3.01%	7.51%
43	$3,832	$154,296	$151,767	7.59%	3.09%
44	$3,947	$178,572	$182,539	13.18%	17.68%
45	$4,066	$230,780	$227,602	26.96%	22.46%
46	$4,188	$273,284	$279,821	16.60%	21.10%
47	$4,313	$324,558	$319,626	17.18%	12.68%
48	$4,443	$324,347	$333,869	-1.43%	3.07%
49	$4,576	$468,840	$467,446	43.14%	38.64%
50	$4,713	$576,743	$596,076	22.01%	26.51%
51	$4,855	$626,650	$620,671	7.81%	3.31%
52	$5,000	$583,855	$606,261	-7.63%	-3.13%
53	$5,150	$794,525	$797,538	35.20%	30.70%
54	$5,305	$858,376	$897,499	7.37%	11.87%
55	$5,464	$917,842	$919,040	6.29%	1.79%
56	$5,628	$1,099,041	$1,141,824	19.13%	23.63%
57	$5,797	$1,081,149	$1,071,628	-2.16%	-6.66%
58	$5,970	$1,260,224	$1,297,402	16.01%	20.51%
59	$6,150	$1,472,708	$1,457,590	16.37%	11.87%
60	$(90,000)	$1,501,892	$1,551,142	8.09%	12.59%
61	$(92,700)	$1,358,497	$1,336,283	-3.38%	-7.88%
62	$(95,481)	$1,490,346	$1,524,548	16.73%	21.23%
63	$(98,345)	$1,577,248	$1,547,096	12.43%	7.93%
64	$(101,296)	$1,348,785	$1,390,684	-8.06%	-3.56%
65	$(104,335)	$1,382,291	$1,365,891	10.22%	5.72%
66	$(107,465)	$1,432,612	$1,475,804	11.41%	15.91%
67	$(110,689)	$1,587,271	$1,572,053	18.52%	14.02%
68	$(114,009)	$1,293,195	$1,350,445	-11.34%	-6.84%
69	$(117,430)	$976,245	$963,892	-15.43%	-19.93%
70	$(120,952)	$1,132,156	$1,159,676	28.36%	32.86%
71	$(124,581)	$1,280,422	$1,262,389	24.10%	19.60%

(Continued)

Table 6.4 (Continued)

Contribution (Withdrawal)	Age	Odd$	Even$	Odd %	Even %
$(128,318)	72	$1,068,410	$1,108,362	-6.54%	-2.04%
$(132,168)	73	$1,030,174	$1,023,763	8.79%	4.29%
$(136,133)	74	$1,031,601	$1,070,403	13.35%	17.85%
$(140,217)	75	$1,183,244	$1,184,856	28.29%	23.79%
$(144,424)	76	$1,005,477	$1,060,362	-2.82%	1.68%
$(148,756)	77	$1,121,475	$1,143,096	26.33%	21.83%
$(153,219)	78	$1,161,564	$1,238,350	17.24%	21.74%
$(157,816)	79	$1,133,894	$1,163,558	11.20%	6.70%
$(162,550)	80	$1,285,448	$1,375,689	27.70%	32.20%
$(167,427)	81	$1,383,309	$1,430,268	20.64%	16.14%
$(172,449)	82	$1,254,420	$1,367,220	3.15%	7.65%
$(177,623)	83	$1,291,711	$1,362,311	17.13%	12.63%
$(182,951)	84	$1,437,371	$1,587,236	25.44%	29.94%
$(188,440)	85	$1,292,814	$1,375,829	3.05%	-1.45%
$(194,093)	86	$1,425,513	$1,591,425	25.28%	29.78%
$(199,916)	87	$1,375,992	$1,487,794	10.55%	6.05%
$(205,913)	88	$1,291,197	$1,479,791	8.80%	13.30%
$(212,091)	89	$1,113,898	$1,240,982	2.69%	-1.81%
$(218,454)	90	$1,238,214	$1,460,250	30.77%	35.27%
$(225,007)	91	$1,271,139	$1,473,716	20.83%	16.33%
$(231,757)	92	$1,365,004	$1,685,791	25.62%	30.12%
$(238,710)	93	$1,494,682	$1,826,182	26.99%	22.49%
$(245,871)	94	$1,455,686	$1,915,246	13.84%	18.34%
$(253,248)	95	$1,192,467	$1,562,693	-0.68%	-5.19%
$(260,845)	96	$819,500	$1,225,238	-9.40%	-4.90%
$(268,670)	97	$473,162	$785,310	-9.48%	-13.98%
$(276,731)	98	$291,939	$702,433	20.19%	24.69%
$(285,032)	99	$43,253	$473,244	12.45%	7.95%
$(293,583)	*100*	*$(249,057)*	*$214,885*	2.94%	7.44%

96

Chapter 7

Comparing Approaches— Managing Wealth versus Managing Return

Receiving a million dollars tax free will make you feel better than being flat broke.

—DOLPH SHARP

What is the difference between managing wealth (the future standard for measuring fiduciary liability) and managing returns? Chapter 6 highlighted the basic contradiction between making the most of (and managing) one's wealth versus seeking various time-weighted, risk-adjusted market-relative returns that so many investors and advisers mindlessly chase. We showed a simple example of how lower returns and higher risk can result in more money (wealth), and also how such timing could play out over an 80-year time horizon with "superior" returns merely alternating between odd and even years. We posited the notion that a real wealth manager should really be focused on managing wealth instead of managing potentially meaningless risk and return numbers. We explained how many advisers who call themselves wealth managers attempt to evade their responsibility to actually manage wealth (and dollar-weighted returns) with the claim that "dollar returns are outside of my control" because savings and spending are determined by the client. Finally, we exposed how the game of *managing returns instead of dollars* enables advisers to make a defendable case for their supposed "value" even if that value ends up destroying the dollar result for the client.

With the basic evidence and mathematical proof of the difference between wealth and returns laid out in Chapter 6, we will now proceed to contrast the fundamental differences between the typical practices used by consultants and investment managers to service trustees, sponsors, retirement plan participants, and individual investors. The elements in typical wealth-advising services—including asset allocation, identification of risk tolerance, solving for savings shortfalls, and the identification of life goals, and so on—will be outlined and contrasted to true wealth management, since how these elements of "service" are normally assembled actually work to contradict wealth maximization.

Finally, we will expose that even if the future were *not* uncertain and we had the luxury of a time machine to know the outcomes of investments in advance (like the clairvoyance we assumed with the odd and even managers in Chapter 6), we will see that the very premises that serve as the foundation of typical investment advisory services often fail to produce superior wealth. If such services do not work with clairvoyance, how can one justify paying for such services with the reality of uncertainty in the future? Obviously, one should not, and if you read on, you will discover how and why real wealth management makes a real difference in wealth.

Asset Allocation

Normally, the way asset allocation is practiced by typical "wealth" (return) advisers, the focus is not really on wealth or your specific goals, but instead on the risk and return characteristics as measured on a simple risk versus return chart, notionally to create a better portfolio for your *risk tolerance*. But as we have already seen in Chapter 6, such "better" portfolios may only be "better" from the standpoint of these meaningless (but defendable) risk and return measures, and actually may end up producing *inferior wealth results.*

To a real wealth manager, though, asset allocation is set not by a risk versus return chart that ignores the real wealth effect on your goals, *but instead is based upon the impact to your wealth relative to the funding status of your unique goals.* To a real wealth manager, the main decision of asset allocation is set *to the minimum risk level necessary* to have sufficient confidence for the goals one is attempting to fund, regardless of whether the investor can "tolerate" more risk or may achieve a potentially higher return (but yet with potentially less wealth). This key premise of real wealth managers, of avoiding needless investment risks even if higher risk is tolerable, produced a huge benefit in the broad market collapse in 2008.

Pension Plans Can Be Overfunded, Why Can't You?

I realize that many in the industry say there is no way you can have too much money. Even if it is obvious to you that you do have too much money for the goals you personally value, often the industry claims that your problem is establishing a means of protecting that "excess" wealth from estate taxation. The solution they would offer is to position you in an unnecessarily risky portfolio to produce even more "excess" returns that you do not need for your goals, while subjecting you to needless risks of putting those otherwise adequately funded goals in jeopardy. Alternatively, these wealth managers will run a Monte Carlo simulation that shows you there is still a 1 percent, 5 percent, or 10 percent chance of "failure" to scare you into taking more risk than needed (without disclosing there is an 80 percent chance of leaving an estate that is 2 to 10 times greater than your estate goal).

Why is it that wealth management plans never seem to be overfunded, yet it is still possible for a pension plan? After all, isn't your personal wealth plan similar to a pension fund? If a pension plan can be overfunded (i.e., more *current* portfolio value than is likely to be needed for the liabilities of the pension—the liabilities of a pension fund are akin to your spending goals), then why can't your *wealth* plan be over-funded? Shouldn't there be a measure of this that is monitored as pension plans are? Shouldn't your wealth manager be able to tell you that if the portfolio results produce more than x dollars over the next year, you will be overfunded? Without such a measure, how could you tell when your wealth plan is overfunded?

To real wealth managers, your wealth plan *can* become overfunded, just like a pension plan can, *if* your adviser (or you) is truly managing wealth instead of optimizing potentially meaningless time-weighted returns and risk. If an adviser isn't going to advise you to adjust your wealth goals (liabilities) in the face of being overfunded, shouldn't he at least advise you to remove some investment risk from the table because you can afford to do so? This is what *should* happen in wealth management, just as it does in pension plans. Doing so is highly uncommon amongst an industry dominated by return managers who choose merely to promote themselves as wealth managers instead of acting like a fiduciary who actually delivers wealth management.

When a pension plan is overfunded, trustees of the pension may act on one or more of the several choices they have *because of the excess MONEY (wealth)* that fortunate timing of market results produced *for the liabilities (spending goals)* of the plan. Pension trustees may reduce future contributions (the equivalent to reducing how much you are saving toward your goals), they may increase the benefits of the plan (equivalent to increasing your spending or estate goals), or they may reduce the portfolio risk (because higher risk is not warranted for the liabilities of the plan), either by adjusting the portfolio allocation or by immunizing a portion of the liabilities.[1] The bottom line is that prudent fiduciaries will act on fortunate market results to reduce contributions, increase benefits, or reduce investment risk. Their actuaries help them with this calculation. Isn't this what a true wealth manager should do for investors as well?

Conversely, unfortunate timing of market results may cause a pension trust to become underfunded. In such cases, the assets of the pension trust are insufficient to confidently support the liabilities of the plan. Prudent trustees would act on this by either increasing contributions to the trust (the personal wealth equivalent of increasing how much you are saving), freezing or limiting the accrual of future liabilities (equivalent to reducing or freezing your retirement spending or estate goals or delaying a portion of these goals), or possibly changing the asset allocation of the trust to increase the potential return, thereby also increasing the risk of the portfolio. These are basic choices, and your personal wealth goals should be treated no differently than a pension plan and should consider all of these choices.

The Fallacy of Risk Tolerance in Setting Asset Allocation

In many of my writings, I have criticized the notion of identifying the pain one can bear (risk tolerance) and then implementing an asset allocation that is designed to actually *experience* that risk. This is, of course, an absurd behavior, but yet it is standard fare for many advisers. No one would rationally accept more pain (risk) merely because they can tolerate it *if* one could confidently fund the *goals he or she personally values* with a lower risk asset allocation. That's why pension plans measure whether they are overfunded! In my paper *The Efficiency Deficiency,*[2] I showed a simple example of how imperceptible the differences in actual historical returns would be for two materially different asset allocation choices with significantly different risk and return characteristics based on Center for Research in Securities Pricing (CRSP) data going back to 1926. The results are shown in Table 7.1.

Clearly most investors can "tolerate" a loss of 1.55 percent in a bad year (although there is no reason to do so if you can confidently exceed your goals with less risk than that). Historically, it would be difficult to imagine someone who could perceive the difference between

Table 7.1 Number of Historical Observations Over 80 Years of Actual History Between Two Materially Different Portfolio Allocations

	Aggressive Portfolio	More Conservative
Allocation	60% Large/40% Small	55% Large/25% Small 18% Bonds/2% Cash
Number of years in the last 80 years that performed:		
Less than –30%	3 (1930, 1931, 1937)	2 (1931 and 1937)
Less than –1.55%	20	19
Greater than +15%	38	38
Between +15% and –1.55%	22	23

these allocations over the last 80 years. When it comes to measuring risk as loss of wealth, we see almost identical results. At the very extreme, we had to go back to 1930 to incur one additional observation of a severe decline of more than a 30 percent loss in the aggressive portfolio that was not present for the more conservative portfolio. Of course, the "100 year flood" of 2008 added one additional observation. The aggressive portfolio was down 36 percent and while the more conservative allocation was down 28 percent.

The Risk Tolerance Game

Between the minor losses of 1.55 percent and the major losses of 30 percent or more that happened more than 70 years ago and just recently for one of the portfolios, various other years had losses for both of these allocations falling somewhere between these two extremes. *This* is what your adviser is often attempting to identify in your **risk tolerance.** To set your asset allocation he will attempt to identify your risk tolerance for pain *between* these two extremes. Yet these extremes are nonetheless clearly outside of your adviser's control and have almost equal chances of occurring, regardless of the asset allocation selected. Despite how useless such effort is and how unmanageable it is in reality, once the magical risk tolerance is identified, the focus moves to "optimizing" the risk and return characteristics. The supposed value becomes selecting "superior" investments, all in ignorance of the client-specific wealth goals and whether being right about any of these "superior" portfolio traits may end up destroying wealth for the unique client's circumstances.

The Wealthcare Process Applied to Over- and Underfunding

A lot of retail investors are pitched how their "wealth will be managed like institutions would manage their portfolios." Just because a pension fund looks at a risk/return chart, or uses a particular money manager, **does not mean** that the trustees of the pension would make the same decisions for your *personal pension* (i.e., your wealth plan), since your liabilities (goals) and current funding level would be different. If you think about it, and you should think often, such a pitch is a misnomer when you consider that competently managed pension trusts monitor their funded status and continuously make adjustments to their contributions, liabilities, and allocation based on their funded status.

The **Wealthcare process** conceptually turns your personal wealth management plan into your own personal institutional quality pension trust. When markets produce fortunate superior results, causing you to be overfunded, the same choices available to trustees of pension plans are evaluated and prioritized. That is, should you reduce contributions (savings), reduce investment risk, or increase benefits (spending) and/or terminal values (estate goals)? In Wealthcare, we identify the specific dollar values that would cause you to be overfunded; these values are monitored, measured, and *known in advance.* In the case of a pension plan, the trustees would weigh the relative value of all of these choices. In the case of your Wealthcare plan, you are the trustee and your adviser would counsel you on the impact of such choices to help determine your unique preferences among those choices. To learn more, contact Wealthcare Capital Management at www.wealthcarecapital.com or call and ask to speak with a Wealthcare specialist at 1-866-566-4786.

How Real Wealth Management Works

Connecting your asset allocation choices to your contributions (savings) and liabilities (spending) based on your funded status over time, instead of just a simple risk and return analysis for risk tolerance, is really how institutional pension funds are competently managed. Of course, the fund's trustees and advisers look at all of the choices, not just asset allocation. But if we were to assume that the choices to reduce contributions or increase benefits would be ignored, and all we did is shift the portfolio allocation to an efficient allocation that brings us as close as possible to our targeted 82 percent confidence level[3] whenever actual market results cause excessive over- or underfunding, **we would discover that we could really begin to manage and maximize wealth,** albeit *not returns and risk* as they are *normally* measured. But then again, wealth management's purpose is to maximize dollar wealth and one's lifestyle, not such potentially meaningless and abstract risk or return numbers. It is also how the Supreme Court has now defined the impact of fiduciary breaches.

The Real Wealth Management Effect

When one is a true wealth manager and knows in advance the current and future portfolio values where funding is either excessive or insufficient for a particular set of contributions and withdrawals, then one can observe the value to monitoring and adjusting the investment policy asset allocation based on the funded status. One can also compare the wealth result to many of the generally accepted rules of thumb that may destroy wealth by ignoring the funded status, yet produce what would normally be considered superior and defendable results.

We will use a simple case as an example for analyzing this effect. Pretend it is 1926 and a 20-year-old widow needs to generate $5,000 a year in annual income adjusted for inflation (about $50,000 in today's dollars) from the proceeds of a $100,000 life insurance policy left to her by her husband, who died in a mining accident. We will then compare the **wealth** result of five asset-allocation approaches as follows:

1. **Long-term (risk tolerance) allocation.** Asset allocation is set once to a policy that considers the long-term nature of the plan, but also heavily weighs the sensitivity to risk of the immediate annual cash needs and the widow's personal sensitivity to investment risk. The allocation is rebalanced annually.

2. **Age-based allocation (target date).** The asset-allocation investment policy is adjusted each year to a simple formula based on the equity exposure being set to 100 percent, less the person's age. This is similar to how many target date funds determine equity risk exposure. Therefore, the portfolio begins with 80 percent equity exposure (age 100 less the current age of 20) and is reduced by 1 percent each year as the person ages. Thus, at age 60 the equity exposure is 40 percent, at age 80 it is 20 percent, and so on.

3. **Stocks for the long run.** This is a 100 percent equity allocation created under the premise that given this is a very long-term plan and "equity risk declines with time," and given that equities produce superior long-term returns, then 100 percent equities is the "right" allocation. (See Jeremy Siegel's book, *Stocks for the Long Run,* McGraw-Hill, 2007.)

4. **Superior selection.** This is a portfolio that has very low risk and the same asset allocation as the long-term (risk tolerance) allocation, but superior investment selection causes it to outperform the asset allocation benchmark net of expenses by 1.5 percent a year. It also assumes there is no timing risk of when superior or inferior performance occurs, as shown in our odd and even choices in Chapter 6; the portfolio simply outperforms by the exact same amount each year. The portfolio has very low risk and very high returns relative to the other portfolios.

5. **Wealth management allocation.** This is a portfolio that begins with one of the six default Financeware portfolio allocations to have

82 percent initial confidence, but the portfolio allocation is adjusted nine times over the course of 80 years (actually, all occurring during the first 20 years because she would be excessively overfunded thereafter) based on the over- and underfunded status.* It has a relatively low return and relatively high risk, and the portfolio returns merely replicate the index result for the allocation.

All of these fictional allocation choices can be examined for our example widow from a wealth perspective. To contrast the difference between a return manager versus a real wealth manager, the first consideration would be how such a return manager would decide between these allocations, especially if the manager could know in advance what the return-based characteristics would be over the next 80 years (remember, we are deciding this in 1926). Let's presume for a moment that the financial adviser had a time machine and could see what the future portfolio results would be for a performance report for each of the portfolios. The common statistics return managers use to make their decisions based on track records in this case would actually be known future results and have no uncertainty of the future result of

---

*For purposes of the demonstration of the mathematics behind tying allocation choices to the funded status for a *particular set* of wealth goals, we use our software's six default portfolio allocations, which are 30, 45, 60, 80, 90, and 100 percent equities. *Overfunding* is defined as more than 90 percent confidence and *underfunding* is defined as less than 75 percent confidence using a Monte Carlo simulation and our capital market assumptions. This **should not** be construed to imply a track record, but instead should be viewed merely as a means of conveying the mathematical dollar effect of adjusting equity risk exposure for a *particular liability stream*, following these simple rules. It is important to note that the shifts to various portfolio allocations are completely dependent on the market's impact on a unique set of investor circumstances and that extreme market environments will cause the confidence level to fall outside the targeted range, and that range cannot be met in all years merely by adjusting the allocation. In such cases, the allocation used is the one that brings us closest to our targeted confidence level. This is why real wealth management would consider adjustments to contributions, withdrawals, timing of either of these, or terminal value in addition to the allocation choice.

Table 7.2 Clairvoyant Statistics

Allocation Choice	Average Stock Allocation	Compound Return	Risk (SD)	Growth of $100
1. Long-term risk tolerance	38%	8.29%	9.55%	$ 58,505
2. Age-based (target date)	41%	8.42%	14.43%	$ 64,172
3. Stocks for the long run	100%	10.36%	20.20%	$265,707
4. Superior selection	38%	9.80%	9.55%	$176,612
5. Wealth management	38%	8.58%	14.39%	$ 72,460

their normal track-record–based criteria, an uncertainty that would otherwise always be present. Yet, even with this clairvoyance, courtesy of the time machine, could he pick a superior approach for the wealth result for our widow? Based on Table 7.2, which would you pick?

These statistics make it pretty clear that there are only two choices that really need to be considered. To the typical return manager, if the client is sensitive to risk, the choice of allocation 4 with its consistent superior selection looks like a no-brainer choice. This must be why so many advisers attempt to produce "superior" risk-adjusted results like this portfolio. Otherwise, if the client with this long-term 80-year horizon could bear the risk of an all-equity portfolio, experts like Jeremy Siegel would argue that the higher return offered by stocks would be a better choice, as in allocation 3. It is interesting how poorly the rule of thumb of setting the equity allocation tied to age of the client, allocation 2, fares. From an efficiency perspective, it has much higher risk for barely any additional return. Isn't it nice that the Department of Labor granted this approach a special exemption from fiduciary liability for automatic selection for 401(k) plans? The 2008 Supreme Court ruling may end up trumping this DOL safe harbor.

Perhaps you are a sophisticated wealth manager and you know that all of the statistics here mean nothing, since the timing of when various returns occur might not have a relationship to any particular client's wealth result. You might know that the dollar-weighted return is what will determine the wealth outcome, that it is unique to each client's

Table 7.3 Clairvoyant Statistics Relative to Real Wealth Management

Allocation Choice	Number of Years in the Next 80 Allocation Had a Higher % Return than Allocation 5	% of Years Allocation Had Higher Return than Allocation 5
1. Long-term risk tolerance	48	60.00%
2. Age-based (target date)	39	48.75%
3. Stocks for the long run	48	60.00%
4. Superior selection	65	81.25%
5. Wealth management	NA	NA

cash flows, but that performance reports from your time machine only give you statistics based on the allocation results over the life of the plan, not on your particular client's situation of unique cash flows that would impact the dollar result. However, your time machine might be able to give you some more interesting information. Although it cannot model your particular client's choice of contributions and withdrawals over the next 80 years, it can show you whether this notion of "wealth management" and measuring funded status more frequently had higher or lower returns relative to the other choices, as shown in Table 7.3.

As a wealth manager, while you cannot model the actual results for your client based on the year-by-year returns, as would be required to understand the dollar wealth result, between the portfolio statistics in Table 7.2 and the number and percentage of years that the allocation choices outperformed the return of the wealth management approach (Table 7.3), you have some pretty compelling knowledge that should be useful, courtesy of your time machine. Only the age-based (target date) approach had more years where returns were lower than the wealth management approach. The other allocation choices outperformed the return of the wealth management approach anywhere from 60 percent to more than 81 percent of the time! Does this new useful information change the allocation choice you would select for your 20-year-old widow in 1926?

Regardless of this additional information, we probably wouldn't change our allocation choice to the wealth management allocation approach. Between the inferior risk and return statistics, and the knowledge that the returns will be higher in 60 to 81 percent of the years, we would still probably choose either stocks for the long run of allocation 3, if the investor could bear the risk of an all-stock portfolio, or attempt to produce superior results through selection, as in allocation 4 if the investor could not tolerate the risk of an all-equity portfolio. All of the other choices clearly *appear* inferior, at least if you are measuring temperature with a ruler, that is.

So, armed with this knowledge, courtesy of our time machine, it should be easy to pick a winning allocation strategy for our widow. It is merely a matter of her tolerance for risk. Correct?

The Wealth Result for the Allocation Choices for Our 20-Year-Old Widow

As you may recall, our 20-year-old widow received $100,000 in life insurance proceeds from her deceased husband and needed a $5,000 annual income stream adjusted for 3 percent inflation each year for the next 80 years. What would the result be for her unique wealth management plan for each of the allocation choices? Some of the results are shown in Table 7.4.

Nice job picking the "superior" alternatives of allocations 3 or 4! Our stocks for the long-run approach didn't run all that long, with the

Table 7.4 Wealth Results for Allocation Choices for the 20-Year-Old Widow

Allocation Choice	Wealth Result	Number of Years Wealth was Less than Allocation #5	% of Years $ Wealth was Less than Allocation #5
1. Long-term risk tolerance	Broke @ 51	78	97.50%
2. Age-based (target date)	Broke @ 50	79	98.75%
3. Stocks for the long run	Broke @ 55	75	93.75%
4. Superior selection	$1,072,678	77	96.25%
5. Wealth management	$4,878,522	NA	NA

widow being broke 35 years into her wealth management plan and another 45 years to go. The excellent risk control and superior return of allocation 4 had our widow dying at age 100 with an estate just over $1 million, which, when adjusted for inflation is about equal to the spending power of the original $100,000. To achieve this "superior" result, all one needed to do was beat allocation 1 *every single year by exactly* 1.5 percent. Good thing we had a time machine, because as we can see, if our attempts failed and all we did was equal the allocation, she would have been broke at age 51. Finally, do we need to poke any more fun at the stupidity of basing the allocation on only the person's age? It doesn't look like it makes sense from *any* perspective (return, risk, percent of years of outperformance, OR wealth!), yet age-based allocations and target date funds are growing in popularity every day because of their "simplicity." Simple stupidity!

However, look at the wealth management results of allocation 5. This superior wealth result was produced not by beating markets; it just assumes the result of the indices like all of the other allocation choices (with the exception of allocation 4, which outperforms by 1.5 percent every single year). At no time did the allocation ever beat itself! The passive allocation choice changed nine times over the course of the 80 years (actually, all in the first 20 years, because she was overfunded thereafter), not based on a risk tolerance, not based on market forecasts, but instead based on the funded status as described in note 3. Despite the allocations *never producing superior returns* to the asset classes used, despite the return being "beat" in 60 to 81 percent of the years (except for the miserable age-based allocation alternative), and despite having far higher risk and far lower return than the next best allocation choice, for this investor's wealth management goals, **the wealth management allocation choice produced four and a half times more wealth!**

Since the return manager industry is not focused on wealth, and thus it unilaterally somehow gets to choose how things are benchmarked (i.e., measuring temperature with a ruler), 80 years hence it would be able to justify costing this widow more than $3.8 million of wealth, albeit with massively superior risk-adjusted returns. To me, this is not ethical. Using an approach that produced superior returns and less risk is defensible as long as you are also willing to measure temperature with a ruler.

If you really wish to be honest, though, you would not play this risk and return game, but would focus on the client's wealth. It is what one can spend. It is what really matters. It is what many are advertising but evading. It isn't rocket science; it is merely a mathematical reality of accepting risk only when one has the capacity to do so, and removing risk when it is not needed for the liabilities, just like any competently managed pension plan does every day. It also requires that one avoid needless risks that introduce uncertainty for *when* superior results might occur. We saw the impact of that in Chapter 6 with the odd and even managers, as well as in Chapter 5 on diversification.

Many investors, plan sponsors, and even advisers that should know better have bought into and accepted what return managers and the product vendors promote and sell. They toss aside the wealth result in ignorance of simple, yet meaningless, risk and return numbers. They become victims of return or risk control product peddlers and wholesalers, merely because they don't know the difference between *real* wealth management and return managers. They are fooled, because it is easy to fool them with the industry promoting a standard that is meaningless to the investor's wealth, yet very profitable for the adviser's and product vendor's wealth. This may be generally accepted. It may be commonplace. It may be legal. To me, though, it is unethical to build a business around creating victims by preying on their ignorance. Ethically managing wealth should be the future of financial advising if that is the value an adviser purports to deliver.

Chapter 8

Market Misbehavior: Over- or Underfunding Investor Goals

If one advances confidently in the direction of his dreams, and endeavors to live the life which he has imagined, he will meet with a success unexpected in common hours.
—HENRY DAVID THOREAU

In Chapter 6, we showed some simple examples of the effects of the difference between time-weighted (return manager) returns and dollar-weighted (wealth manager) returns. Chapter 7 scrutinized a real-life investor example and demonstrated how some of the "best" generally accepted and even clairvoyantly "successful" approaches of asset allocation ended up costing a widow investor millions of dollars of wealth. It even showed how over 80 years of actual historical results, a wealth management approach with higher risk and a lower time-weighted return that only equaled the performance of the asset classes used, ended up producing millions more in wealth than an approach that exceeded the market benchmark returns by 1.5 percent a year with less risk.

Matching the main decision of asset allocation policy to your funded status, removing needless investment risks when you are overfunded *for your goals* due to strong market results (we call this overfunded status the "sacrifice zone" because you are needlessly sacrificing either by accepting unnecessary exposure to investment risk, or sacrificing goals you could otherwise confidently fund) is a key decision that is normally evaded or simply ignored by return managers who shamelessly advertise themselves as wealth managers. Likewise, accepting additional investment risk *only when needed* to compensate for an underfunded status due to poor market results (we call this the uncertainty zone because the confidence level is insufficient for the goals one is funding) is the *only* proper time to accept a portfolio that may expose you to your tolerance for risk, or maybe even more.

Return Managers Abusing Monte Carlo Simulation

The very mathematics *real wealth managers* use to measure funded status are manipulated by return managers and assembled into misleading presentations. Monte Carlo simulation has come in vogue for such return managers, generally under the packaging of measuring or increasing one's odds of success of supposed "wealth management plans" defined in the way return managers like to define it (i.e., measuring temperature with a ruler), which is often a plan to scare you into sacrificing your lifestyle. Notionally, measuring such odds of success should give the consumer some confidence in the adviser's advice. Calling it *odds of success* is very misleading because the goals as they are normally modeled have almost *no chance* of working out as planned. How can something that has such high odds of success have almost no chance of working out as planned?

Such odds assume that the investor and adviser *never* pay attention to what is happening to the funded status over the *entire* planning horizon. Ask yourself this: Would you change your savings rate, spending rate, asset allocation, or estate goals if your portfolio declined by 50 percent over the course of the next two or three years and your new confidence level based on this current portfolio value dropped to only a 25 percent chance of success? Of course you would! You would shrink, delay or freeze goals, increase the potential return by accepting more risk, increase the contributions you are making toward savings, or choose among any of the other options you might have. You might even delay buying that new Lexus for an extra year. Long-term Monte Carlo (or geometric mean) confidence levels (or odds of "success") **assume you would not change anything.**

Would Something Change in Your Life if You Had an Extra Million or Two?

Likewise, if your portfolio doubled in just a few years, wouldn't you consider spending a bit more? How about reducing the investment risk you are taking, or how much you are contributing to savings? Might you increase your gifting to charity or your kids if you had a spare million or two? How Monte Carlo simulations, with their typical odds of success, are normally run assume you would ignore the fact you had millions more and would do nothing in response to that excess wealth. *That* is clearly something to have confidence in, isn't it? NOT!

The root of this problem stems from the history of the financial planning industry. For decades, what planners have attempted to do is plan your financial future. In the old days before Monte Carlo or geometric mean simulations were used, it was easy for a client to see that the planner's projections were completely unreliable. The old versions would project out how much money a client would have 20 to 30 years hence as an exact dollar amount, based on a simple return assumption. But, all it would take would be a bad year or two to expose to the client that the planner couldn't forecast what the portfolio would be worth next year, yet alone 30 years from now. Just put yourself in the shoes of a client starting with $1 million and planning on retiring in a few years based on the advice of such a planner at the beginning of this decade. The planner would have shown you that your $1 million would grow to $1,259,712 over the next three years based on a conservative 8 percent assumption. The reality of the bear market turned your $1 million balanced portfolio into $877,707. Now it is time to retire! Oops! Where am I going to come up with that missing $382,000?

Such planners rapidly adopted Monte Carlo (and geometric mean) "odds of success" simulators. The *odds of success* such engines demonstrate that there is a wide range of potential outcomes. Take our 20-year-old widow from Chapter 7 as an example.

In Figure 8.1, we see *the bottom half* of the trials that were run for our 20-year-old widow based on our initial advice in 1926. Table 8.1 shows the range of ending values in deciles.

So, we see in these results that our widow with 83 percent initial confidence (or the idiotic notion of "odds of success"), assuming NOTHING EVER CHANGES, would have about equal chances of being broke

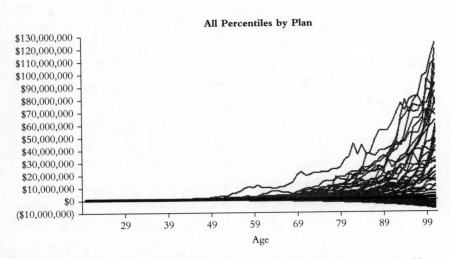

All Percentiles by Plan

Figure 8.1 Simulation trials of 50th to 100th percentiles for our 20-year-old widow

Table 8.1   Ending Values of Simulations by Decile for our 20-Year-Old Widow with $100,000 Initial Portfolio, $5,000 Inflation-adjusted Spending and 83% Confidence Level Based on a Portfolio with 80% Equity Exposure

Percentile	Ending Value	Plan "Failure" Age	Return
0	$12,285,385,311		16.32%
10	$ 1,211,520,308		12.92%
20	$ 518,547,009		12.50%
30	$ 341,030,507		11.32%
40	$ 217,427,944		11.26%
50	$ 125,289,697		11.66%
60	$ 67,676,866		9.95%
70	$ 31,383,768		9.00%
80	$ 6,794,821		7.67%
90	–$ 4,020,177	54	8.89%
100	–$ 7,286,223	33	7.39%

before age 54, or a billionaire. Both are 10 percent chances falling at the 90th and 10th percentiles. She has a one-in-five chance of being outside of the range of bankruptcy or a billionaire. Clearly, we need fatter distribution tails than this! We also observe that she has a 50 percent chance of having more than $125 million and even a 70 percent chance of having more than $31 million. ***Obviously, nothing in her plan would change if she had an extra $30 million, $100 million, or $1 billion.*** Pretty stupid assumption, isn't it?

But this is exactly what is assumed and modeled in those "odds of success" plans.

Real wealth managers constantly manage wealth, not just these erroneous odds of success based on idiotic assumptions. Figure 8.2 and Table 8.2 show us the *range of dollar values necessary* for our widow to remain within 75 to 90 percent confidence over her life and the first five years of her plan, respectively.

From the scale on Figure 8.2 alone, you can observe that a wealth manager has quite a task, managing billions of dollars of uncertainty into

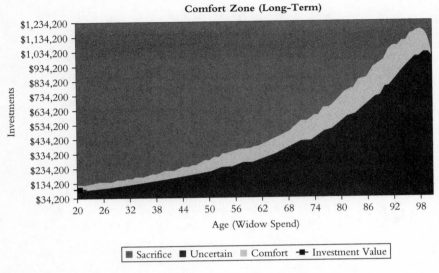

Figure 8.2 Dollar values necessary to avoid over- and underfunding

Table 8.2 Range of Dollar Values Necessary

Next	Sacrifice (Overfunded)	Sacrifice Chance	Uncertain (Underfunded)	Uncertain Chance	Chance Outside
1 year	$120,278	22.5%	$ 91,225	16.6%	39.1%
3 years	$131,719	36.3%	$ 97,112	25.1%	61.4%
5 years	$139,258	45.6%	$102,903	25.8%	71.4%

about a $1 million range of outcomes over 80 years of uncertainty. Table 8.2 shows *how unlikely it is* that our widow's "highly confident" initial odds of success will play out. There is a 71.4 percent chance her wealth plan will become over- or underfunded within just the next five years! **There is no chance** (well . . . maybe if we ran a million simulations instead of a thousand there would be SOME chance) the market will behave in a manner that would not require a change in the plan at some point along the way, and **only a 1 in 1,000 chance** that the markets will be so well behaved that we could avoid the need to change the plan for 38 years (the longest simulated trial that avoided over- and underfunding).

118

No Confidence in Monte Carlo Confidence Levels

I get e-mails all the time about fat tails, "Black Swans," and, recently, about how we don't need Monte Carlo to calculate the odds of success. A recent article in the *Journal of Financial Planning* quoted my paper "Understanding Monte Carlo Simulation"[1] to make a case for why compound returns are just as good a measure of odds of success as Monte Carlo simulations. What the author missed was my main point from the paper: **". . . to get to the highest possible confidence of achieving their goals. THIS IS AN ABUSE OF CLIENTS."** (The formatting of bold all caps was maintained from the original paper—maybe I should have used a larger font for this key point?)

The confidence level of a Monte Carlo simulation (or a geometric mean confidence level for that matter) is not of much value by itself, unless you really would be stupid enough to make no use of an extra million or two that you happen to have lying around (something that is almost certain to happen at some point in any wealth management plan that ignores spending, saving, or asset allocation policy changes that would otherwise be prudent to address and something that a true wealth manager would do).

Conversely, such confidence measures over lifelong wealth management plans also assume you would completely ignore the reality that a black swan with a fat tail swooped down upon your wealth and carried much of it away.

Although the author of that *Journal of Financial Planning* article[2] accurately represented that one can use Monte Carlo simulation **or** geometric mean method to reasonably estimate the odds of exceeding a certain dollar amount (his "odds of success") at *one date* in the future (based on the idiotic notion that no one would ever change his plan *based on dollar effect* to their plan along the way), he missed the key point that doing so is abusive to clients, as I emphasized in the paper his article referenced.

This isn't meant to imply that there is anything wrong with Monte Carlo simulation confidence levels (or geometric mean confidence levels,

119

for that matter); instead, it is the manner in which they are used that can be misleading, and painful to the ultimate investor—an opinion we share with the author of the article, but for completely different reasons.

"High Confidence" with Practically No Chance of Happening

In Chapter 7 we examined the wealth results over 80 years of actual historical returns as applied to a 20-year-old widow with an ongoing, inflation-adjusted spending need. The wealth management approach of adjusting only the asset allocation based on an unchanging spending policy in reaction to funded status produced millions more wealth than clairvoyantly selected superior-return-based allocations. If one were to look at the confidence levels at the initial inception of a lifelong wealth management plan, is there a means of identifying *the odds of markets producing results over the life of the plan that **would avoid** becoming excessively overfunded or underfunded at any time over the entire plan?* Think about this question for a moment. The question being asked *is not* what is initially shown as the confidence level, which as it is normally used, represents the odds of meeting all of the investor's goals over his life **and** ending up with an estate that is *larger* than his initial estate goal. In reality, that approach represents only two sample points—the start date of "now" and end date of death—and EVERYTHING that might happen in between is really ignored. Sure, it models all of the cash flows and varying year-by-year market results (unless you are using a geometric mean method), but *it does not* model what your confidence level would be in each year, of each trial. **It assumes no action would be taken no matter WHAT the result**, and you would keep everything unchanged until the plan end.

How is that for unrealistic? In some trials, you end up with massive amounts of excess wealth, and you don't use it for anything. Sure, *that* is going to happen. In some, you end up with excess wealth and you keep taking needless risks that ultimately are experienced in the form of losing money, so you end up only close to your original goals. In some trials, devastating markets would have you close to the brink of "failure," but fortunate timing of a recovery gets you back to your original goals. And, in some trials, it assumes that the results are very poor and you go ahead and keep right on spending the same thing you planned on 20 years ago, despite having a black swan with a fat tail carrying your wealth away.

If you think about this, what in essence most of those "odds of success" peddlers are saying is, "You should trust me **now** because with your *current* goals and *current* assets and planned savings, you have X percent "odds of success" **based on the assumption that you ignore what your odds would be at any point in the future . . . But trust my odds today anyway.**"

If, as clients, we are expected to really and truly have some sense of comfort in the confidence levels (odds of success) shown to us by our advisers (regardless of whether Monte Carlo or geometric mean based), shouldn't we also know the likelihood of whether the markets would produce results that would maintain us somewhere in that initial confidence range? Phrased another way, we might ask, "Despite the high odds of the initial advice, *how likely is it that the plan being modeled would not change* due ONLY to the behavior of markets over the life of the plan?" Or inversely, what are the odds of the markets being so well behaved that the adviser would not be forced to change his advice if he were to remain consistent with his initial premises? It turns out the answer to this is knowable.

Despite high initial odds, the odds of the markets behaving in a manner that would *not* cause advisers to change their advice are near zero.

We saw this in the results for our widow. There was only a 1-in-1,000 chance of the markets behaving according to plan for 38 years and over a 71 percent chance the markets would behave in an unruly manner over the first five years of the plan. To a true wealth manager, you have to look at the short-term misbehavior of markets to know this. You cannot calculate this behavior by the smooth assumption of geometric means, which might accurately represent the odds over the life of the presumably unchangeable plan, but you need Monte Carlo simulation to expose the dollar wealth effect of potential short-term market behaviors. For example, assume the range of compound returns for our widow over 80 years was between 7.39 percent and 16.32 percent (see Table 8.2). If I created a geometric return distribution, I would likely come to a statistical equivalent of our initial 83 percent confidence using a Monte Carlo simulation, just as the author of the *Journal of Financial Planning* article stated, *over the entire life of the unchanging plan.* If I apply these compound returns to our widow for the first five years of the plan as it would be modeled with a geometric return method, it would mislead us into thinking there is no chance she would become underfunded in the first five years. But with Monte Carlo simulation and the dollar impact of the short-term uncertainty it exposes, we see there is a 25.8 percent chance of becoming underfunded. There is a reasonable difference between zero chance and a 25 percent chance! We would become overfunded with the maximum 16.32 percent geometric mean return in the first five years, but the short-term impact of the Monte Carlo simulator showed us as having a 45 percent chance of becoming overfunded. The return of 12.10 percent needed to become overfunded using the geometric mean would have showed only about a 25 percent chance. The geometric mean method would therefore show only a 25 percent of becoming under- or overfunded, while Monte Carlo simulation would show the odds being nearly *three times* that level.

To be fair, you could reasonably estimate all of this using geometric means. To do so, you would have to calculate the distribution of returns for each year and year's end. Guess what—at that point, it is the same thing as doing the Monte Carlo simulation!

Return managers sometimes discuss the notion of **risk capacity,** even though they attempt to manage returns instead of wealth. Take, for example, another sample client. Like our widow in the previous example, he also is 20 years old. Unlike the widow, who needs a continuous income, he is in savings mode, not spending mode. He saves

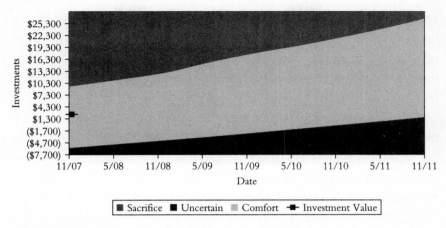

Figure 8.3 Initial comfort zone for a 20-year-old saver in 1926 with 84 percent confidence (FWC Growth allocation, 90% equities)

Table 8.3 Chance of Falling Outside of the (Short-term) Comfort Zone

Next	Overfunded		Underfunded		
	Sacrifice	Chance	Uncertain	Chance	Outside
1 Year	$12,365	0.0%	−$4,225	0.0%	0.0%
3 Years	$21,092	0.0%	−$ 374	0.0%	0.0%
5 Years	$31,498	0.6%	$4,259	0.0%	0.6%

$2,000 a year, adjusted for inflation, and plans to retire at age 65 on $29,000 in inflation-adjusted income (about $110,000 in actual dollars, at age 65). Being young, with a lot of years of saving ahead of him, he can afford to take a lot of investment risk. If we run the initial confidence level based on our "growth" model (90 percent equity exposure) we discover that he has 84 percent initial confidence and that there is almost no chance of falling outside of the comfort zone in the next five years, as shown in Figure 8.3 and its corresponding table, Table 8.3.

We see some pretty interesting things in the table of chances of falling out of the comfort zone over the next five years for this client, shown in Figure 8.3 and Table 8.3. For example, in the next three years, to fall below 75 percent confidence, he would have to lose 100 percent of each of his contributions AND be in debt $374. Imagine how one would have to calculate this using geometric means! Five years into his plan, after having saved $2,000 a year for five years adjusted for inflation ($10,618), his portfolio would have to decline to $4,259 to fall below 75 percent confidence. If you compare *his* ability to maintain his funded status in this obviously wide range of tolerance as compared to the sensitivity of our spending widow (see Figure 8.4 and Table 8.4), we can clearly see what is often referred to as *risk capacity*. Our saver has almost no chance of becoming over- or underfunded, while the

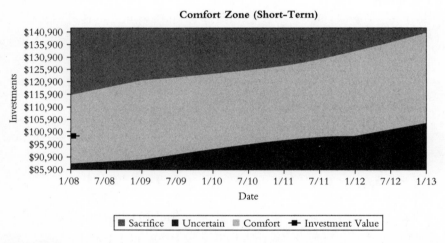

Figure 8.4 Initial comfort zone for 20-year-old widow in 1926 with 83% confidence (Balanced Growth Allocation, 80% Equities)

Table 8.4 Corresponding Table to Figure 8.4

Next	Sacrifice (Overfunded)	Chance	Uncertain (Underfunded)	Chance	Outside
1 year	$120,278	22.5%	$ 91,225	16.6%	39.1%
3 years	$131,719	36.3%	$ 97,112	25.1%	61.4%
5 years	$139,258	45.6%	$102,903	25.8%	71.4%

widow has more than a 71 percent chance of the markets behaving in a way that would cause an excessive funding variance within the next five years.

The 20-year-old saver has the capacity to compound at MINUS 100 percent for the first three years (plus be a bit in debt) and he would still have 75 percent confidence. Our widow would drop to 75 percent confidence if her compound return over the next three years was less than +2.27 percent. Do you think there is a difference here? Even though these allocations both have about the same odds of compounding at more than 2.27 percent (81 versus 83 percent) over three years, there is a *huge* difference on the effect to the client's wealth management plan.

Even if we assume that the investor would ignore the misbehavior of the markets over the entire 80-year horizon, we see that the odds of our widow being close to her initial goals of meeting her inflation-adjusted spending policy and maintaining the spending power of her portfolio is almost zero.

At the 82nd percentile result, she would have an estate that is nearly *three times* her target estate value, and at the 84th percentile, she would have run out of money at age 90. The 83rd percentile result would have left her with an estate worth about 50 percent more than she desired. How is this for long odds?

In the next chapter we will examine the detailed supporting data of the timing of the allocation shifts based on the wealth management approach of monitoring the funded status for our widow versus the other clairvoyantly "successful" allocation methods from Chapter 7. We will also explore how sensitive the widow's wealth management plan is to just one year's investment result, and the timing of her husband's unfortunate death. Finally, we will provide the detailed back-up of year-by-year values and returns for the allocations used in the Chapter 7 examples.

Chapter 9

The Data: Seeing the Effect of Real Markets on Client Goals

It is sheer madness to live in want in order to be wealthy when you die.

—JUVENAL

n Chapter 6, we showed some simple examples of the effects of the difference between time-weighted (return manager) returns and dollar-weighted (wealth manager) returns. Chapter 7 assessed a real-life client example and demonstrated how some of the "best" generally accepted and even clairvoyantly "successful" approaches of asset allocation ended up costing a widow investor millions of dollars of wealth. Chapter 8 examined how unlikely it is that markets would behave in a manner that would have avoided over- and underfunding, even though the initial odds were very high. It also exposed how sensitive a *real* wealth management plan is to the unique cash flows of the

127

investor based on the risk capacity of the plan. Finally, it uncovered how unrealistic and abusive Monte Carlo simulations (or geometric mean odds) can be to the client because of erroneous and impossible assumptions of the client sticking to their original plan, no matter what happens, despite equal odds of being broke or being a billionaire.

I released Chapter 7 as an educational adviser e-mail in 2007. After its release, I received a number of e-mails and phone calls asking for the documentation of the detailed data that supports the results for a real wealth management plan for our 20-year-old widow, as well as the other four allocation methodologies we compared and contrasted in our example plan.

So, Here It Is . . .

Before you analyze this information, it might be helpful to review what would have happened based on our original advice in 1926 that had high *initial* confidence as we discussed in the Monte Carlo simulation in Chapter 8. Keep in mind that a real wealth manager will not force, coerce, or guilt the widow to stick with an old plan that becomes over- or underfunded based on the market's behavior. Instead, a real wealth manager monitors and offers continuous choices an investor should implement to increase or decrease funding or spending policy, target estate values, asset allocation policy, and so on. Therefore, this example is not very realistic because it assumes that nothing is changed over the course of the widow's life *no matter what* happens, as discussed in Chapter 8. As a reminder, our 20-year-old widow came to us in 1926 after her husband died in a mining accident. Her only assets were the proceeds of a $100,000 insurance policy and she had an income need of $5,000 a year (about $50,000 in today's dollars) adjusted for inflation. She ended up living to age 100, so those insurance proceeds needed to provide for 80 years of income need (see Table 9.1).

If we would have ignored the funded status along the way, things would have worked out just about perfectly according to plan, with

Table 9.1   Result of Initial Advice Based on Actual History

Initial Advice for Widow and History's Results

Year	Widow's Age	Beginning Value	Spending Need	Return in $	Return in %	Ending Value	Allocation	Equity Exposure
1926	20	$ 100,000		$ 7,496	7.50%	$ 107,496	Bal Growth	80%
1927	21	$ 107,496	$ (5,000)	$ 29,045	27.02%	$ 131,540	Bal Growth	80%
1928	22	$ 131,540	$ (5,150)	$ 44,915	34.15%	$ 171,305	Bal Growth	80%
1929	23	$ 171,305	$ (5,305)	$ (27,907)	−16.29%	$ 138,094	Bal Growth	80%
1930	24	$ 138,094	$ (5,464)	$ (30,343)	−21.97%	$ 102,287	Bal Growth	80%
1931	25	$ 102,287	$ (5,628)	$ (37,508)	−36.67%	$ 59,151	Bal Growth	80%
1932	26	$ 59,151	$ (5,796)	$ (2,513)	−4.25%	$ 50,842	Bal Growth	80%
1933	27	$ 50,842	$ (5,970)	$ 33,426	65.75%	$ 78,298	Bal Growth	80%
1934	28	$ 78,298	$ (6,149)	$ 5,391	6.88%	$ 77,539	Bal Growth	80%
1935	29	$ 77,539	$ (6,334)	$ 29,101	37.53%	$ 100,306	Bal Growth	80%
1936	30	$ 100,306	$ (6,524)	$ 35,519	35.41%	$ 129,301	Bal Growth	80%
1937	31	$ 129,301	$ (6,720)	$ (43,290)	−33.48%	$ 79,292	Bal Growth	80%
1938	32	$ 79,292	$ (6,921)	$ 20,963	26.44%	$ 93,333	Bal Growth	80%
1939	33	$ 93,333	$ (7,129)	$ 630	0.68%	$ 86,835	Bal Growth	80%
1940	34	$ 86,835	$ (7,343)	$ (5,329)	−6.14%	$ 74,163	Bal Growth	80%
1941	35	$ 74,163	$ (7,563)	$ (6,330)	−8.54%	$ 60,270	Bal Growth	80%
1942	36	$ 60,270	$ (7,790)	$ 13,662	22.67%	$ 66,142	Bal Growth	80%
1943	37	$ 66,142	$ (8,024)	$ 24,374	36.85%	$ 82,493	Bal Growth	80%
1944	38	$ 82,493	$ (8,264)	$ 20,313	24.62%	$ 94,542	Bal Growth	80%
1945	39	$ 94,542	$ (8,512)	$ 36,728	38.85%	$ 122,758	Bal Growth	80%
1946	40	$ 122,758	$ (8,768)	$ (8,787)	−7.16%	$ 105,204	Bal Growth	80%
1947	41	$ 105,204	$ (9,031)	$ 3,727	3.54%	$ 99,899	Bal Growth	80%
1948	42	$ 99,899	$ (9,301)	$ 2,844	2.85%	$ 93,442	Bal Growth	80%
1949	43	$ 93,442	$ (9,581)	$ 14,683	15.71%	$ 98,544	Bal Growth	80%
1950	44	$ 98,544	$ (9,868)	$ 26,882	27.28%	$ 115,557	Bal Growth	80%
1951	45	$ 115,557	$ (10,164)	$ 17,628	15.25%	$ 123,022	Bal Growth	80%
1952	46	$ 123,022	$ (10,469)	$ 13,761	11.19%	$ 126,314	Bal Growth	80%
1953	47	$ 126,314	$ (10,783)	$ (1,955)	−1.55%	$ 113,576	Bal Growth	80%
1954	48	$ 113,576	$ (11,106)	$ 50,642	44.59%	$ 153,112	Bal Growth	80%
1955	49	$ 153,112	$ (11,440)	$ 34,273	22.38%	$ 175,945	Bal Growth	80%
1956	50	$ 175,945	$ (11,783)	$ 8,181	4.65%	$ 172,344	Bal Growth	80%
1957	51	$ 172.344	$ (12.136)	$ (13,958)	−8.10%	$ 146,249	Bal Growth	80%
1958	52	$ 146,249	$ (12,500)	$ 58,310	39.87%	$ 192,059	Bal Growth	80%
1959	53	$ 192,059	$ (12,875)	$ 20,480	10.66%	$ 199,664	Bal Growth	80%
1960	54	$ 199,664	$ (13,262)	$ 3,204	1.60%	$ 189,606	Bal Growth	80%
1961	55	$ 189,606	$ (13,660)	$ 43,962	23.19%	$ 219,909	Bal Growth	80%
1962	56	$ 219,909	$ (14,069)	$ (14,778)	−6.72%	$ 191,061	Bal Growth	80%
1963	57	$ 191,061	$ (14,491)	$ 35,900	18.79%	$ 212,470	Bal Growth	80%
1964	58	$ 212,470	$ (14,926)	$ 33,453	15.74%	$ 230,996	Bal Growth	80%
1965	59	$ 230,996	$ (15,374)	$ 40,536	17.55%	$ 256,158	Bal Growth	80%
1966	60	$ 256,158	$ (15,835)	$ (16,263)	−6.35%	$ 224,061	Bal Growth	80%

(Continued)

Table 9.1 (Continued)

Year	Widow's Age	Beginning Value	Spending Need	Return in $	Return in %	Ending Value	Allocation	Equity Exposure
1967	61	$ 224,061	$ (16,310)	$ 76,953	34.34%	$ 284,703	Bal Growth	80%
1968	62	$ 284,703	$ (16,799)	$ 45,544	16.00%	$ 313,448	Bal Growth	80%
1969	63	$ 313,448	$ (17,303)	$ (34,296)	−10.94%	$ 261,848	Bal Growth	80%
1970	64	$ 261,848	$ (17,823)	$ 2,645	1.01%	$ 246,671	Bal Growth	80%
1971	65	$ 246,671	$ (18,357)	$ 33,681	13.65%	$ 261,995	Bal Growth	80%
1972	66	$ 261,995	$ (18,908)	$ 32,883	12.55%	$ 275,970	Bal Growth	80%
1973	67	$ 275,970	$ (19,475)	$ (40,905)	−14.82%	$ 215,590	Bal Growth	80%
1974	68	$ 215,590	$ (20,059)	$ (39,581)	−18.36%	$ 155,949	Bal Growth	80%
1975	69	$ 155,949	$ (20,661)	$ 54,881	35.19%	$ 190,169	Bal Growth	80%
1976	70	$ 190,169	$ (21,281)	$ 56,815	29.88%	$ 225,703	Bal Growth	80%
1977	71	$ 225,703	$ (21,920)	$ 6,204	2.75%	$ 209,987	Bal Growth	80%
1978	72	$ 209,987	$ (22,577)	$ 21,512	10.24%	$ 208,922	Bal Growth	80%
1979	73	$ 208,922	$ (23,254)	$ 45,863	21.95%	$ 231,531	Bal Growth	80%
1980	74	$ 231,531	$ (23,952)	$ 66,514	28.73%	$ 274,093	Bal Growth	80%
1981	75	$ 274,093	$ (24,671)	$ 7,581	2.77%	$ 257,004	Bal Growth	80%
1982	76	$ 257,004	$ (25,411)	$ 62,258	24.22%	$ 293,851	Bal Growth	80%
1983	77	$ 293,851	$ (26,173)	$ 69,962	23.81%	$ 337,641	Bal Growth	80%
1984	78	$ 337,641	$ (26,958)	$ 15,192	4.50%	$ 325,875	Bal Growth	80%
1985	79	$ 325,875	$ (27,767)	$ 90,158	27.67%	$ 388,266	Bal Growth	80%
1986	80	$ 388,266	$ (28,600)	$ 57,153	14.72%	$ 416,818	Bal Growth	80%
1987	81	$ 416,818	$ (29,458)	$ 4,938	1.18%	$ 392,298	Bal Growth	80%
1988	82	$ 392,298	$ (30,342)	$ 63,509	16.19%	$ 425,465	Bal Growth	80%
1989	83	$ 425,465	$ (31,252)	$ 95,405	22.42%	$ 489,619	Bal Growth	80%
1990	84	$ 489,619	$ (32,190)	$ (25,595)	−5.23%	$ 431,834	Bal Growth	80%
1991	85	$ 431,834	$ (33,155)	$ 133,246	30.86%	$ 531,925	Bal Growth	80%
1992	86	$ 531,925	$ (34,150)	$ 60,748	11.42%	$ 558,523	Bal Growth	80%
1993	87	$ 558,523	$ (35,174)	$ 71,603	12.82%	$ 594,952	Bal Growth	80%
1994	88	$ 594,952	$ (36,230)	$ 3,853	0.65%	$ 562,575	Bal Growth	80%
1995	89	$ 562,575	$ (37,317)	$ 181,921	32.34%	$ 707,179	Bal Growth	80%
1996	90	$ 707,179	$ (38,436)	$ 124,313	17.58%	$ 793,056	Bal Growth	80%
1997	91	$ 793,056	$ (39,589)	$ 203,471	25.66%	$ 956,938	Bal Growth	80%
1998	92	$ 956,938	$ (40,777)	$ 151,453	15.83%	$ 1,067,614	Bal Growth	80%
1999	93	$1,067,614	$ (42,000)	$ 200,678	18.80%	$ 1,226,292	Bal Growth	80%
2000	94	$1,226,292	$ (43,260)	$ (43,215)	−3.52%	$ 1,139,818	Bal Growth	80%
2001	95	$1,139,818	$ (44,558)	$ (28,921)	−2.54%	$ 1,066,339	Bal Growth	80%
2002	96	$1,066,339	$ (45,895)	$(155,299)	−14.56%	$ 865,145	Bal Growth	80%
2003	97	$ 865,145	$ (47,271)	$ 248,758	28.75%	$ 1,066,631	Bal Growth	80%
2004	98	$1,066,631	$ (48,690)	$ 130,091	12.20%	$ 1,148,032	Bal Growth	80%
2005	99	$1,148,032	$ (50,150)	$ 57,541	5.01%	$ 1,155,423	Bal Growth	80%
2006	100	$1,155,423	$ (51,655)	$ 153,001	13.24%	$ 1,256,769	Bal Growth	80%

just a little bit of excess money in spending power at her death, despite a Great Depression that caused no change in the widow's spending habits. But, what if her husband had died one year earlier? How much impact would that have? (See Table 9.2.)

As evidenced in Table 9.2, moving her income need just one year earlier had the widow broke at the same time as our "stocks for the long run" portfolio. Think about the effect of this. All we are doing is moving forward the $5,000 income need by one year, the equivalent of a one-time 5 percent underperformance. Some may argue that one additional year of inflation adjusts all of the spending need, but let's assume she could skip the first-year inflation adjustment to remove that from the equation (see Table 9.3).

Skipping a 3 percent inflation adjustment to our widow's spending need *once* over the course of the last 80 years delayed the depletion of her portfolio **by eight years**. This is why wealth managers constantly tweak their advice. It is also why I get so frustrated with active *return* managers who argue they should measure temperature with a ruler. **The difference of *a one-time 5 percent underperformance* was the difference between maintaining the spending policy over her entire life, along with maintaining the purchasing power of her portfolio, versus being broke 44 years earlier! Can you afford to take that risk? As a fiduciary, are you prepared to accept this sort of liability?**

Any attempt to exceed the market's results will introduce a risk of potentially underperforming, as we extensively covered in Chapter 5, and as we can see from this example. Also, just *one year* of inferior results can cost you 44 *years* of lifestyle, depending on *when* it happens, assuming you ignore your funded status and merely stick to your long-term plan. Outperforming *could* also buy you a superior lifestyle, *provided* that you act on it and do not introduce the risk of underperforming after having received the benefit of your lucky or skillful superior results. However, return managers cannot control *when* superior or inferior results will occur. That is why they measure and manage returns, and NOT wealth. So why take these bets in the first place if you don't need to? The real wealth manager does not.

Table 9.2 Widow's Result if Widowed One Year Earlier

Initial Advice for Widow and History's Results—Husband Passes One Year Earlier

Year	Widow's Age	Beginning Value	Spending Need	Return in $	Return in %	Ending Value	Allocation	Equity Exposure
1926	20	$100,000	$ (5,000)	$ 7,496	7.50%	$ 102,495.51	Bal Growth	80%
1927	21	$102,496	$ (5,150)	$ 27,694	27.02%	$125,039.46	Bal Growth	80%
1928	22	$125,039	$ (5,305)	$ 42,695	34.15%	$162,429.87	Bal Growth	80%
1929	23	$162,430	$ (5,464)	$(26,461)	−16.29%	$130,505.06	Bal Growth	80%
1930	24	$130,505	$ (5,628)	$(28,676)	−21.97%	$ 96,201.58	Bal Growth	80%
1931	25	$ 96,202	$ (5,796)	$(35,277)	−36.67%	$ 55,128.37	Bal Growth	80%
1932	26	$ 55,128	$ (5,970)	$ (2,342)	−4.25%	$ 46,816.16	Bal Growth	80%
1933	27	$ 46,816	$ (6,149)	$ 30,780	65.75%	$ 71,446.51	Bal Growth	80%
1934	28	$ 71,447	$ (6,334)	$ 4,919	6.88%	$ 70,031.65	Bal Growth	80%
1935	29	$ 70,032	$ (6,524)	$ 26,283	37.53%	$ 89,791.23	Bal Growth	80%
1936	30	$ 89,791	$ (6,720)	$ 31,795	35.41%	$114,866.96	Bal Growth	80%
1937	31	$114,867	$ (6,921)	$(38,457)	−33.48%	$ 69,488.45	Bal Growth	80%
1938	32	$ 69,488	$ (7,129)	$ 18,371	26.44%	$ 80,730.81	Bal Growth	80%
1939	33	$ 80,731	$ (7,343)	$ 545	0.68%	$ 73,933.45	Bal Growth	80%
1940	34	$ 73,933	$ (7,563)	$ (4,537)	−6.14%	$ 61,833.14	Bal Growth	80%
1941	35	$ 61,833	$ (7,790)	$ (5,278)	−8.54%	$ 48,765.63	Bal Growth	80%
1942	36	$ 48,766	$ (8,024)	$ 11,054	22.67%	$ 51,796.25	Bal Growth	80%
1943	37	$ 51,796	$ (8,264)	$ 19,087	36.85%	$ 62,619.42	Bal Growth	80%
1944	38	$ 62,619	$ (8,512)	$ 15,420	24.62%	$ 69,526.80	Bal Growth	80%
1945	39	$ 69,527	$ (8,768)	$ 27,010	38.85%	$ 87,769.43	Bal Growth	80%
1946	40	$ 87,769	$ (9,031)	$ (6,282)	−7.16%	$ 72,456.62	Bal Growth	80%
1947	41	$ 72,457	$ (9,301)	$ 2,567	3.54%	$ 65,721.70	Bal Growth	80%
1948	42	$ 65,722	$ (9,581)	$ 1,871	2.85%	$ 58,011.90	Bal Growth	80%
1949	43	$ 58,012	$ (9,868)	$ 9,116	15.71%	$ 57,259.47	Bal Growth	80%
1950	44	$ 57,259	$(10,164)	$ 15,620	27.28%	$ 62,715.32	Bal Growth	80%

Year	Age	Balance	Withdrawal	Amount	%	Balance	Strategy	%
1951	45	$ 62,715	$(10,469)	$ 9,567	15.25%	$ 61,813.61	Bal Growth	80%
1952	46	$ 61,814	$(10,783)	$ 6,914	11.19%	$ 57,945.09	Bal Growth	80%
1953	47	$ 57,945	$(11,106)	$ (897)	-1.55%	$ 45,941.91	Bal Growth	80%
1954	48	$ 45,942	$(11,440)	$ 20,485	44.59%	$ 54,987.22	Bal Growth	80%
1955	49	$ 54,987	$(11,783)	$ 12,308	22.38%	$ 55,512.78	Bal Growth	80%
1956	50	$ 55,513	$(12,136)	$ 2,581	4.65%	$ 45,957.75	Bal Growth	80%
1957	51	$ 45,958	$(12,500)	$ (3,722)	-8.10%	$ 29,735.15	Bal Growth	80%
1958	52	$ 29,735	$(12,875)	$ 11,856	39.87%	$ 28,715.31	Bal Growth	80%
1959	53	$ 28,715	$(13,262)	$ 3,062	10.66%	$ 18,515.72	Bal Growth	80%
1960	54	$ 18,516	$(13,660)	$ 297	1.60%	$ 5,153.34	Bal Growth	80%
1961	55	$ 5,153	$(14,069)	$ 1,195	23.19%	BROKE	Bal Growth	80%
1962	56	BROKE	$(14,491)	$ 519	-6.72%		Bal Growth	80%
1963	57		$(14,926)		18.79%		Bal Growth	80%
1964	58		$(15,374)		15.74%		Bal Growth	80%
1965	59		$(15,835)		17.55%		Bal Growth	80%
1966	60		$(16,310)		-6.35%		Bal Growth	80%
1967	61		$(16,799)		34.34%		Bal Growth	80%
1968	62		$(17,303)		16.00%		Bal Growth	80%
1969	63		$(17,823)		-10.94%		Bal Growth	80%
1970	64		$(18,357)		1.01%		Bal Growth	80%
1971	65		$(18,908)		13.65%		Bal Growth	80%
1972	66		$(19,475)		12.55%		Bal Growth	80%
1973	67		$(20,059)		-14.82%		Bal Growth	80%
1974	68		$(20,661)		-18.36%		Bal Growth	80%
1975	69		$(21,281)		35.19%		Bal Growth	80%
1976	70		$(21,920)		29.88%		Bal Growth	80%
1977	71		$(22,577)		2.75%		Bal Growth	80%
1978	72		$(23,254)		10.24%		Bal Growth	80%
1979	73		$(23,952)		21.95%		Bal Growth	80%

(Continued)

133

Table 9.2 (Continued)

Year	Widow's Age	Beginning Value	Spending Need	Return in $	Return in %	Ending Value	Allocation	Equity Exposure
1980	74		$(24,671)		28.73%		Bal Growth	80%
1981	75		$(25,411)		2.77%		Bal Growth	80%
1982	76		$(26,173)		24.22%		Bal Growth	80%
1983	77		$(26,958)		23.81%		Bal Growth	80%
1984	78		$(27,767)		4.50%		Bal Growth	80%
1985	79		$(28,600)		27.67%		Bal Growth	80%
1986	80		$(29,458)		14.72%		Bal Growth	80%
1987	81		$(30,342)		1.18%		Bal Growth	80%
1988	82		$(31,252)		16.19%		Bal Growth	80%
1989	83		$(32,190)		22.42%		Bal Growth	80%
1990	84		$(33,155)		-5.23%		Bal Growth	80%
1991	85		$(34,150)		30.86%		Bal Growth	80%
1992	86		$(35,174)		11.42%		Bal Growth	80%
1993	87		$(36,230)		12.82%		Bal Growth	80%
1994	88		$(37,317)		0.65%		Bal Growth	80%
1995	89		$(38,436)		32.34%		Bal Growth	80%
1996	90		$(39,589)		17.58%		Bal Growth	80%
1997	91		$(40,777)		25.66%		Bal Growth	80%
1998	92		$(42,000)		15.83%		Bal Growth	80%
1999	93		$(43,260)		18.80%		Bal Growth	80%
2000	94		$(44,558)		-3.52%		Bal Growth	80%
2001	95		$(45,895)		-2.54%		Bal Growth	80%
2002	96		$(47,271)		-14.56%		Bal Growth	80%
2003	97		$(48,690)		28.75%		Bal Growth	80%
2004	98		$(50,150)		12.20%		Bal Growth	80%
2005	99		$(51,655)		5.01%		Bal Growth	80%
2006	100		$(53,204)		13.24%		Bal Growth	80%

Table 9.3 Skipping One Year of Inflation Adjustment

Initial Advice for Widow and History's Results—Husband Passes One Year Earlier, Skip 1st Year Inflation Adjustment

Year	Widow's Age	Beginning Value	Spending Need	Return in $	Return in %	Ending Value	Allocation	Equity Exposure
1926	20	$100,000	$ (5,000)	$ 7,496	7.50%	$102,495.51	Bal Growth	80%
1927	21	$102,496	$ (5,000)	$ 27,694	27.02%	$125,189.46	Bal Growth	80%
1928	22	$125,189	$ (5,150)	$ 42,746	34.15%	$162,785.59	Bal Growth	80%
1929	23	$162,786	$ (5,305)	$ (26,519)	−16.29%	$130,961.96	Bal Growth	80%
1930	24	$130,962	$ (5,464)	$ (28,776)	−21.97%	$ 96,722.00	Bal Growth	80%
1931	25	$ 96,722	$ (5,628)	$ (35,468)	−36.67%	$ 55,626.78	Bal Growth	80%
1932	26	$ 55,627	$ (5,796)	$ (2,363)	−4.25%	$ 47,467.29	Bal Growth	80%
1933	27	$ 47,467	$ (5,970)	$ 31,208	65.75%	$ 72,704.83	Bal Growth	80%
1934	28	$ 72,705	$ (6,149)	$ 5,006	6.88%	$ 71,561.09	Bal Growth	80%
1935	29	$ 71,561	$ (6,334)	$ 26,857	37.53%	$ 92,084.70	Bal Growth	80%
1936	30	$ 92,085	$ (6,524)	$ 32,607	35.41%	$118,168.26	Bal Growth	80%
1937	31	$118,168	$ (6,720)	$ (39,563)	−33.48%	$ 71,886.06	Bal Growth	80%
1938	32	$ 71,886	$ (6,921)	$ 19,005	26.44%	$ 83,969.93	Bal Growth	80%
1939	33	$ 83,970	$ (7,129)	$ 567	0.68%	$ 77,408.32	Bal Growth	80%
1940	34	$ 77,408	$ (7,343)	$ (4,751)	−6.14%	$ 65,315.04	Bal Growth	80%
1941	35	$ 65,315	$ (7,563)	$ (5,575)	−8.54%	$ 52,177.21	Bal Growth	80%
1942	36	$ 52,177	$ (7,790)	$ 11,827	22.67%	$ 56,214.87	Bal Growth	80%
1943	37	$ 56,215	$ (8,024)	$ 20,716	36.85%	$ 68,907.05	Bal Growth	80%
1944	38	$ 68,907	$ (8,264)	$ 16,968	24.62%	$ 77,610.64	Bal Growth	80%

(Continued)

Table 9.3 (Continued)

Year	Widow's Age	Beginning Value	Spending Need	Return in $	Return in %	Ending Value	Allocation	Equity Exposure
1945	39	$ 77,611	$ (8,512)	$ 30,151	38.85%	$ 99,249.09	Bal Growth	80%
1946	40	$ 99,249	$ (8,768)	$ (7,104)	−7.16%	$ 83,377.62	Bal Growth	80%
1947	41	$ 83,378	$ (9,031)	$ 2,953	3.54%	$ 77,300.46	Bal Growth	80%
1948	42	$ 77,300	$ (9,301)	$ 2,200	2.85%	$ 70,199.29	Bal Growth	80%
1949	43	$ 70,199	$ (9,581)	$ 11,031	15.71%	$ 71,649.30	Bal Growth	80%
1950	44	$ 71,649	$ (9,868)	$ 19,545	27.28%	$ 81,326.59	Bal Growth	80%
1951	45	$ 81,327	$(10,164)	$ 12,406	15.25%	$ 83,568.95	Bal Growth	80%
1952	46	$ 83,569	$(10,469)	$ 9,348	11.19%	$ 82,448.02	Bal Growth	80%
1953	47	$ 82,448	$(10,783)	$ (1,276)	−1.55%	$ 70,389.14	Bal Growth	80%
1954	48	$ 70,389	$(11,106)	$ 31,386	44.59%	$ 90,668.37	Bal Growth	80%
1955	49	$ 90,668	$(11,440)	$ 20,295	22.38%	$ 99,524.01	Bal Growth	80%
1956	50	$ 99,524	$(11,783)	$ 4,628	4.65%	$ 92,368.94	Bal Growth	80%
1957	51	$ 92,369	$(12,136)	$ (7,481)	−8.10%	$ 72,751.51	Bal Growth	80%
1958	52	$ 72,752	$(12,500)	$ 29,006	39.87%	$ 89,257.54	Bal Growth	80%
1959	53	$ 89,258	$(12,875)	$ 9,518	10.66%	$ 85,900.21	Bal Growth	80%
1960	54	$ 85,900	$(13,262)	$ 1,379	1.60%	$ 74,017.08	Bal Growth	80%
1961	55	$ 74,017	$(13,660)	$ 17,162	23.19%	$ 77,519.16	Bal Growth	80%
1962	56	$ 77,519	$(14,069)	$ (5,209)	−6.72%	$ 58,240.46	Bal Growth	80%
1963	57	$ 58,240	$(14,491)	$ 10,943	18.79%	$ 54,692.26	Bal Growth	80%
1964	58	$ 54,692	$(14,926)	$ 8,611	15.74%	$ 48,377.24	Bal Growth	80%
1965	59	$ 48,377	$(15,374)	$ 8,489	17.55%	$ 41,492.71	Bal Growth	80%
1966	60	$ 41,493	$(15,835)	$ (2,634)	−6.35%	$ 23,023.32	Bal Growth	80%

Year	#				%		Fund	
1967	61	$ 23,023	$(16,310)	$ 7,907	34.34%	$ 14,620.38	Bal Growth	80%
1968	62	$ 14,620	$(16,799)	$ 2,339	16.00%	$ 159.72	Bal Growth	80%
1969	63	$ 160 BROKE	$(17,303)	$ (17)	−10.94%	BROKE	Bal Growth	80%
1970	64		$(17,823)		1.01%		Bal Growth	80%
1971	65		$(18,357)		13.65%		Bal Growth	80%
1972	66		$(18,908)		12.55%		Bal Growth	80%
1973	67		$(19,475)		−14.82%		Bal Growth	80%
1974	68		$(20,059)		−18.36%		Bal Growth	80%
1975	69		$(20,661)		35.19%		Bal Growth	80%
1976	70		$(21,281)		29.88%		Bal Growth	80%
1977	71		$(21,920)		2.75%		Bal Growth	80%
1978	72		$(22,577)		10.24%		Bal Growth	80%
1979	73		$(23,254)		21.95%		Bal Growth	80%
1980	74		$(23,952)		28.73%		Bal Growth	80%
1981	75		$(24,671)		2.77%		Bal Growth	80%
1982	76		$(25,411)		24.22%		Bal Growth	80%
1983	77		$(26,173)		23.81%		Bal Growth	80%
1984	78		$(26,958)		4.50%		Bal Growth	80%
1985	79		$(27,767)		27.67%		Bal Growth	80%
1986	80		$(28,600)		14.72%		Bal Growth	80%
1987	81		$(29,458)		1.18%		Bal Growth	80%
1988	82		$(30,342)		16.19%		Bal Growth	80%
1989	83		$(31,252)		22.42%		Bal Growth	80%
1990	84		$(32,190)		−5.23%		Bal Growth	80%

(Continued)

137

Table 9.3 (Continued)

Year	Widow's Age	Beginning Value	Spending Need	Return in $	Return in %	Ending Value	Allocation	Equity Exposure
1991	85		$(33,155)		30.86%		Bal Growth	80%
1992	86		$(34,150)		11.42%		Bal Growth	80%
1993	87		$(35,174)		12.82%		Bal Growth	80%
1994	88		$(36,230)		0.65%		Bal Growth	80%
1995	89		$(37,317)		32.34%		Bal Growth	80%
1996	90		$(38,436)		17.58%		Bal Growth	80%
1997	91		$(39,589)		25.66%		Bal Growth	80%
1998	92		$(40,777)		15.83%		Bal Growth	80%
1999	93		$(42,000)		18.80%		Bal Growth	80%
2000	94		$(43,260)		−3.52%		Bal Growth	80%
2061	95		$(44,558)		−2.54%		Bal Growth	80%
2002	96		$(45,895)		−14.56%		Bal Growth	80%
2003	97		$(47,271)		28.75%		Bal Growth	80%
2004	98		$(48,690)		12.20%		Bal Growth	80%
2005	99		$(50,150)		5 01%		Bal Growth	80%
2006	100		$(51,655)		13.24%		Bal Growth	80%

Was It a Black Swan?

We see this effect in our original case study where a *return manager* outperforming by 1.5 percent a year with certainty each and every year (no risk of underperforming the benchmark in *any* year) ended up costing the widow millions. Contrast this to a wealth manager who adjusted only the allocation based on funded status in a portfolio that only equaled the index results, and produced millions more wealth.

Remember that all of these results are fictitious from the perspective of a real wealth manager, because the *only* thing that is changed is the allocation risk level of the investment policy. Real wealth managers would treat the wealth management plan like a prudent pension fiduciary would, adjusting funding, spending, terminal values, and allocation in various combinations in a continuous advising process based on what the investor personally values.

We also know that despite using real historical returns, none of the scenarios where the widow "went broke" would have actually occurred, either. The widow would have intuitively become more conservative in her spending policy and adjusted her lifestyle with or without a wealth manager to guide the way. She wouldn't spend her portfolio down to the last nickel just because an old plan said the odds of it working out in the end had high confidence. But such scare tactics do help return managers maximize the fees they can earn on excessively large and overfunded portfolios!

If we look at Table 9.4, which documents the returns, dollar values, and spending need used in all of the calculations, as well as the confidence levels and the nine shifts of allocation policy that would have been made along the way for our widow (erroneously assuming the only choice exposed was allocation policy), we see some interesting things.

First, one might observe that despite the multibillion-dollar range of uncertainty we exposed in Chapter 8 with a forever unchanging allocation and spending policy, we see that there were only 2 years in the last 80 (widow's age 27 and 28 during the Great Depression)

Table 9.4 Wealth Management Allocation Only Shifts for Widow

Widow's Age	Beginning Value	Spending Need	Return in $	Return in %	Year End Value	Change to This FWC Allocation at Year End	Confidence Level	Confidence Level on New Allocation	Equity Exposure
21	$ 100,000	$ (5,000)	$ 7,496	7.50%	$ 102,496	Bal Growth	83		80%
22	$ 102,496	$ (5,150)	$ 27,694	27.02%	$ 125,039	Bal Growth	84		80%
23	$ 125,039	$ (5,305)	$ 24,602	19.68%	$ 144,337	Bal Income	91	83	45%
24	$ 144,337	$ (5,464)	$ (3,949)	−2.74%	$ 134,924	Risk Averse	92	83	30%
25	$ 134,924	$ (5,628)	$ (13,105)	−9.71%	$ 116,191	Bal Income	73	86	45%
26	$ 116,191	$ (5,796)	$ (42,607)	−36.67%	$ 67,788	Bal Growth	68	83	80%
27	$ 67,788	$ (5,970)	$ (4,794)	−7.07%	$ 57,024	Aggressive	35	50	100%
28	$ 57,024	$ (6,149)	$ 51,060	89.54%	$ 101,934	Aggressive	31		100%
29	$ 101,934	$ (6,334)	$ 8,994	8.82%	$ 104,595	Aggressive	75		100%
30	$ 104,595	$ (6,524)	$ 46,732	44.68%	$ 144,802	Aggressive	77		100%
31	$ 144,802	$ (6,720)	$ 67,003	46.27%	$ 205,086	Aggressive	88		100%
32	$ 205,086	$ (6,921)	$ (24,283)	−11.84%	$ 173,882	Risk Averse	97	94	30%
33	$ 173,882	$ (7,129)	$ 23,023	13.24%	$ 189,776	Risk Averse	78		30%
34	$ 189,776	$ (7,343)	$ 5,065	2.67%	$ 187,499	Risk Averse	83		30%
35	$ 187,499	$ (7,563)	$ (1,303)	−0.70%	$ 178,633	Risk Averse	80		30%
36	$ 178,633	$ (7,790)	$ (8,176)	−4.58%	$ 162,667	Bal Income	71	85	45%
37	$ 162,667	$ (8,024)	$ 28,893	17.76%	$ 183,536	Balanced	72	81	60%
38	$ 183,536	$ (8,264)	$ 53,381	29.08%	$ 228,653	Balanced	87		60%
39	$ 228,653	$ (8,512)	$ 23,855	10.43%	$ 243,996	Risk Averse	95	87	30%

40	$ 243,996	$ (8,768)	16.01%	$ 39,070	$ 274,299	Risk Averse	90	30%
41	$ 274,299	$ (9,031)	−2.14%	$ (5,867)	$ 259,402	Risk Averse	95	30%
42	$ 259,402	$ (9,301)	1.83%	$ 4,747	$ 254,847	Risk Averse	91	30%
43	$ 254,847	$ (9,581)	2.08%	$ 5,298	$ 250,564	Risk Averse	89	30%
44	$ 250,564	$ (9,868)	7.24%	$ 18,135	$ 258,831	Risk Averse	84	30%
45	$ 258,831	$(10,164)	10.76%	$ 27,844	$ 276,511	Risk Averse	86	30%
46	$ 276,511	$(10,469)	5.95%	$ 16,453	$ 282,495	Risk Averse	89	30%
47	$ 282,495	$(10,783)	5.12%	$ 14,469	$ 286,180	Risk Averse	89	30%
48	$ 286,180	$(11,106)	1.28%	$ 3,650	$ 278,723	Risk Averse	89	30%
49	$ 278,723	$(11,440)	18.28%	$ 50,947	$ 318,231	Risk Averse	85	30%
50	$ 318,231	$(11,783)	8.12%	$ 25,852	$ 332,300	Risk Averse	92	30%
51	$ 332,300	$(12,136)	1.73%	$ 5,758	$ 325,922	Risk Averse	93	30%
52	$ 325,922	$(12,500)	1.40%	$ 4,574	$ 317,996	Risk Averse	91	30%
53	$ 317,996	$(12,875)	14.54%	$ 46,244	$ 351,365	Risk Averse	90	30%
54	$ 351,365	$(13,262)	4.09%	$ 14,377	$ 352,480	Risk Averse	93	30%
55	$ 352,480	$(13,660)	7.08%	$ 24,972	$ 363,793	Risk Averse	92	30%
56	$ 363,793	$(14,069)	9.91%	$ 36,047	$ 385,771	Risk Averse	92	30%
57	$ 385,771	$(14,491)	0.68%	$ 2,607	$ 373,887	Risk Averse	95	30%
58	$ 373,887	$(14,926)	8.21%	$ 30,707	$ 389,667	Risk Averse	91	30%
59	$ 389,667	$(15,374)	8.43%	$ 32,843	$ 407,136	Risk Averse	95	30%
60	$ 407,136	$(15,835)	7.67%	$ 31,225	$ 422,526	Risk Averse	96	30%
61	$ 422,526	$(16,310)	0.57%	$ 2,429	$ 408,645	Risk Averse	96	30%
62	$ 408,645	$(16,799)	14.18%	$ 57,939	$ 449,784	Risk Averse	93	30%

(Continued)

141

Table 9.4 (Continued)

Widow's Age	Beginning Value	Spending Need	Return in $	Return in %	Year End Value	Change to This FWC Allocation at Year End	Confidence Level	Level on New Allocation	Equity Exposure
63	$ 449,784	$(17,303)	$ 40,710	9.05%	$ 473,190	Risk Averse	97		30%
64	$ 473,190	$(17,823)	$ (18,879)	−3.99%	$ 436,489	Risk Averse	98		30%
65	$ 436,489	$(18,357)	$ 42,888	9.83%	$ 461,020	Risk Averse	93		30%
66	$ 461,020	$(18,908)	$ 46,948	10.18%	$ 489,060	Risk Averse	95		30%
67	$ 489,060	$(19,475)	$ 37,747	7.72%	$ 507,332	Risk Averse	98		30%
68	$ 507,332	$(20,059)	$ (13,018)	−2.57%	$ 474,254	Risk Averse	99		30%
69	$ 474,254	$(20,661)	$ (14,578)	−3.07%	$ 439,014	Risk Averse	96		30%
70	$ 439,014	$(21,281)	$ 79,028	18.00%	$ 496,761	Risk Averse	90		30%
71	$ 496,761	$(21,920)	$ 93,075	18.74%	$ 567,917	Risk Averse	96		30%
72	$ 567,917	$(22,577)	$ 13,952	2.46%	$ 559,292	Risk Averse	99		30%
73	$ 559,292	$(23,254)	$ 36,176	6.47%	$ 572,214	Risk Averse	99		30%
74	$ 572,214	$(23,952)	$ 65,966	11.53%	$ 614,228	Risk Averse	99		30%
75	$ 614,228	$(24,671)	$ 85,627	13.94%	$ 675,184	Risk Averse	100		30%
76	$ 675,184	$(25,411)	$ 50,975	7.55%	$ 700,749	Risk Averse	100		30%
77	$ 700,749	$(26,173)	$ 179,354	25.59%	$ 853,930	Risk Averse	100		30%
78	$ 853,930	$(26,958)	$ 117,784	13.79%	$ 944,756	Risk Averse	100		30%
79	$ 944,756	$(27,767)	$ 94,309	9.98%	$1,011,297	Risk Averse	100		30%
80	$1,011,297	$(28,600)	$ 221,160	21.87%	$1,203,857	Risk Averse	100		30%
81	$1,203,857	$(29,458)	$ 169,492	14.08%	$1,343,890	Risk Averse	100		30%

82	$1,343,890	$(30,342)	$ 32,325	2.41%	$1,345,874	Risk Averse	100	30%
83	$1,345,874	$(31,252)	$ 133,851	9.95%	$1,448,473	Risk Averse	100	30%
84	$1,448,473	$(32,190)	$ 233,575	16.13%	$1,649,858	Risk Averse	100	30%
85	$1,649,858	$(33,155)	$ 63,169	3.83%	$1,679,871	Risk Averse	100	30%
86	$1,679,871	$(34,150)	$ 342,864	20.41%	$1,988,585	Risk Averse	100	30%
87	$1,988,585	$(35,174)	$ 169,701	8.53%	$2,123,111	Risk Averse	100	30%
88	$2,123,111	$(36,230)	$ 236,288	11.13%	$2,323,170	Risk Averse	100	30%
89	$2,323,170	$(37,317)	$ (49,343)	-2.12%	$2,236,511	Risk Averse	100	30%
90	$2,236,511	$(38,436)	$ 482,447	21.57%	$2,680,522	Risk Averse	100	30%
91	$2,680,522	$(39,589)	$ 218,691	8.16%	$2,859,624	Risk Averse	100	30%
92	$2,859,624	$(40,777)	$ 414,742	14.50%	$3,233,590	Risk Averse	100	30%
93	$3,233,590	$(42,000)	$ 374,943	11.60%	$3,566,533	Risk Averse	100	30%
94	$3,566,533	$(43,260)	$ 235,149	6.59%	$3,758,422	Risk Averse	100	30%
95	$3,758,422	$(44,558)	$ 224,077	5.96%	$3,937,941	Risk Averse	100	30%
96	$3,937,941	$(45,895)	$ 69,442	1.76%	$3,961,488	Risk Averse	100	30%
97	$3,961,488	$(47,271)	$ 136,117	3.44%	$4,050,334	Risk Averse	100	30%
98	$4,050,334	$(46,690)	$ 461,252	11.39%	$4,462,896	Risk Averse	100	30%
99	$4,462,896	$(50,150)	$ 335,699	7.52%	$4,748,445	Risk Averse	100	30%
100	$4,748,445	$(51,655)	$ 181,732	3.83%	$4,878,522	Risk Averse	100	30%

where the confidence level for the plan couldn't be adjusted to targeted adequate funding levels by shifting *only* the asset allocation (other than the overfunding periods in the last 60 years). Clearly, in such an environment, the spending policy would and *should* be adjusted.

We also observe how unrealistic this is, because it assumes the widow wouldn't adjust her spending at the young age of 59, despite having excessive confidence and a spending need of only 3.7 percent of the current portfolio value. It only gets worse from there. By age 80, she would only be spending 2.8 percent of the portfolio value, and by age 99 she would be at only 1 percent. In reality, a *real wealth manager* would have told her to spend more.

Of course, this is what would happen if people really never thought about things—but they do, which is what makes the assumption that there would be no adjustments over a lifetime so unrealistic.

So, what were the returns and portfolio values for the other allocation choices? Was it a "Black Swan" with a fat tail that swooped down upon the portfolio, which caused most of the other allocation choices to fail? Was there an outlier in the bell curve (by the way, our bell is warped because we use a log normal distribution, not a normal distribution) that caused the other allocations to fail, like our initial plan would have, if the timing of her husband's death had moved by only one year?

Table 9.5 shows us the returns for each year, for the five allocation choices for our widow. One would notice in the shaded area that there **were not** outlier returns immediately preceding the time periods where the widow ran out of money with these choices. Well . . . maybe there were outliers, but they were more likely to the upside, not downside. The *worst* loss of any of these portfolios in the shaded area was for the 100 percent stock allocation with a 10.78 percent decline. That is hardly a Black Swan. **Two of the seven years before the widow ran out of money with allocation #3, stocks for the long run, she would have experienced returns of more than 40 percent!**

In Table 9.6, we can observe the *dollar* impact of these returns on the widow's wealth.

Table 9.5 Returns for the Allocation Choices

Asset Allocation Alternatives—Returns

Widow's Age	#1- Long Term (Risk "Tolerance") Allocation	#2-Age Based Allocation (Target Date)	#3- Stocks for the Long Run	# 4- Superior Selection	#5- Wealth Management Allocation
21	5.96%	6.68%	11.62%	7.46%	7.50%
22	14.55%	25.66%	37.49%	16.05%	27.02%
23	16.45%	33.08%	43.61%	17.95%	19.68%
24	−5.90%	−18.36%	−8.42%	−4.40%	−2.74%
25	−7.28%	−21.47%	−24.90%	−5.78%	−9.71%
26	−18.59%	−34.91%	−43.34%	−17.09%	−36.67%
27	2.61%	−3.18%	−8.19%	4.11%	−7.07%
28	34.73%	65.81%	53.99%	36.23%	89.54%
29	8.67%	8.61%	−1.44%	10.17%	8.82%
30	20.95%	33.55%	47.67%	22.45%	44.68%
31	19.20%	33.22%	33.92%	20.70%	46.27%
32	−15.67%	−30.07%	−35.03%	−14.17%	−11.84%
33	15.64%	23.43%	31.12%	17.14%	13.24%
34	2.65%	1.29%	−0.41%	4.15%	2.67%
35	−1.22%	−4.32%	−9.78%	0.28%	−0.70%
36	−3.67%	−6.70%	−11.59%	−2.17%	−4.58%
37	12.43%	19.85%	20.34%	13.93%	17.76%
38	20.80%	33.03%	25.90%	22.30%	29.08%
39	13.60%	21.31%	19.75%	15.10%	10.43%
40	20.60%	32.11%	36.44%	22.10%	16.01%
41	−2.96%	−5.31%	−8.07%	−1.46%	−2.14%
42	1.98%	2.60%	5.71%	3.48%	1.83%
43	2.05%	2.17%	5.50%	3.55%	2.08%
44	8.62%	11.89%	18.79%	10.12%	7.24%

(Continued)

Table 9.5 (Continued)

Widow's Age	#1- Long Term (Risk "Tolerance") Allocation	#2-Age Based Allocation (Target Date)	#3- Stocks for the Long Run	# 4- Superior Selection	#5- Wealth Management Allocation
45	13.42%	19.66%	31.71%	14.92%	10.76%
46	6.85%	9.84%	24.02%	8.35%	5.95%
47	5.61%	7.36%	18.37%	7.11%	5.12%
48	0.78%	−0.21%	−0.99%	2.28%	1.28%
49	22.58%	30.25%	52.62%	24.08%	18.28%
50	9.85%	13.58%	31.56%	11.35%	8.12%
51	1.94%	2.70%	6.56%	3.44%	1.73%
52	0.13%	−2.17%	−10.78%	1.63%	1.40%
53	18.80%	24.36%	43.36%	20.30%	14.54%
54	5.01%	6.35%	11.96%	6.51%	4.09%
55	6.68%	5.60%	0.47%	8.18%	7.08%
56	12.04%	14.06%	26.89%	13.54%	9.91%
57	−0.37%	−1.37%	−8.73%	1.13%	0.68%
58	9.75%	10.92%	22.80%	11.25%	8.21%
59	9.76%	10.44%	16.48%	11.26%	8.43%
60	9.80%	10.60%	12.45%	11.30%	7.67%
61	−0.39%	−0.72%	−10.06%	1.11%	0.57%
62	18.69%	19.36%	23.98%	20.19%	14.18%
63	10.75%	10.82%	11.06%	12.25%	9.05%
64	−5.92%	−5.84%	−8.50%	−4.42%	−3.99%
65	8.50%	8.83%	4.01%	10.00%	9.83%
66	11.02%	10.85%	14.31%	12.52%	10.18%
67	8.12%	7.84%	18.98%	9.62%	7.72%
68	−5.00%	−3.83%	−14.66%	−3.50%	−2.57%
69	−5.34%	−3.70%	−26.47%	−3.84%	−3.07%
70	21.15%	18.81%	37.20%	22.65%	18.00%

71	21.80%	19.95%	23.84%	23.30%	18.74%
72	3.18%	2.80%	−7.18%	4.68%	2.46%
73	7.29%	6.35%	6.56%	8.79%	6.47%
74	13.43%	10.86%	18.44%	14.93%	11.53%
75	15.96%	12.32%	32.42%	17.46%	13.94%
76	7.04%	7.90%	−4.91%	8.54%	7.55%
77	26.64%	27.33%	21.41%	28.14%	25.59%
78	15.70%	12.50%	22.51%	17.20%	13.79%
79	9.04%	11.05%	6.27%	10.54%	9.98%
80	23.27%	21.81%	32.16%	24.77%	21.87%
81	14.38%	14.61%	18.47%	15.88%	14.08%
82	1.67%	2.32%	5.23%	3.17%	2.41 %
83	11.04%	8.47%	16.81%	12.54%	9.95%
84	16.78%	14.79%	31.49%	18.28%	16.13%
85	2.06%	6.43%	−3.17%	3.56%	3.83%
86	22.95%	18.27%	30.55%	24.45%	20.41 %
87	9.62%	8.02%	7.67%	11.12%	8.53%
88	12.17%	11.40%	9.99%	13.67%	11.13%
89	−2.18%	−4.01%	1.31%	−0.68%	−2.12%
90	23.77%	18.60%	37.43%	25.27%	21.57%
91	9.25%	4.07%	23.07%	10.75%	8.16%
92	16.08%	10.15%	33.36%	17.58%	14.50%
93	11.56%	10.37%	28.58%	13.06%	11.60%
94	8.31%	0.26%	21.04%	9.81%	6.59%
95	5.07%	11.22%	−9.11%	6.57%	5.96%
96	1.76%	3.74%	−11.88%	3.26%	1.76%
97	1.57%	14.42%	−22.10%	3.07%	3.44%
98	14.61%	1.80%	28.69%	16.11%	11.39%
99	8.73%	5.27%	10.87%	10.23%	7.52%
100	4.06%	3.12%	4.89%	5.56%	3.83%

Table 9.6 Widow's Portfolio Value Based on Each of the Allocation Policy Choices

Asset Allocation Alternatives—Portfolio Values

Widow's Age	#1- Long Term (Risk "Tolerance") Allocation	#2- Age Based Allocation (Target Date)	#3- Stocks for the Long Run	#4- Superior Selection	#5- Wealth Management Allocation
21	$100,955	$101,680	$106,624	$ 102,455	$ 102,496
22	$110,496	$122,621	$141,446	$ 113,751	$ 125,039
23	$123,364	$157,874	$197,823	$ 128,861	$ 144,337
24	$110,626	$123,423	$175,712	$ 117,732	$ 134,924
25	$ 96,946	$ 91,300	$126,338	$ 105,300	$ 116,191
26	$ 73,128	$ 53,634	$ 65,791	$ 81,509	$ 67,788
27	$ 69,066	$ 45,960	$ 54,431	$ 78,888	$ 57,024
28	$ 86,903	$ 70,058	$ 77,668	$ 101,319	$ 101,934
29	$ 88,100	$ 69,754	$ 70,214	$ 105,286	$ 104,595
30	$100,035	$ 86,631	$ 97,160	$ 122,401	$ 144,802
31	$112,526	$108,692	$123,399	$ 141,022	$ 205,086
32	$ 87,967	$ 69,092	$ 73,255	$ 114,112	$ 173,882
33	$ 94,600	$ 78,148	$ 88,925	$ 126,547	$ 189,776
34	$ 89,764	$ 71,810	$ 81,217	$ 124,456	$ 187,499
35	$ 81,106	$ 61,147	$ 65,707	$ 117,242	$ 178,633
36	$ 70,341	$ 49,260	$ 50,300	$ 106,909	$ 162,667
37	$ 71,061	$ 51,015	$ 52,508	$ 113,779	$ 183,536
38	$ 77,574	$ 59,599	$ 57,843	$ 130,882	$ 228,653
39	$ 79,612	$ 63,787	$ 60,757	$ 142,134	$ 243,996
40	$ 87,245	$ 75,498	$ 74,127	$ 164,779	$ 274,299
41	$ 75,634	$ 62,456	$ 59,113	$ 153,346	$ 259,402
42	$ 67,830	$ 54,777	$ 53,186	$ 149,381	$ 254,847
43	$ 59,637	$ 46,385	$ 46,531	$ 145,096	$ 250,564

Age				
44	$ 54,908	$ 42,033	$ 45,408	$ 149,907	$ 258,831
45	$ 52,113	$ 40,132	$ 49,644	$ 162,112	$ 276,511
46	$ 45,212	$ 33,612	$ 51,098	$ 165,171	$ 282,495
47	$ 36,967	$ 25,302	$ 49,700	$ 166,140	$ 286,180
48	$ 26,148	$ 14,142	$ 38,102	$ 158,819	$ 278,723
49	$ 20,614	$ 6,980	$ 46,713	$ 185,627	$ 318,231
50	$ 10,861	BROKE	$ 49,674	$ 194,904	$ 332,300
51	BROKE		$ 40,794	$ 189,481	$ 325,922
52			$ 23,895	$ 180,077	$ 317,996
53			$ 21,382	$ 203,762	$ 351,365
54			$ 10,676	$ 203,774	$ 352,480
55			BROKE	$ 206,781	$ 363,793
56				$ 220,719	$ 385,771
57				$ 208,729	$ 373,887
58				$ 217,282	$ 389,667
59				$ 226,370	$ 407,136
60				$ 236,121	$ 422,526
61				$ 222,426	$ 408,645
62				$ 250,525	$ 449,784
63				$ 263,909	$ 473,190
64				$ 234,419	$ 436,489
65				$ 239,503	$ 461,020
66				$ 250,580	$ 489,060
67				$ 255,223	$ 507,332
68				$ 226,225	$ 474,254
69				$ 196,877	$ 439,014
70				$ 220,186	$ 496,761
71				$ 249,562	$ 567,917
72				$ 238,673	$ 559,292
73				$ 236,401	$ 572,214
74				$ 247,746	$ 614,228
75				$ 266,328	$ 675,184

(Continued)

149

Table 9.6 (Continued)

Widow's Age	#1- Long Term (Risk "Tolerance") Allocation	#2- Age Based Allocation (Target Date)	#3- Stocks for the Long Run	#4- Superior Selection	#5- Wealth Management Allocation
76				$ 263,661	$ 700,749
77				$ 311,692	$ 853,930
78				$ 338,345	$ 944,756
79				$ 346,232	$1,011,297
80				$ 403,391	$1,203,857
81				$ 437,974	$1,343,890
82				$ 421,524	$1,345,874
83				$ 443,142	$1,448,473
84				$ 491,939	$1,649,858
85				$ 476,312	$1,679,871
86				$ 558,618	$1,988,585
87				$ 585,539	$2,123,111
88				$ 629,358	$2,323,170
89				$ 587,768	$2,236,511
90				$ 697,842	$2,680,522
91				$ 733,293	$2,859,624
92				$ 821,423	$3,233,590
93				$ 886,667	$3,566,533
94				$ 930,359	$3,758,422
95				$ 946,901	$3,937,941
96				$ 931,920	$3,961,488
97				$ 913,283	$4,050,334
98				$1,011,722	$4,462,896
99				$1,065,108	$4,748,445
100				$1,072,678	$4,878,522

What Does This Mean for You?

So what does all of this evidence mean when it comes to wealth management? Does it mean a *real wealth management* approach will always produce more wealth than would otherwise be realized with a *return management* approach? No, that would be a misleading claim and an overstatement of the mathematical facts. *In retrospect*, there will always be better decisions that could have been made. That does not make it rational to project making superior decisions in the future while ignoring the uncertainty such decisions introduce.

Does the evidence presented contrasting the effect of dollar weighted funding level measurements and allocation shifts mean that managing funded status is a better market timing strategy that produces superior returns? No, it does not, because the funded status is unique to each individual's cash flows *and risk capacity,* and in reality, there will be many more changes made in the wealth management plan than just the asset allocation.

The evidence merely shows there is a vast amount of uncertainty in the market's behavior. Think about the multibillion-dollar range of uncertainty for our widow with $100,000. *When* different results occur affects different people in different ways, sometimes with no effect, and sometimes with an effect that would cause a change to something other than their allocations. Why are planners so stuck on being able to forecast things? Don't investors *want* advice about their choices to improve their lifestyle because of green swans, or prudent tweaks they should make in the face of possible black swans?

Return managers measure something that is often meaningless to wealth. They may or may not be successful at producing superior risk-adjusted returns. However, as shown here, even if superior risk-adjusted returns are achieved it may still be irrelevant in terms of actual wealth a person has, or can spend.

The abuses of the "odds of success" crowd cost many investors dearly. They focus only on finding black swans (not green ones, where there is more wealth and choices). But it is time to stop playing these ridiculous games by pretending that 85 percent or 90 percent confidence is "better" than 83 percent or 75 percent. There are so many *tiny,* insignificant savings and spending policy decisions that are far more manageable than the vast continuous uncertainty of the markets, and these decision levers are what real wealth managers can utilize to provide realistic and meaningful advice. **That does not mean that the advice will never change.**

The future of financial advising is dependent on advisers and fiduciaries recognizing this. Do you?

Chapter 10

Superior Results with True Wealth Management

Most people would rather be certain they're miserable than risk being happy.
—ROBERT ANTHONY

In Chapter 6, we showed some simple examples of the effects of the difference between time-weighted (return manager) returns and dollar-weighted (wealth manager) returns. Chapter 7 illustrated a real-life client example and demonstrated how some of the "best" generally accepted and even clairvoyantly "successful" approaches of asset allocation ended up costing a widow investor millions of dollars of wealth. Chapter 8 examined *how unlikely* it is that markets would behave in a manner that would have avoided over- and underfunding, even though the initial odds were very high. Chapter 9 provided the detailed back-up data for the returns and allocation shifts for our sample widow in Chapter 7. It also demonstrated how sensitive her wealth plan was to just **one year** of timing for a cash flow inflation adjustment or just one year of inferior investment results.

In this last chapter of Part Two of this book, we will demonstrate that the superior dollar result of *real wealth management* is NOT due to mean reversion, lucky market timing, or exposing an investor to excessive investment risk (all assumptions of return managers, not wealth managers). To demonstrate this, we will apply the same rules we used for our 20-year-old widow example—adjusting only the asset allocation but unrealistically not investor's goals or spending policy—to another investor who is also 20 years old but is saving for a retirement that is 45 years away (referred to as a saver). To keep a level playing field, both will start with the same 82 percent initial confidence level for their wealth management plans with a portfolio allocation that begins with 80 percent equity exposure in 1926.

A Real Wealth Management Plan

The first step in this process is to examine the allocation shifts of a wealth management plan for our 20-year-old saver to observe whether, like the widow, he experiences superior *wealth* results relative to other clairvoyantly selected "superior" investment strategies. His situation back in 1926 is that he is 20 years old and starts with $2,000 in annual savings (keep in mind this is over $21,000 in today's dollars), adjusted each year for 3 percent inflation until retirement at age 65, with a $103,000 inflation-adjusted retirement income to age 100. This case is very similar to the saver we introduced in Chapter 8 when we examined risk capacity relative to our widow and how unlikely it was the market would behave in a manner that would cause an allocation change for him in the near term, yet it was very likely for the widow. We slightly lowered the income goal for our saver in this case to match both the initial confidence level and allocation at inception in 1926 to the widow's so we could contrast the difference in allocation shifts over time on a completely level playing field.

As would be expected for a plan with such high risk capacity, a 100 percent stock allocation in the "stocks for the long run" portfolio would actually almost double the results of the wealth management plan. But, keep in mind, in the wealth management plan the rules we apply are to avoid needless risk exposure to the equity markets, and over the life of our saver we average only 53 percent equity exposure versus a lifetime of being 100 percent exposed to equities.

Also, as might be expected for a plan with very high risk capacity, using a fixed allocation over the entire life of the plan with a 45-year accumulation period is too conservative and produces an inferior geometric mean result, albeit with very low investment risk. Despite the wealth management plan producing only 0.46 percent higher compound return with 5.5 percent higher risk, the wealth result compounds over time to be more than **21 times** the wealth result of constant-weighted allocation that is unchanged over the entire plan horizon.

Also, like the widow's example, the *target date/lifecycle* approach is once again about the worst choice that could be made for the saver. Starting with 80 percent equities and reducing the equity exposure by 1 percent a year at each birthday (as is the common rule of thumb for this approach) not only exposed our saver to fairly high risk and a low return, but **had him broke** at age 90, versus having $26.7 million at the end of the wealth management plan. The *theory of target date/lifecycle* approaches is to use the calendar **as a proxy** to consider risk capacity of withdrawals, but since it ignores the funded status, the shifts in allocation will frequently go the wrong direction from what makes sense based on the market's uncertain behavior, and thus is the worst dollar result for both our widow and the saver.

Understanding Risk Capacity versus Risk Tolerance

Unlike our widow, for our saver with extraordinarily high risk capacity, none of these results is significantly different than what would have been predicted by return managers. However, many return managers argue that their value lies in superior selection and their ability to outperform and/or reduce investment risk. In our saver's case, his high risk capacity during much of his plan exposes a significant difference

Table 10.1 Wealth Management Choices for Our 20-Year-Old Saver

	Wealth Management	Superior Selection
Compound return	9.78%	10.07%
Risk (SD)	18.54%	12.98%
Growth of $100	$174,519	$216,166
Wealth at age 100	$26,743,678	$22,731,344

from our widow in the excess returns that need to be produced to come close to competing with a real wealth management plan. If we take the average equity exposure of the real wealth management plan of 53 percent and assume that the superior selection skills outperform the allocation policy by 0.75 percent each and every year (completely ignoring the risk of ever underperforming at the wrong time for the investor), we can observe in Table 10.1 that the higher returns and lower risk added no value, and once again, **cost the investor more than $4 million of wealth.**

So, despite the high risk capacity and long-term accumulation of our saver's wealth management plan, we again observe how misleading "successful" management of returns (and risk) is from the perspective of wealth. It is easy for return managers to sell this because investors are not aware of it, and make the erroneous assumption that there is some benefit to producing higher returns with lower risks. After all, if the growth of $100 is significantly more with superior selection, shouldn't that improve my wealth management results? As we can see for the saver, the superior risk adjusted results cost him dearly . . . millions. **Is having $4 million less wealth a benefit with the same spending?**

Think about how much "conventional wisdom" has suckered financial advisers into buying this *lack of any real value proposition* promoted by brokerage firms, money managers, and mutual fund complexes into standard "best practices."

How many times have you seen a risk versus return chart like the one in Figure 10.1? The "superior selection" square on the risk/return chart

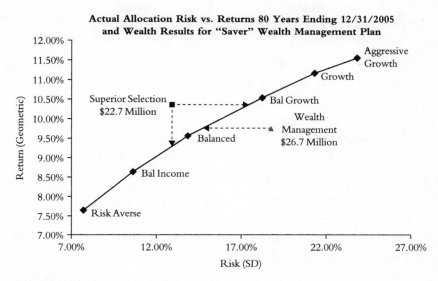

Figure 10.1 Historical risk versus return

shows a great benefit for the return managers who promote risk-adjusted returns instead of wealth management. Sometimes return managers would sell such a portfolio based on how much it is above the efficient frontier, often drawing a line from the square straight down to the efficient frontier and showing that "excess return" as being their "value."

Product Vendors' Sleight of Hand

Even more ironic to me is how many advisers buy the story from the product vendors who are swindling them into a sales pitch that goes something like, "*We* are not seeking *excess returns*, we are about **risk control** and we seek investment results that only match market results with less investment risk." Of course, to sell this story they use a horizontal line that goes directly to the right from the square to the efficient frontier, supposedly demonstrating that they comply with their sales pitch of only equaling efficient market results with "less risk." How can investors (or worse, sophisticated financial advisers) be suckered into buying this? It is almost like a bad magician's sleight of hand in misdirecting the attention of the observer by choosing to guide their gaze based only on whether they focus vertically (the outperformance pitch) or horizontally (the risk control pitch). They are the same story! They are just packaged differently!

The one thing that is not normally shown on such risk/return charts is what the *wealth* effect is to the client. In this case, however, we expose the fraud of the return manager's sales spin by showing the ending wealth result for a specific client and the $4 million price to our saver's wealth derived from the return manager's approach of producing higher returns with lower risk. (The returns are all geometric/compound returns and the risk is standard deviation of annual returns.)

On a complete efficient frontier, there are more than just the model portfolio dots; there are an infinite number of portfolios that make up that efficient frontier line. (The portfolio model "dots" are the actual results of Financeware Macro Model allocations used throughout this chapter as described in end note 3 in Chapter 7.) If we were to choose merely the efficient portfolio that matched return for the superior selection portfolio (where the horizontal right arrow hits the efficient frontier), we would discover that such an efficient but "inferior" portfolio that had more risk and the same return would have produced $30.2 million, or $7.5 million more wealth than the less risk and same return "superior selection" portfolio! (See Figure 10.2.)

Likewise, demonstrating the value of true wealth management, if I chose the portfolio on the efficient frontier that matched the return of the wealth management plan, but was obviously more "efficient" (where the arrow goes left from our wealth management plan triangle in Figure 10.3), I would discover the wealth result to be only $16.2 million, a full $10.5 million of wealth less than that "inefficient" real wealth management portfolio with more risk, and the same return (see Figure 10.3).

It is personally very frustrating to see how such charts are used every day in the investment product selling industry to demonstrate fictitious value and also are used to justify vastly uncertain choices in product selection (often with certain high expenses). When one considers that the

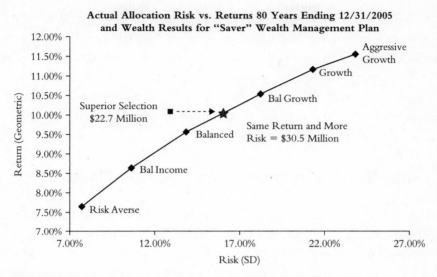

Figure 10.2 Higher risk and same return produce higher wealth

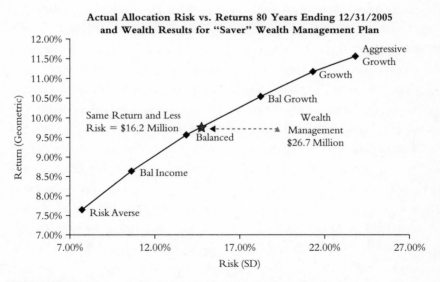

Figure 10.3 Same return and lower risk produce less wealth

way such sales presentations are normally assembled is based on uncertain future results based on the track record of what happened, instead of *what would have happened as in this analysis,* it makes me want to scream!

The bottom line of this contrast, though, is the reality of what we showed in the widow's case, our saver's case, and where we started this entire series; it is the premise of the fundamental difference between managing returns and managing wealth.

It Is Not Hard to Understand if You Are Objective

Personally, I am confused as to why people don't get this. To me, it does not seem complicated to understand the simple realities of the difference in these two approaches. I know it is conceptually easier to ignore the reality of the numerous year-by-year variable results and data points to an oversimplified "bottom line" risk and return number. But, when we know that doing so may be meaningless for *what one is trying to achieve,* you would think that there would be a large enough universe of advisers out there who are sophisticated enough to expose the fallacy so that the game would ultimately come to an end. Yet, currently it thrives and even grows despite the fiction on which it is based. The Supreme Court's ruling, though, may very well change this since fiduciary liability is henceforth going to be measured on dollars of wealth in an individual participant's plan balance instead of theoretical rates of return.

Were these two superior wealth results of the widow and saver due to "mean reversion" or exceptionally lucky timing? Or, is this merely the nature of continuously managing the future uncertainty based on a unique set of goals (liability stream) as competently managed pension trusts do?

As one might expect with a wealth management plan for a young saver with high risk capacity, there are fewer allocation shifts relative to the widow's plan (seven versus nine). In fact, this high risk capacity plan of our saver (see Table 10.2) *caused only 1 allocation shift in the first 20 years of the plan,* despite a very wild Great Depression bear market and post-Depression rebound. That is risk capacity! Our widow had all nine of her allocation shifts occurring in the first 20 years of her plan. Think about

Table 10.2 Details of Saver's Plan and Allocation Shifts

Saver's Age	Beginning Value	Savings (Spending Need)	Return in $	Return in %	Year End Value	Allocation	Confidence Level	Confidence on New Allocation	Equity Exposure
21	$ 2,000	$ 2,000	$ 150	7.5%	$ 4,150	Bal Growth	77		80%
22	$ 4,150	$ 2,060	$ 1,121	27.0%	$ 7,331	Bal Growth	79		80%
23	$ 7,331	$ 2,122	$ 2,503	34.1%	$ 11,956	Bal Growth	80		80%
24	$ 11,956	$ 2,185	$ (1,948)	−16.3%	$ 12,194	Bal Growth	81		80%
25	$ 12,194	$ 2,251	$ (2,679)	−22.0%	$ 11,766	Bal Growth	77		80%
26	$ 11,766	$ 2,319	$ (4,314)	−36.7%	$ 9,770	Bal Growth	75		80%
27	$ 9,770	$ 2,388	$ (415)	−4.2%	$ 11,743	Bal Growth	69	80	80%
28	$ 11,743	$ 2,460	$ 10,515	89.5%	$ 24,717	Aggressive	78		100%
29	$ 24,717	$ 2,534	$ 2,181	8.8%	$ 29,432	Aggressive	84		100%
30	$ 29,432	$ 2,610	$ 13,150	44.7%	$ 45,191	Aggressive	83		100%
31	$ 45,191	$ 2,688	$ 20,911	46.3%	$ 68,789	Aggressive	85		100%
32	$ 68,789	$ 2,768	$ (30,418)	−44.2%	$ 41,140	Aggressive	90		100%
33	$ 41,140	$ 2,852	$ 13,079	31.8%	$ 57,071	Aggressive	83		100%
34	$ 57,071	$ 2,937	$ (62)	−0.1%	$ 59,946	Aggressive	82		100%
35	$ 59,946	$ 3,025	$ (4,755)	−7.9%	$ 58,216	Aggressive	82		100%
36	$ 58,216	$ 3,116	$ (6,145)	−10.6%	$ 55,187	Aggressive	79		100%
37	$ 55,187	$ 3,209	$ 16,560	30.0%	$ 74,957	Aggressive	74		100%
38	$ 74,957	$ 3,306	$ 38,145	50.9%	$ 116,407	Aggressive	77		100%
39	$ 116,407	$ 3,405	$ 38,811	33.3%	$ 158,623	Aggressive	83		100%
40	$ 158,623	$ 3,507	$ 81,383	51.3%	$ 243,513	Aggressive	86		100%

(Continued)

Table 10.2 (Continued)

Saver's Age	Beginning Value	Savings (Spending Need)	Return in $	Return in %	Year End Value	Allocation	Confidence Level	Confidence on New Allocation	Equity Exposure
41	$ 243,513	$ 3,612	$ (12,593)	-5.2%	$ 234,532	Balanced	91	81	60%
42	$ 234,532	$ 3,721	$ 6,610	2.8%	$ 244,863	Balanced	77		60%
43	$ 244,863	$ 3,832	$ 6,087	2.5%	$ 254,782	Balanced	75		60%
44	$ 254,782	$ 3,947	$ 40,034	15.7%	$ 298,764	Bal Growth	70	80	80%
45	$ 298,764	$ 4,066	$ 81,500	27.3%	$ 384,329	Bal Growth	82		80%
46	$ 384,329	$ 4,188	$ 58,629	15.3%	$ 447,146	Bal Growth	84		80%
47	$ 447,146	$ 4,313	$ 50,017	11.2%	$ 501,476	Bal Growth	88		80%
48	$ 501,476	$ 4,443	$ (7,761)	-1.5%	$ 498,158	Bal Growth	87		80%
49	$ 498,158	$ 4,576	$ 222,123	44.6%	$ 724,857	Bal Growth	85		80%
50	$ 724,857	$ 4,713	$ 89,073	12.3%	$ 818,643	Bal Income	91	85	45%
51	$ 818,643	$ 4,855	$ 20,643	2.5%	$ 844,141	Bal Income	86		45%
52	$ 844,141	$ 5,000	$ (11,346)	-1.3%	$ 837,796	Bal Income	86		45%
53	$ 837,796	$ 5,150	$ 185,780	22.2%	$ 1,028,726	Bal Income	80		45%
54	$ 1,028,726	$ 5,305	$ 61,709	6.0%	$ 1,095,740	Bal Income	88		45%
55	$ 1,095,740	$ 5,464	$ 62,001	5.7%	$ 1,163,205	Bal Income	88		45%
56	$ 1,163,205	$ 5,628	$ 161,810	13.9%	$ 1,330,642	Bal Income	85		45%
57	$ 1,330,642	$ 5,797	$ (19,763)	-1.5%	$ 1,316,676	Bal Income	89		45%
58	$ 1,316,676	$ 5,970	$ 149,461	11.4%	$ 1,472,107	Bal Income	86		45%
59	$ 1,472,107	$ 6,150	$ 157,098	10.7%	$ 1,635,355	Bal Income	87		45%

Age	Balance	Withdrawal	Return	New Balance	Strategy			Allocation
60	$ 1,635,355	$ 6,334	10.7%	$ 1,816,736	Bal Income	90		45%
61	$ 1,816,736	$ 6,524	−1.5%	$ 1,796,214	Bal Income	89		45%
62	$ 1,796,214	$ 6,720	20.4%	$ 2,170,131	Bal Income	85	88	45%
63	$ 2,170,131	$ 6,921	9.1%	$ 2,373,471	Risk Averse	92		30%
64	$ 2,373,471	$ 7,129	−4.0%	$ 2,285,905	Risk Averse	89		30%
65	$ 2,285,905	$(103,000)	9.8%	$ 2,407,511	Risk Averse	80		30%
66	$ 2,407,511	$(106,090)	10.2%	$ 2,546,591	Risk Averse	82		30%
67	$ 2,546,591	$(109,273)	7.7%	$ 2,633,874	Risk Averse	90		30%
68	$ 2,633,874	$(112,551)	−2.6%	$ 2,453,737	Risk Averse	89		30%
69	$ 2,453,737	$(115,927)	−3.1%	$ 2,262,382	Risk Averse	78		30%
70	$ 2,262,382	$(119,405)	23.3%	$ 2,669,865	Bal Income	67	79	45%
71	$ 2,669,865	$(122,987)	22.4%	$ 3,146,222	Bal Income	90		45%
72	$ 3,146,222	$(126,677)	2.5%	$ 3,096,837	Risk Averse	97	96	30%
73	$ 3,096,837	$(130,477)	6.5%	$ 3,166,670	Risk Averse	94		30%
74	$ 3,166,670	$(134,392)	11.5%	$ 3,397,341	Risk Averse	96		30%
75	$ 3,397,341	$(138,423)	13.9%	$ 3,732,525	Risk Averse	98		30%
76	$ 3,732,525	$(142,576)	7.5%	$ 3,871,749	Risk Averse	98		30%
77	$ 3,871,749	$(146,853)	25.6%	$ 4,715,856	Risk Averse	99		30%
78	$ 4,715,856	$(151,259)	13.8%	$ 5,215,064	Risk Averse	100		30%
79	$ 5,215,064	$(155,797)	10.0%	$ 5,579,851	Risk Averse	100		30%
80	$ 5,579,851	$(160,471)	21.9%	$ 6,639,633	Risk Averse	100		30%
81	$ 6,639,633	$(165,285)	14.1%	$ 7,409,146	Risk Averse	100		30%

(Continued)

163

Table 10.2 (Continued)

Saver's Age	Beginning Value	Savings (Spending Need)	Return in $	Return in %	Year End Value	Allocation	Confidence Level	Confidence on New Allocation	Equity Exposure
82	$ 7,409,146	$(170,243)	$ 178,215	2.4%	$ 7,417,118	Risk Averse	100		30%
83	$ 7,417,118	$(175,351)	$ 737,653	9.9%	$ 7,979,420	Risk Averse	100		30%
84	$ 7,979,420	$(180,611)	$1,286,728	16.1%	$ 9,085,537	Risk Averse	100		30%
85	$ 9,085,537	$(186,029)	$ 347,863	3.8%	$ 9,247,370	Risk Averse	100		30%
86	$ 9,247,370	$(191,610)	$1,887,398	20.4%	$10,943,158	Risk Averse	100		30%
87	$10,943,156	$(197,359)	$ 933,862	8.5%	$11,679,661	Risk Averse	100		30%
88	$11,679,661	$(203,279)	$1,299,870	11.1%	$12,776,251	Risk Averse	100		30%
89	$12,776,251	$(209,378)	$ (271,359)	−2.1%	$12,295,514	Risk Averse	100		30%
90	$12,295,514	$(215,659)	$2,652,315	21.6%	$14,732,170	Risk Averse	100		30%
91	$14,732,170	$(222,129)	$1,201,930	8.2%	$15,711,972	Risk Averse	100		30%
92	$15,711,972	$(228,793)	$2,278,768	14.5%	$17,761,947	Risk Averse	100		30%
93	$17,761,947	$(235,657)	$2,059,546	11.6%	$19,585,836	Risk Averse	100		30%
94	$19,585,836	$(242,726)	$1,291,336	6.6%	$20,634,446	Risk Averse	100		30%
95	$20,634,446	$(250,008)	$1,230,226	6.0%	$21,614,663	Risk Averse	100		30%
96	$21,614,663	$(257,508)	$ 381,153	1.8%	$21,738,308	Risk Averse	100		30%
97	$21,738,308	$(265,234)	$ 746,928	3.4%	$22,220,003	Risk Averse	100		30%
98	$22,220,003	$(273,191)	$2,530,414	11.4%	$24,477,226	Risk Averse	100		30%
99	$24,477,226	$(281,386)	$1,841,177	7.5%	$26,037,017	Risk Averse	100		30%
100	$26,037,017	$(289,828)	$ 996,489	3.83%	$26,743,678	Risk Averse	100		30%

this. Despite them being the same age and starting with the same allocation, the widow had no allocation shifts for the last 60 years of what became an excessively overfunded plan, while during this same period the saver had six of his seven allocation shifts occurring. The superior *wealth management* results for both our widow and saver were created by shifts in asset allocation that overlapped only once in the last 80 years.

Both plans ended up being excessively overfunded by age 72, so the last 29 years had them both in the most conservative, risk-averse allocation. However, in the first 51 years of these plans, they had the same allocation in only 27 percent (14 of 51) of the years, as seen in Table 10.3.

We can also observe some of the massive differences in the allocations for the widow and saver with allocations in some periods being at the opposite extremes of 30 percent and 100 percent equities (at ages 32 to 35 and 39 to 40), all based merely on management of the liabilities and funded status like competent pension trusts do.

Table 10.3 Allocations of Widow and Saver for First 51 Years

		Widow		Saver	
Year	Age	Allocation	Equity %	Allocation	Equity %
1	21	Bal Growth	80%	Bal Growth	80%
2	22	Bal Growth	80%	Bal Growth	80%
3	23	Bal Income	45%	Bal Growth	80%
4	24	Risk Averse	30%	Bal Growth	80%
5	25	Bal Income	45%	Bal Growth	80%
6	26	Bal Growth	80%	Bal Growth	80%
7	27	Aggressive	100%	Bal Growth	80%
8	28	Aggressive	100%	Aggressive	100%
9	29	Aggressive	100%	Aggressive	100%
10	30	Aggressive	100%	Aggressive	100%
11	31	Aggressive	100%	Aggressive	100%
12	32	Risk Averse	30%	Aggressive	100%
13	33	Risk Averse	30%	Aggressive	100%
14	34	Risk Averse	30%	Aggressive	100%
15	35	Risk Averse	30%	Aggressive	100%
16	36	Bal Income	45%	Aggressive	100%

(Continued)

Table 10.3 (Continued)

Year	Age	Widow		Saver	
		Allocation	Equity %	Allocation	Equity %
17	37	Balanced	60%	Aggressive	100%
18	38	Balanced	60%	Aggressive	100%
19	39	Risk Averse	30%	Aggressive	100%
20	40	Risk Averse	30%	Aggressive	100%
21	41	Risk Averse	30%	Balanced	60%
22	42	Risk Averse	30%	Balanced	60%
23	43	Risk Averse	30%	Balanced	60%
24	44	Risk Averse	30%	Bal Growth	80%
25	45	Risk Averse	30%	Bal Growth	80%
26	46	Risk Averse	30%	Bal Growth	80%
27	47	Risk Averse	30%	Bal Growth	80%
28	48	Risk Averse	30%	Bal Growth	80%
29	49	Risk Averse	30%	Bal Growth	80%
30	50	Risk Averse	30%	Bal Income	45%
31	51	Risk Averse	30%	Bal Income	45%
32	52	Risk Averse	30%	Bal Income	45%
33	53	Risk Averse	30%	Bal Income	45%
34	54	Risk Averse	30%	Bal Income	45%
35	55	Risk Averse	30%	Bal Income	45%
36	56	Risk Averse	30%	Bal Income	45%
37	57	Risk Averse	30%	Bal Income	45%
38	58	Risk Averse	30%	Bal Income	45%
39	59	Risk Averse	30%	Bal Income	45%
40	60	Risk Averse	30%	Bal Income	45%
41	61	Risk Averse	30%	Bal Income	45%
42	62	Risk Averse	30%	Bal Income	45%
43	63	Risk Averse	30%	Risk Averse	30%
44	64	Risk Averse	30%	Risk Averse	30%
45	65	Risk Averse	30%	Risk Averse	30%
46	66	Risk Averse	30%	Risk Averse	30%
47	67	Risk Averse	30%	Risk Averse	30%
48	68	Risk Averse	30%	Risk Averse	30%
49	69	Risk Averse	30%	Risk Averse	30%
50	70	Risk Averse	30%	Bal Income	45%
51	71	Risk Averse	30%	Bal Income	45%

Mean Reversion?

After releasing Chapter 7 of this book as an educational adviser e-mail, I heard from an adviser, who is no longer a client of ours, responding to the data illustrating the superior wealth result for the widow by saying: *"Hidden in your philosophy **and what makes the numbers work** is the principle of reversion to mean in the markets."*

Of course, when he said this (what is now an obviously erroneous statement in the face of the evidence in Table 10.3), he was not yet privy to the data that exposed the fact that *only one* of the allocation shifts of two superior *wealth* strategies occurred in the same year and that in 73 percent of the years the allocations were different before both plans were excessively overfunded.

This is the evidence that one needs to ascertain whether the adviser is a return manager instead of a wealth manager. He was so convinced that returns and risk (the dogma of what he has been trained to sell) are more important than wealth that he came up with a return manager assumption to defend a factual result he either did not like or which contradicted his return manager training. Many advisers do this daily. After all, it is conventional "wisdom" and many "advanced" training programs show the value generated by creating über efficient (and often expensive) portfolios. It is used to justify expenses, both those of the product vendors using advisers as their source of "distribution" and the adviser's fees for advice through inheritance, since it is supposedly the source of the adviser's primary value. It is still no different, though, than measuring temperature with a ruler. The investor who ends up with less wealth (albeit with *potentially* "better" risk-adjusted returns) is the victim of this game.

Please remember that *none* of these results, despite being based on actual history for the last 80 years, would have actually occurred because of the individual choices a real wealth manager (or investor who is not brain dead) would have made along the way. Decisions would have been made throughout the life of the plan, such as reducing or increasing savings, increasing or decreasing estate targeted value, changing the amount or timing of planned spending, *or (not just)* adjusting investment risk through asset allocation. Part Two of this book merely exposes the difference in only the allocation choice (isolating the single choice to be investment risk) between managing meaningless risk and return numbers versus the discipline of one who is truly focused on managing wealth. **The results and benefits of considering *more than* just allocation policy can help investors make the most of their life.**

I normally close thought pieces by saying that this is the future of financial advising. The reality of this true wealth management discipline we have been attempting to teach to advisers for almost 10 years is that it is not all that new—it is conceptually similar to the same old process used by sophisticated pension trustees for decades.

But, most of the industry cannot let go of the "magic" of risk versus return charts and "superior" risk-adjusted returns, which may end up actually destroying the investor's wealth, even if the track record plays out going forward. The product vendors sell stories that people (both investors and advisers) want to hear and believe in, regardless of whether or not there is any wealth benefit to it. They profit from it handsomely by preying on such victims (many of those victims being the advisers themselves, who recite the sales spin without even realizing they are misleading their clients) enough to maintain a media message that positions their fiction as if it were fact.

We are content with truth. This, in all reality, is *probably not* the future of financial advising (at least the foreseeable future), but it is what an honest, ethical, *wealth manager* delivers, just as a meteorologist uses a thermometer to measure the temperature instead of a ruler. As the lawsuits in ERISA plans start to be based on participant balances instead of meaningless returns, the long-term outcome will likely be an evolution toward truly measuring and managing wealth, but this is likely decades away from becoming the standard. There is simply too much inertia in existing practices, and while this continues, wealth will be destroyed.

Part Three

PRACTICAL SOLUTIONS AND RESOURCES FOR MEETING FIDUCIARY OBLIGATIONS

Having identified the changes needed in procedures for fiduciaries in Part One, and the new measures of liabilities that fiduciaries face and why these measures have changed in Part Two, we now move on in Part Three to give you some final practical solutions to the problems you may face.

Chapter 11 will identify how some of the "safest" fiduciary actions are no longer so safe, and what you can do about getting ahead of the curve to avoid needless liability.

Chapter 12 will identify some free resources that fiduciaries can use to help mitigate their risks and help to document procedural prudence in the future landscape for participant-directed plans.

Chapter 13 will visit the ongoing debate of active versus passive management, which rests in the notion of skill versus luck.

From a perspective of the emerging landscape of wealth-based liability for fiduciaries based on the 2008 Supreme Court ruling, knowing whether your safe harbors are indeed safe, accessing the free tools to protect your liability, and documenting your rationale for skill versus luck decisions are critical to your participants' benefits, and your protection as a fiduciary.

Chapter 11

Safe Harbors that Are Unsafe (Particularly Section 404(C))

When participant-directed defined contribution plans started to grow in popularity, many trustees and fiduciary advisers became concerned about their obligations under ERISA since there was no telling whether participants would make sound decisions. ERISA puts a lot of responsibility on fiduciaries for expert prudence as it relates to investments and the risk posed by what any single participant might do for their own account actually stymied some of the growth of participant directed plans due to trustees' liability concerns.

Enter section 404(c), a safe harbor that appeased many of the fiduciaries' concerns. The DOL initially released this code over 20 years ago and released the "final" preamble and regulation over 15 years ago. Since then, the number of defined contribution plans has burgeoned, and according to Larkspur Data Resources, only 27 percent of the more than 600,000 defined contribution plans choose not to comply with section 404(c).

At the highest level, this code was appealing to fiduciaries, as they viewed it from the perspective of eliminating their personal responsibility for investment results. Specifically, it stated in part:

Section 404(c) of the Employee Retirement Income Security Act of 1974 (ERISA or the Act) provides that if a pension plan that provides for individual accounts permits a participant or beneficiary to exercise control over assets in his account and that participant or beneficiary in fact exercises control over assets in his account, then the participant or beneficiary shall not be deemed to be a fiduciary by reason of his exercise of control and no person who is otherwise a fiduciary shall be liable for any loss, or by reason of any breach, which results from such exercise of control.

This language makes it is easy to see why employers rushed to adopt 404(c)-compliant plans and granted participants control over investment discretion. The impression left with fiduciaries from this section of the code is they could, in essence, wash their hands of having responsibility for investment results, a liability they had otherwise always accepted in the past. There are, however, some conditions that must be met for a plan to be 404(c) compliant. Also, remember this is an optional election; fiduciaries do not have to comply with 404(c) if they wish to maintain their fiduciary responsibility.

At the highest level, complying with 404(c) seemed reasonably easy to accomplish, clear, and straightforward. To be 404(c) compliant, as it appeared on the surface, all the trustees needed to do was make sure participants had sufficient information to make an informed decision, and provide sufficient investment alternatives with differing characteristics so that a participants could materially control the risk and return of their portfolio balance. One might argue this could be accomplished with a money market fund, a bond fund, and a stock fund. Participants concerned with safety against losses could put all of their money in the money market fund. Those who wanted long-term growth despite the risk of losses could put all their money in the stock fund. Most investors, of course, should have a blend of these alternatives, accomplishing an almost limitless array of portfolio risk and return characteristics, and if educated properly, they would do so.

However, in a courtroom, it isn't very easy to prove that you have provided participants "sufficient information to make an informed decision," and proving that you educated participants became an industry in itself.

Late in 2008, the Department of Labor sought comments on proposed regulations about fee disclosures to plan participants. Unfortunately, as of this writing it appears as though these new regulations will not be adopted. Hopefully my new book *Stop the Retirement Rip-off* will continue to be a catalyst to more fully disclose retirement plan expenses and risks to participants. In fact, without full expense disclosure to participants, it is hard to argue that *any* plan is actually compliant with 404(c). The very fact that the Department of Labor proposed new fee-disclosure regulations to both plan sponsors (February 2008) and participants (September 2008) must inherently mean that fee information has not been generally available. *Stop the Retirement Rip-off* is designed for retirement plan participants to explain in detail the hidden fees they may be paying, how to find them, and how to get the trustees to fix them if they are excessive.

But, if 404(c)-compliant plans are breaching their duties for compliance on "sufficient information to make an informed decision" on fees (to the point that the Department of Labor is proposing regulations to actually force plans to expose these previously hidden fees), how come there are not more enforcement actions? Could anyone reasonably argue that you can make an informed decision without knowing the costs?

This is one area that will be a lightning rod for lawsuits against fiduciaries. We already know 80 percent plus of all 401(k) participants are not aware of what, if anything, they are paying for their retirement accounts.[1] How can 73 percent of all plans be compliant with 404(c), yet 80 percent plus of participants be uninformed about their fees, and thus obviously insufficiently educated about their plan expense?

404(c) Election by Trustees Backfires

In an attempt to limit their personal liability, fiduciaries have rushed to adopt plans under 404(c) and grant participant-direction. **Yet that election has put them on the hook for potentially more liability than they eliminated.** In a 404(c) plan with excessive fees, not only are the trustees at risk for violating ERISA's "costs are reasonable" language (Chapter 4) but in addition, if the expenses were not fully and clearly disclosed to participants, they are in breach of their 404(c) election that they thought was protecting them.

What about the investment choices themselves? How much liability have the trustees eliminated by offering a number of investment alternatives that allow each participant to construct a portfolio with risk and return characteristics suitable for their personal situation under section 404(c)?

It is clear to me that the 404(c) safe harbor does not apply to the selection of investment alternatives that are offered to participants. The proposed regulations about fee disclosures introduced in September 2008 by the DOL in fact explicitly stated that 404(c) *does not* exempt fiduciaries from investment responsibilities of ERISA for the alternatives offered participants. Yet, many trustees assumed that they were free from the burden of investment selection by electing this option, and thus became complacent in their selection of the offerings of investment alternatives for their plans. Many fiduciaries trusted biased product sellers that peddled their own funds, or received revenue sharing from competitors' funds to appear "objective" without exercising prudent fiduciary care. They merely looked at the product seller star rankings and suggested offerings, ignored that the seller of the products was not taking fiduciary responsibility for the selection of products, signed a document saying they were ultimately responsible, and ended up victimizing the plan participants. This all happened to the product seller's delight, because they could market 404(c) compliance to trustees as something that was comforting in relieving their personal liability. The way this was sold to trustees is they don't have to worry about investment selection for the alternatives because the product seller "provides participant education and sufficient alternatives to comply with 404(c)" yet does not take full fiduciary responsibility for doing so.

The trustees that bought into this marketing spin by product sellers and nonfiduciaries from an investment option perspective of 404(c) have another problem when it comes to lawsuits from participants beyond poor fee disclosure.[2]

The intent, and the specific language of 404(c), never explicitly said that the offering of investment alternatives of the plan were exempt from ERISA fiduciary prudence standards. This left many plan sponsors falling victim to a confusing array of issues in the selection of their product vendor.

Imagine you are the trustee of a participant-directed defined contribution plan and you hear a presentation from a vendor that goes something like this:

Mr. Trustee, we here at Acme Retirement Plan Services offer a broad array of investment alternatives that enable you to have a 404(c)-compliant retirement plan. We provide participant education to your employees at least twice a year through in-person employee education seminars. We provide a quarterly educational newsletter to participants to keep them informed. Fact sheets of fund offerings with recent track records are included in the quarterly employee statements, and are available online. Recorded educational webinars are also available online, and we offer free advice software to all participants, enabling them to model and choose the right portfolio and savings rates for their goals. Finally, to the extent that we are managing assets in any of our funds, we are a fiduciary to you and the plan participants.

We even offer competitors' funds to show how objective we are in serving you and your participants' best interests. These things in combination—404(c)-compliant investment alternatives from numerous investment managers, participant education, disclosure information, and our role as a fiduciary—dramatically limit your personal liability as a trustee.

You have no idea how many trustees have been victimized by a sales pitch similar to this one. Here is what the seller of this retirement plan platform is not telling you (but might be disclosing in fine print of lengthy documents):

1. As trustee, you are responsible for the ultimate selection of the investment alternatives offered, not us.
2. The competitors' funds we offer (or any of the funds, for that matter) pay us a revenue-sharing fee that comes from your participants' plan balances that could be avoided with lower-cost institutional share classes.
3. In addition to being responsible for the selection of alternatives offered in your plan, you are also responsible for making sure the fees are reasonable, and we will make it hard for you to figure that out.
4. Our education will be misleading and will not fully disclose expenses and the risk of underperforming by our fund selection you are stuck accepting responsibility for, but it will sound impressive and sophisticated.
5. You will feel better, and so long as no sophisticated ERISA attorney brings a suit against you, we will back you up fully. However, you are personally still on the hook for all prudent fiduciary ERISA regulations, and most of our plans really wouldn't survive ERISA or 404(c) compliance audits. It isn't our fault, since you as trustee are the one that is ultimately responsible, and it says that right in our agreement with you. If you as trustee screw something up, we will not stand behind you and we will be focused on defending ourselves against you.

The real facts versus the sales pitch are quite a bit different, aren't they? The DOL is attempting to tackle some of these problems. Early in 2008, it proposed new regulations requiring more disclosure in a more understandable format to plan trustees. In the summer of 2008, DOL proposed new regulations for fee disclosures to participants.

Of course, the product vendor industry lobbying and commenting on this higher level of clear information has been negative. Groups like the Investment Company Institute (ICI) and various insurance trade associations have commented that additional disclosure rules are not needed because everything is already disclosed, so it is superfluous. Yet, they claim the cost of additional disclosure (for things that are supposedly already disclosed) is burdensome and costly! They close with the chant that too much information will confuse participants and claim such confusion will limit participation in retirement plans, causing a greater social burden in the future. Nice, huh? People wouldn't invest in their retirement if they actually knew what they were paying for it, and according to these trade industry lobbyists, participants already know it because they are already disclosing it. How's that for a logical quandary?

New Fee Disclosure Regulations Explicitly Clarify the Lack of a 404(c) Safe Harbor Exemption from ERISA

What is most interesting to me about the recent fee disclosure regulations to participants proposed by the Department of Labor is that they explicitly made a point of covering a topic completely unrelated to fee disclosures, but instead are using the new proposed regulations to also make a point to clarify section 404(c).

The proposed regulations state:

> The Department also is taking this opportunity to reiterate its long held position that the relief afforded by section 404(c) and the regulation thereunder does not extend to a fiduciary's duty to

prudently select and monitor designated investment managers and designated investment alternatives under the plan. Accordingly, it is the Department's view that a fiduciary breach or an investment loss in connection with the plan's selection of a designated investment alternative is not afforded relief under section 404(c) because it is not the result of a participant's or beneficiary's exercise of control. The Department is proposing to amend paragraph (d)(2) (entitled "Limitation on liability of plan fiduciaries") of § 2550.404c–1 to add a new subparagraph (iv) providing that, "[P]aragraph (d)(2)(i) does not relieve a fiduciary from the duty to prudently select and monitor any designated investment manager or designated investment alternative offered under the plan."

If these proposed regulations are adopted (which currently seems unlikely), this has profound implications for trustees and other fiduciaries. In fact, even if they are not adopted, it is clear that the DOL in this statement that ALL of the ERISA requirements apply to the selection of investment alternatives, even under 404(c) by the inclusion of the comment that the DOL wants to "reiterate its long-held belief."

Might this be a sign that the DOL is going to step up evaluation? Will the trustees be able to prove compliance that the costs are reasonable? That the risk of underperforming the investment policy benchmark was worth the hope of outperforming? That the assets are used for the sole benefit of participants? That participants have adequate information to make an informed decision?

I have seen few plans that I could argue all of these standards were met, and welcome the opportunity to pursue such plans as an expert witness against them on behalf of participants.

The bottom line on this safe harbor, though, is that the only thing 404(c) really provides (if you can truly comply) is that a trustee is not on the hook for stupid decisions by a participant for their personal account, *provided* all the conditions of ERISA were met for the investment options offered and the education was sufficient, unbiased, and truly effective in educating the participant. That is a very tough hurdle to meet, and it means that many fiduciaries have a false sense of security in their supposedly limited liability of having a 404(c) plan.

Go back over the previous chapters and review the pillars of sole benefit, reasonable costs, diversification, and to avoid the risk of large losses. *None* of these provisions of ERISA are excluded from the criteria of evaluating fiduciaries and their prudence (or lack thereof), according to what the DOL is attempting to reiterate with its new proposed participant disclosure regulations.

This means that the hapless comfort fiduciaries thought they had now subjects them to liability for not only complying with the requirements of 404(c), but also the very foundations of procedural prudence ERISA required in the first place. They probably have been misled into believing that their responsibility for the old ERISA standards no longer applied with their new "safe harbor" plans, yet the DOL is saying otherwise.

Is more enforcement on the horizon? It probably is, if you take the DOL comments seriously. Will this expand the basis and universe of potential participant lawsuits based on their individual plan balances based on the February 2008 Supreme Court ruling? No doubt about it, because any attorney that has a reasonable case for an individual's personal plan balance impairment will also seek to use the evidence of a lack of compliance with the overall plan requirements, including 404(c).

This doesn't mean that electing section 404(c) is a bad thing for fiduciaries. It is, in fact, a prudent thing to do, if your investments are selected and offered to participants on the basis of the four pillars of retirement plans.

Chapter 12

Tools and Resources for Fiduciaries

t is very popular amongst the providers of 401(k) and other retirement plan platforms to offer "education" in various forms. Sometimes it comes in the form of a seminar, other times in printed materials, and still others via webinars or conference calls.

As mentioned earlier, the content for such education going forward is going to become Exhibit A in the plaintiff's case against fiduciaries. Much of this supposed education is focused on asset allocation.

Target date funds with their glide path ease to a targeted year of retirement have become the easy de facto standard, despite the mismatch and destruction to individual wealth they create. *When* you retire is only *one* of the multiple variables that go into the equation of your asset allocation decision, so target date funds are leaving a misleading sense of comfort. The DOL has blessed these products nonetheless, although trustees need to remember, they are still measured from a perspective of a prudent expert and are *required* to provide sufficient information and education to make an informed decision. Target date funds as shown in Chapters 6 to 10 will not survive the scrutiny of a plethora of trial lawyers chasing the ERISA ambulance.

So, while the various forms of seminars and printed materials might make it sound easy for the participant to merely pick a date, and let the fund manage their asset allocation toward that retirement date, and while it is currently a popular thing to do, the impairment of each individual's plan balance and the price for focusing only on date, not funded status, goals, or *any* of the other equally valid inputs (as defined benefit plans would normally measure), will become a future liability for trustees.

Risk-tolerance questionnaires and scoring systems will also contribute to that liability, subjecting risk-taker personalities to needless investment risks, or scaring hyperconservative investors into a portfolio that produces a negative or near-zero real return out of fear.

Much of the basic seminar and printed materials about asset allocation concepts permeate the educational content. There will be many cases of "false and misleading" information being given in this "educational" content. This is particularly true when the investment selections offered for the allocation models shown in the content materially underperform their benchmark, or have excessive fees.

Educational content thus must not focus on single variables, like retirement date; risk questionnaires should not be focused only on risk tolerance and/or time horizon (liquidity needs should be part of the risk scoring model); and *all educational content should be consistent with the investment policy for the plan.* Any content focused on specific investments should fairly and equally disclose inconsistency with any of the four pillars of retirement plans, and not hide the balancing of the choice in fine print disclosure. Finally, if personalized advice is available that improves on the easy, off-the-shelf answers communicated in the content, it should be obvious to a participant that such personalized advice that is more inclusive of their overall financial situation and goals would likely be better advice than any default options (or overly simplified scoring systems for investment selection) and how they can obtain that advice.

Independent Retirement Plan Consultants

As we covered earlier, ERISA and the associated prudent fiduciary procedures designed for defined benefit plans created an entire industry of retirement plan consultants to assist fiduciaries in fulfilling their obligations.

Independent consultants are not affiliated with financial product manufacturing, distribution, custody, or brokerage services and charge a consulting fee for their services. The fee may be in the form of a flat "hard dollar" retainer, a percentage of assets, hourly rates, or ala carte pricing for various services (e.g., $2,000 to do an investment manager search). The services commonly offered by such consultants normally include things such as establishing risk tolerance(s), model asset allocation(s), investment manager searches and universe ("peer") ratings, performance reporting, and manager "research" focused on the investment manager's "people, process, and philosophy" commonly referred to by such consultants as **the three Ps of investment management.**

In the context of a defined benefit plan, where the company was at risk for gambles they made on asset allocation and manager selection bets, and ultimately was on the hook for the cost of the consultant because the liabilities of the plan were a fixed, promised benefit to each participant regardless of investment results and costs to the trust, there was little liability to participants created by anything that such consultants did. But, in the context of such consultants delivering services to any participant-directed plan, or perhaps even any defined contribution plan without participant direction where the participants' benefits are at risk for the actual experience they have in the investment results, these "independent consultants" have huge conflicts of interest and generally evade responsibility to the trustees for any of their specific advice. In fact, their services normally evade giving any specific advice and any responsibility for said advice, despite selling their services as a fiduciary.

Confusion about Fiduciary Status and Conflicts of Interest

Under ERISA, amongst trustees and even advisers, there is a lot of confusion about what being a fiduciary necessarily means. Anyone that is paid for a service to the plan—for example, a custodian merely holding the securities, a record keeper merely performing bookkeeping services, or a retirement plan consultant—are all fiduciaries *in some capacity*. But, this fiduciary responsibility does not necessarily mean that trustees are protected in any material form. **In fact, in the case of many retirement plan consultants, they actually INCREASE the fiduciary risk to trustees.**

For example, while record keepers are compensated for services to the trust, thus making them a named fiduciary, it would be difficult to point blame (and ultimate responsibility) to them for investment results when they were removed from the choice of investments, provided they still accurately accounted for the participant balances, their service contract's fiduciary role for which they were retained. Clearly, they would have some responsibility for making sure participant records were accurate, but if they were not involved in selection of the investment alternatives, there is no way trustees could point to their named fiduciary record keeper when investment results failed to meet ERISA requirements.

Most retirement plan consultants have used this fiduciary by name, but not in real responsibility, in creating their contracts for services they provide trustees. First, like the record keepers, such retirement plan consultants are, by definition, named fiduciaries because they are providing services to a plan for compensation. However, although trustees know that such consultants are actively involved in the choices and decisions for asset allocation and investment selection, most of the independent retirement plan consultants evade ultimate responsibility for investment decisions. **This enables them to sell a service to trustees for investment advice, sell themselves with the label of a fiduciary to the trustees for this investment advice, and yet avoid taking any material responsibility for the advice.**

For example, take the simple service of a consultant doing a manager search for the trustees. The trustees might be looking for a large-cap domestic core investment manager. The consultant establishes with the trustees various criteria they will use in the screening process for alternatives *the trustees* will select. The retirement plan consultant will ask questions of the trustees for the search criteria they would prefer—like whether the portfolio is managed by a team, or an individual, the number of years the firm has been in business, whether the track record has been audited, the minimum assets under management, risk and return characteristics of the track record, and so on. The consultant does not establish these criteria, and does not normally take responsibility for such. The responsibility in most contracts is placed squarely on the trustees.

The consultant then does a search through a "universe of peers" and normally offers three or more investment managers that most closely meet the criteria the *trustees* established. Normally, such searches are presented at meetings of trustees with the consultant. The consultant shows various reports (mostly focused on **past performance** relative to a benchmark and the universe peers) and discusses other various qualitative information about the firms such as "the three Ps" of people, process, and philosophy. Sometimes, representatives from the various investment firms are also brought in to meet with the trustees. The trustees deliberate (normally with the consultant present) and choose one of the firms the consultant offered. They often even ask the consultant directly, "Which firm would you suggest we select?" Although the consultant often verbally answers the question with, "Based on your criteria, it seems as though Acme Capital Management would be the best fit for what you are seeking," they will *not* put this advice in writing, nor will they accept responsibility for the selection of this management firm to comply with the investment policy or the investment results of the manager. They will charge a fee, though, to monitor the firm they do not take responsibility for selecting. The contract most consultants use evades this responsibility and places it back in the hands of the trustees. So, this begs the question, what services are the trustees really getting for this consulting fee, and did they really protect themselves from much fiduciary liability to hire a named fiduciary that isn't responsible for the *perceived* advice they delivered? Such contracts to me are a sham—a material misrepresentation.

As for the conflicts of interest by such "independent" consultants, one has to step back to really understand that their self-interest is to sell their services. Unlike consultants that you should know have material conflicts by being tied to investment products, brokerage or custody services, as a trustee—you would think— that the independent consultant should be providing independent objective advice (despite them not being willing to take ultimate responsibility for any of the hiring or firing decisions). But, the very premise of their services, regardless of how they price it, has a material conflict of interest inherent in within it.

Take a well-designed participant-directed 401(k), 403(b) or 457 plan as an example. Would you really need a consultant to monitor the performance of index funds where there is mountains of free public information on their performance and when you have a record keeper that reports participant-level daily valuations and returns as well as at the plan level? My company's record keeper includes this performance information and participant record keeping for a cost of $30 a year per participant in addition to all government filings for the plan, compliance testing, and web-based participant statements. Why would I pay a consultant potentially thousands of dollars for this duplicate information?

If I had such a plan, why would I pay a consultant to search for managers? Wouldn't I select the lowest-cost alternatives for the indices in my investment policy available through my custodian (subject to evaluation of tracking error)? In fact, if you look at the services offered by many "independent" (and especially those not so independent) retirement plan consultants as it relates to investment advice, we can see *they have a material conflict of interest in convincing you to risk materially underperforming the investment policy they write for you (yet again to not accept responsibility) by attempting to select and search for "better" managers.* The consultant has a conflict in that you would not pay them for a generic investment policy statement that any participant-directed plan *should use*; if you are truly going to meet the needs of any potential plan participant and comply with all aspects of ERISA and 404(c).

You would not pay a retirement plan consultant for manager searches if you weren't succumbing to the gamble of risking underperforming in the hope of outperforming, nor would you have to pay the consultant to monitor the people, process, and philosophy if you were prudently avoiding the risk in the first place, as ERISA suggests.

If the consultant takes responsibility for selecting the investment alternatives not only to comply with whatever is written in their "custom" investment policy, but also the actual results, then the consultant may be worth the investment. But there is clearly a conflict with a consultant that encourages you to risk underperforming, packages a bunch of services like searches and performance reporting to help cover your butt for when things go wrong, but does not take responsibility for the results. In fact, the very services they sell can actually *increase* your fiduciary liability, instead of reducing it as they promote, relative to a well-designed plan.

ERISA 3(21)(A) Fiduciaries versus ERISA 3(38) and 405(d)(1) Fiduciaries

The fiduciary label is tossed around a lot in sales presentations to trustees, but the label is misleading. Although it might be obvious to trustees that some advisers accept no fiduciary responsibility whatsoever, there is a NOT-so-subtle difference between the *type* of fiduciary you as a trustee are engaging, and it is completely dependent on the contract the firm is executing with you and for what services you are contracting.

Fiduciaries under ERISA section 3(21)(A) are fiduciaries in name only, leaving the trustees responsible for the "advice" delivered by the consultant. Consultants that act in *both* ERISA 3(38) and 405(d)(1) capacity ("investment manager" *and* "independent fiduciary"), *may* offer you some greater protection. As an example, investment manager fiduciaries under *only* section 3(38), **might or might not** have material responsibility to the trustees. Although any investment manager that acts with discretion on behalf of the trust, even if it is only for one of the investment alternatives, is a 3(38) fiduciary and may even be an "independent fiduciary" under 405(d)(1), that does not mean he or she is protecting you as a trustee *from all of the decisions*. The responsibility of fiduciaries in such a case is limited to the investment funds they manage; the trustees are *still* responsible for having selected that fund and asset class. The investment managers can protect themselves from liability for the management of that fund and may even be able to use the investment policy statement of the plan against the trustees.

The only way for trustees to transfer the majority of their liability to a hired fiduciary is to contract with a fiduciary that acts with discretion on *all plan assets* and alternatives, excepting perhaps brokerage windows, also known as self-directed brokerage accounts.

IF you hire a fiduciary under ERISA 3(38) and 405(d)(1) and the fiduciary accepts discretion for selecting which investment classes, funds, lifestyle portfolios, and investment options that are available for your plan, *and* if the fiduciary admits this in the contract, you now have materially reduced your fiduciary risk and *the fiduciary* will have to deal with the lawsuit from the participant when a fund materially underperforms its benchmark in the investment policy statement.

Fund Ratings—The Problems with Peers

So much of what trustees evaluate and consultants sell to trustees is the relative peer ranking and monitoring of investment alternative selections. Throughout this book, though, we have demonstrated how past performance is not indicative of future results and, perhaps more importantly, even if such "superior" risk and return measures played out in the future, whether or not such results would actually improve the wealth of a participant is still uncertain.

Yet, there exists an entire fund rating and consulting industry, and it is a large industry. Although we have already discussed how if past performance isn't meaningful or predictive, then it is questionable as to what conclusions one should draw from it, that fact has not reduced the temptation to drive forward by looking backward. At least, if one were a prudent expert under ERISA, you would certainly be skeptical of how much weight past performance would have on your decisions.

Say you are looking for a large-cap value manager. Your friendly consultant (or web site, for that matter) maintains a database of investment managers and funds and creates rules to classify managers and funds into peer groups. This is where the first problem occurs. These rules that establish which peer group a fund belongs are different among many consultants and databases.

For example, some focus only on the holdings of the portfolio, which in the case of an active manager (or even an index fund that is a subasset class) will change. Some do what is called performance-based style analysis that doesn't normally classify the manager into any specific asset class or subasset class, but statistically calculates a blend of asset classes that explain most of the variance of returns. Some use only a correlation measure, and still others ignore some or all of the quantitative measures and let investment managers and funds actually self-select the universe to which they would like to belong! Some merely subjectively interpret a questionnaire the manager completes to decide which peer group the manager belongs. Still others combine some or even all of these traits to assemble their peer group.

To many managers and fund databases, the ultimate goal is to find a peer group label to stuff the manager in so they can proceed with their next step of ranking them against one another. These various peer-ranking methods have numerous problems. First, aren't there, or should there not be, a number of funds or managers that do not belong in any of the peer groups? In essence, shouldn't the peer group process itself acknowledge that some funds are just completely uncertain and there is no way to really consider them a peer of anything? Most peer groups don't do this because it gets in the way of their sales.

Also, if you are going to use the peer ranking as one of your criteria for selection as trustee (and you shouldn't for various reasons outlined here), it is equally important to define in your investment policy the rules that you will use (or that your consultant or database uses) to create peer groups. The differences among different methods of assembling a supposed "peer group" can be astonishing.

Imagine you have a consultant that relies on Morningstar criteria and shows you "five-star" funds to select. Five-star funds generally fall in the top 10 percent of the Morningstar peer group based on risk-adjusted returns. Another consultant has different rules and shows that the same fund fell at the 55th percentile in his peer group for the same fund.

I've seen this inconsistency among competing consultants over and over again through the years. For example, in Acme Consultants' large-cap value peer group (as Acme defines it), a fund or manager falls into the top quartile of their large-cap value peer group universe. Yet, in the Smith and Jones retirement consulting database, the same manager falls in the bottom quartile of the Smith and Jones large-cap value universe. If your investment policy statement says that you will pick managers in the top half of their respective peer group, or top quartile, or whatever, and the policy does not define the construction rules of the peer group, you are at risk from any participant discovering a peer group rating that violates your own investment policy!

Of course, many firms revise these rules and expand the number of peer groups on a regular basis. Depending on the rules of how the peer groups are created, managers and funds can bounce around to different peer groups. This phenomenon does not meet the standards of ERISA expert-level prudence in my opinion. There is too much statistical noise and too many unmeasured variances in portfolios that are, by their nature, moving targets to even create a truly valid peer group. The number of funds in the peer universe constantly changes, thus expanding and contracting the peer group size, which would obviously affect any fund's relative ranking. There is also a known bias in nearly all peer group universes academically researched called *survivorship bias*. This is the result of funds that close, change their style, or go out of business, and are thus removed from the peer group, creating a bias based on what is left in the universe. Most peer groups only include those funds that actually survived, not all the funds that may have been selected along the way.

There has been progress by some in the industry to try to eliminate all of this peer group noise. For example, Ron Surz of PPCA, Inc.

has created a unique means of creating a manager universe. Instead of surveying thousands of managers, he allows you to create a universe of what all potential managers *might* do. In essence, you set the criteria, for example, to be S&P 500 as the universe of stocks from which your large-cap manager can select securities, and Surz simulates the statistical range of outcomes for what any manager could create with this rule. This is a lot timelier than waiting a month for survey data to come back and eliminates biases on the construction of the peer group. Unfortunately, he has not found a way to do this for fixed-income managers or balanced managers, but it is a more valid approach than the typical noisy and potentially misleading peer groups of the past.

A bigger question, though, is whether a peer group rating is the right thing for you as a fiduciary to consider in the first place. Does it belong in your investment policy? With the way managers move around amongst various peer groups with ratings that go up and down on a regular basis, did your consultants include peer ratings in your policy statement to justify their existence? Are high-star ratings really just marketing, or do they have any material predictive value? And, what does it take to get a high peer ranking? Is what it takes consistent with ERISA?

Fundgrading from an ERISA Perspective

In Chapter 5 we covered in detail the explicit language in ERISA about diversification and introduced our free web site for fiduciaries and consumers, www.fundgrades.com. As a fiduciary, at a minimum you should use this free service to give yourself some ammunition when your consultant promotes various funds to you. As a consultant, you should use this free service before you suggest funds to trustees.

If you create a login in the web site, it is easy for you to quickly add each of the funds you offer as standard options for your plans and see the grades for all of the four pillars of ERISA. Our suggested current fund offerings are shown in Figure 12.1.

My 401(k) Report Card

	Portfolio Grades					
	Overall	Diversification	Expense	Relative Risk	Return	Risk of Material Underperformance
Last 3 Years	A−	A+	A+	C+	C	A+
Prior 3 Years	A−	A+	A+	B−	C	A
Last 6 Years	A−	A+	A+	C+	C	A+

Note: The following grades are based on the last three years of data.

	Ticker	Description	Asset Class	Fund Grades					
				Overall	Divers.	Expense	Relative Risk	Return	UnderPer. Risk
ⓘ	NMPAX	Columbia Mid Cap Index Fund Z	Mid-Cap Blend	A−	A+	A	C+	C	A+
ⓘ	DFIGX	DFA Intermediate Govt Fx Inc	Interm. Govt Bonds	B+	B+	A+	A−	C	C−
ⓘ	FSMAX	Fidelity Spartan 500 Idx Adv	Large-Cap Blend	A−	A+	A+	C+	C	A+
ⓘ	FSIIX	Fidelity Spartan Intl Index Inv	Developed Intl Stock	B−	A−	A−	C+	C	C
ⓘ	FSTMX	Fidelity Spartan Total Mkt Idx...	Total Domestic Equity	A−	A+	A	C+	C	A+
ⓘ	VIGRX	Vanguard Growth Index Inv	Total Domestic Growth	B+	A+	A+	B−	C	B−
ⓘ	VBLTX	Vanguard Long-Term Bond Index...	Long Govt/ Corp	B+	A+	A	C	C	A−
ⓘ	VGSIX	Vanguard REIT Index Inv	Real Estate/ REITs	B+	A	A+	C	C+	B
ⓘ	VBISX	Vanguard Short-Term Bond Index...	Interm. Govt/ Credit	B	B−	A	A−	C	C+
ⓘ	NAESX	Vanguard Small-Cap Index Inv	Small-Cap Blend	B	B+	A+	B−	C	C+
ⓘ	VIVAX	Vanguard Value Index Inv	Total Domestic Value	B+	A	A+	C+	C	B

Figure 12.1   Grades of suggested fund options from fundgrades.com

Money market funds are not included in this list, nor are our lifestyle portfolios. Fundgrades allows you to create various portfolios, and they can be graded as well, based on how all the funds are grouped and weighted, as in our "balanced" portfolio shown in Figure 12.2.

As mentioned in Chapter 5, to get a high return grade relative to an asset class, the fund must, by definition, violate the diversification rules of ERISA. ***The only way one could materially beat a benchmark is by materially not owning it.*** When less than 3 percent of all funds receive an overall honor roll grade in our system (B or better), and with the ability for fiduciaries, whether consultants or trustees, to have

My 401(k) Report Card

	Portfolio Grades					
	Overall	Diversification	Expense	Relative Risk	Return	Risk of Material Underperformance
Last 3 Years	B+	A+	A+	C−	C	B
Prior 3 Years	A−	A+	A+	C+	C	A
Last 6 Years	A−	A+	A+	C	C	A−

Note: The following grades are based on the last three years of data.

	Ticker	Description	Asset Class	Fund Grades					
				Overall	Divers.	Expense	Relative Risk	Return	UnderPer. Risk
ⓘ	NMPAX	Columbia Mid Cap Index Fund Z[4]	Mid-Cap Blend	A−	A+	A	C+	C	A+
ⓘ	DFIGX	DFA Intermediate Govt Fx Inc	Interm. Govt Bonds	B+	B+	A+	A−	C	C−
ⓘ	FSMAX	Fidelity Spartan 500 Idx Adv[4]	Large-Cap Blend	A−	A+	A+	C+	C	A+
ⓘ	FSIIX	Fidelity Spartan Intl Index Inv	Developed Intl Stock	B−	A−	A−	C+	C	C
ⓘ	FSTMX	Fidelity Spartan Total Mkt Idx...	Total Domestic Equity	A−	A+	A	C+	C	A+
ⓘ	VIGRX	Vanguard Growth Index Inv[4]	Total Domestic Growth	B+	A+	A+	B−	C	B−
ⓘ	VBLTX	Vanguard Long-Term Bond Index...	Long Govt/ Corp	B+	A+	A	C	C	A−
ⓘ	VGSIX	Vanguard REIT Index Inv[4]	Real Estate/ REITs	B+	A	A+	C	C+	B
ⓘ	VBISX	Vanguard Short-Term Bond Index...	Interm. Govt/ Credit	B	B−	A	A−	C	C+
ⓘ	NAESX	Vanguard Small-Cap Index Inv[4]	Small-Cap Blend	B	B+	A+	B−	C	C+
ⓘ	VIVAX	Vanguard Value Index Inv[4]	Total Domestic Value	B+	A	A+	C+	C	B

[4]This fund was not included in portfolio grading because it has a zero dollar amount.

Figure 12.2 Portfolio grades for our balanced portfolio

free access to this information, taking a few minutes to get past the star ratings and evaluating your investment options on fundgrades is a free insurance policy documenting additional prudence. This is especially true if you document inconsistencies and why you accepted any inconsistencies, or if you change your investment options to comply with the ERISA procedural prudence measures used in fundgrades.

Chapter 13

The Skill versus Luck Debate

We have already highlighted throughout much of this book the risks that are introduced by attempting to outperform investment policy benchmarks and how difficult it is to justify this attempt, as well as the risks to fiduciaries for violating the diversification requirements of ERISA that such attempts, by definition, require.

A good friend of mine, Dr. Michael Edesess, Ph.D., commented on a recent debate in www.advisorspectives.com on this very topic. Dr. Edesess's elegantly simple conclusion was that the question is not whether skill or luck exists, but instead, whether or not skill can be identified in advance.

Advisor Perspectives, which is run by Robert Huebscher, frequently interviews high-profile industry and academic experts on various investment topics. Robert Huebscher's educational e-mail is distributed to many thousands of financial advisers, and he is unafraid to give equal time to both sides of any story. He also encourages feedback to anything that he publishes to generate open debate. The topic of skill versus luck was introduced a short time ago when he interviewed and wrote a brief synopsis of some of Russ Wermers' (Associate Professor of Finance, University of Maryland–Robert H. Smith School of Business, Department of Finance) work, which attempted to calculate what he calls "The False Discovery Rate," or FDR.

The content of the series of articles that generated debate on the topic follow. The owner of the copyright, *Advisor Perspectives*, graciously permitted them to be used in this book. This initial article effectively launched a firestorm.

Article #1: The False Discovery Rate (FDR)—Luck versus Skill in Active Mutual Funds

By Robert Huebscher

August 5, 2008

A recurring question in the topic of active versus passive management is the degree to which active mutual fund managers who outperform their benchmark can be considered to have done so through skill versus luck. An academic study, described in an article by Mark Hulbert in the *New York Times* several weeks ago, answers this question through a new statistical technique.

The study's authors are Russ Wermers, a professor of finance at the University of Maryland, Laurent Barras of the Swiss Finance Institute, and Oliver Scaillet of the University of Geneva. We spoke with Professor Wermers on July 25, 2008.

The False Discovery Rate

If all active fund managers were to choose stocks by throwing darts, inevitably some small percentage would deliver alpha, even over some large period of time. However, they would do so through random luck. Fund managers are not dart throwers, yet some percentage of them will nonetheless deliver alpha through luck. Wermers' tool, known as the False Discovery Rate (FDR), identifies the size of the group delivering alpha through skill, and well as the size of the group failing to deliver alpha through lack of skill.

The FDR technique begins by segregating fund returns into three groups: negative alpha, zero alpha, and positive alpha. The zero alpha group consists of those funds that earn returns just sufficient to match their benchmark, net of expenses. They deliver zero alpha to their investors. Based on the number of funds that exhibit an alpha close to zero, which are almost all funds without skills, the FDR technique estimates the number of funds without skills that end up with positive (or negative) alphas simply by luck (good or bad). Then, it is simply a matter of subtracting the actual size of the positive alpha group from the expected size (based on luck alone) to determine the size of the group of funds that delivered alpha through skill. A similar procedure is used to determine the size of the group that deliver negative alpha (net of expenses) through lack of skills.

The study used the Center for Research in Securities Prices (CRSP) data, and matched it with Thomson's CDA data for fund investment-objective information.

The data are free of survivorship bias and only funds with at least 60 months of returns were included. Share classes were consolidated (dollar weighted) into a single fund. Sales loads were not modeled (if they were, it is likely an even smaller percentage of funds would have delivered alpha).

Key Findings

Over the 32-year period studied by Wermers and his co-authors, from 1975 to 2006, only 0.6% of funds delivered positive alpha through skill, as opposed to luck alone. The FDR cannot determine which funds delivered alpha through skill; it can only estimate the size of this group. Those select few funds (approximately 12 out of the 2,076 studied) will remain anonymous.

Of the remaining funds, 24.0% are unskilled and 75.4% are zero alpha (delivering excess returns sufficient to only cover fees and expenses). A very interesting finding is that the proportion of skilled managers decreases over time, specifically from 1990 to 2006. In 1990, 14.4% of funds fell into the "skilled" category, while 9.2% were in the unskilled category. These numbers were 0.6 % and 24.0%, respectively, in 2006. As the study notes, "although the number of actively managed funds has dramatically increased, skilled managers (those capable of picking stocks well enough to overcome their trading costs and expenses) have become increasingly rare." The decay in alpha is shown in the graph below [see Figure13.1]:

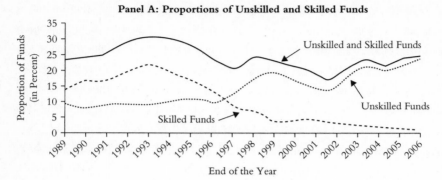

Figure 13.1 Declining alpha of active management

Funds were categorized into three investment objectives: Growth, Growth & Income, and Aggressive Growth. Wermers noted that this categorization was the only one consistently available for the 32-year time period he and his coauthors studied.

The funds in the Aggressive Growth category exhibited the greatest degree of skill. These funds tilt toward small cap, low book-to-market, and momentum stocks. The Growth & Income category, which includes traditional value and core funds, had no funds that exhibited skill, along with a substantial portion that were unskilled, a finding that the study terms "remarkable."

Another curious finding concerns the relationship between skill and fund size. In general, larger funds were more prevalent in the high alpha "right tail" of the data. We asked Wermers about this, since intuition would suggest that smaller "boutique" funds would exhibit greater skill, and that skill would erode as fund size grows and managers are forced to invest in a smaller universe of stocks.

Wermers believes that these findings are inconclusive, though, since the vast majority of right-tail funds are there by luck alone—a more detailed examination of the funds within the right and left tails is underway.

Implications for Advisors

Mark Hulbert posed the question of why skill declined over the 32-year period, and offered three possibilities: high fees and expenses, increased market efficiency, and the movement of skilled mutual fund managers to the hedge fund industry.

The study showed that over their entire histories, 9.6% of funds produced truly positive alphas before expenses, while almost none produced significantly positive alphas after expenses. This indicated to the authors that, even though expenses for actively managed funds declined over the period studied, expenses eliminated the good performance of a lot of managers who appeared to have true stock picking skills. Given that only 0.6% of funds produced alpha over this period, skills are dropping faster than expenses.

Wermers said that "expenses are too high, relative to the ability of fund managers to generate alphas." He added that a "prescription is to pay close attention to the expenses charged by funds, as higher expenses do not seem to be associated with higher skills."

We concur, as does the overwhelming body of academic studies on mutual fund expenses. Regarding the possibility that the market has become more efficient over this period, Wermers noted that several recent studies have shown this to be true.

The FDR test has not yet been applied to hedge fund or separately managed account databases. If it did, and it revealed a similar decay in skill, that would support the hypothesis that the market has become more efficient.

We believe the fundamental reason for the decline in skill is the movement of skilled managers to the hedge funds, and this factor overwhelms any other possible explanation. The hedge fund industry is the most profitable industry ever conceived, and its performance-based fees insure that skilled managers will be handsomely compensated. By contrast, very few mutual funds utilize performance-based fees. The asset-based fees in the mutual fund industry will naturally select for those managers who cannot succeed in the hedge fund industry.

One aspect of the fund's methodology troubled us. We believe a more meaningful question to ask is whether fund managers possess skill, not whether the fund possesses skill. This could be answered by applying the FDR test at the manager level, not the fund level. Wermers noted that the referees from the *Journal of Finance* who reviewed the study raised the same issue, and he plans to add these findings once he completes the analysis.

The final question is whether the study proves that it is "almost hopeless" to find skilled active managers, as Mark Hulbert notes in his article. Wermers thinks not. He said, "There is a role for smart sophisticated advisors to make a difference, because it is so hard to find a skilled active manager." He added that advisors should also be prepared to say when it is appropriate for clients to go passive. "Advisors add value by looking at management, strategies, track records, expenses, and all other factors to determine whether skilled managers really work hard to find good active alpha," he said.

My Synopsis of the Article The article in *Advisor Perspectives* that was based on an interview with Wermers basically applies some common sense to evaluating managers. Clearly some managers may have skill, but based on the sheer number of them there will be numerous managers that had no skill and were just lucky. Wermers is merely attempting to statistically estimate how much luck is likely to exist in a universe of managers instead of the industry standard that automatically credits any outperformance as skill.

But, when *Advisor Perspectives* distributes such content to many thousands of financial advisers, and you have an editor that welcomes debate, you are bound to get some comments.

Enter a response to this article by C. Thomas Howard, Ph.D., professor, Reiman School of Finance, University of Denver. He wrote the following in response to the article about Wermers's research that concluded the exact opposite.

Article #2: Response to *Luck versus Skill in Active Mutual Funds*

The following letter is in response to our article *"Luck versus Skill in Active Mutual Funds,"* which appeared on August 5, 2008.

August 5, 2008
C. Thomas Howard, Ph.D.
Professor, Reiman School of Finance
University of Denver

The Barras, Scaillet, and Wermers (BSW) paper featured in this *AP* article builds on a long line of studies that conclude active equity managers add no value net of management fees. It also provides additional depressing evidence that manager skill (as defined by a positive alpha) seems to have all but vanished in recent years.

What is surprising to me is that fund performance results point in exactly the opposite direction. Using a more inclusive 1980–2008 active U.S. equity open end mutual fund data base than did BSW, I find that:

- The average fund alpha is characterized by an upward sloping time trend.
- Currently, my best estimate is that the average active U.S. equity fund out-performs the S&P 500 by roughly 100bp after fees. So, unlike times past, it is now a rational decision to invest in the average active manager rather than in an index.
- As the average fund alpha has increased over time, the average fund standard deviation has decreased. Thus alphas are improving while risk is declining.
- Over the first six months of 2008, a difficult market environment indeed, the average after fees fund alpha was a whopping 463bp (annualized).

These observations point to increasing managerial skill among active U.S. equity managers rather than decreasing skill as claimed by BSW. It also argues for investing in a portfolio of active managers rather than in an index.

Evidence and Data

My data are all active U.S. equity open end mutual funds that existed during any month over the 28 1/2 year period January 1980 through June 2008 as reported by Thomson Financial. I exclude index, mixed asset, target date, and alloca-tion funds. Monthly fund returns, net of automatically deducted management and other fees, are calculated by averaging the returns across all share classes existing in that month. The final sample is comprised of 4,207 funds and 482,443 fund/month observations. At the end of 1982 there were 300 funds, with the number increasing to a peak of 2,617 at the end of 2003, and then declining to 2,117 as of June 2008. Thus, there has been a roughly 20% drop in the number of funds since 2003.

Annual alphas, based on S&P 500 benchmark returns, are calculated by summing the average monthly fund alphas within each year. The resulting annual alphas are shown below [see Figure 13.2], along with the alpha time trend.

Average annual alphas are highly volatile, with some years very negative and others very positive. The average alpha over all fund/month observations is −82bp, similar to what others have found. However, the time trend is positive, with a slope of 14bp annually. The implication is that managers are becoming more skilled over time.

There is also support for the notion, observed by others, that manager skill is more valuable during challenging economic times. Fund alpha averaged 232bp over the eight economically difficult years of 1982, 1983, 1990, 1991, 2000, 2001, 2007, and 2008. In contrast, average fund alpha plummeted during the super-charged economy of the late 1990s. In fact, the fund underperformance observed over 1982 to 2008 can be turned into superior performance when 1995 to 1999 is

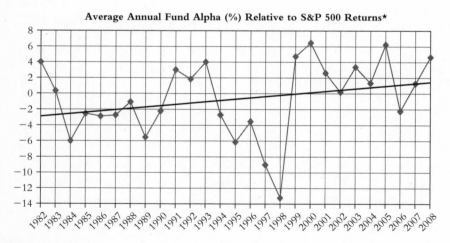

Average Annual Fund Alpha (%) Relative to S&P 500 Returns*

Figure 13.2 Trend in alpha relative to the S&P 500

*For 2008, annualized sum over first 6 months

eliminated, resulting in an average fund alpha of 20bp. While the late 90s were an amazing time economically, they were not at all kind to equity fund managers.

Below is a graph of the average fund 36-month trailing annual standard deviations as of the end of each year, along with the time trend. [See Figure 13.3.] Note that there is a downward trend (−8bp annually), implying average fund risk declined over this period.

Together, these two graphs reveal average fund performance has improved over this nearly 30-year time period while average fund volatility has declined. This represents a strong case for increasing manager skill.

So Why Did BSW Come to Such a Different Conclusion?

I and BSW are using essentially the same data over the same time period, so our diametrically opposed conclusions are driven by different methodologies. My results are based on straightforward, intuitive calculations. BSW employs complicated statistical techniques that distort the conclusions reached, as I argue below.

- In using the Carhart four-factor risk model, BSW needs at least 60 months of historical data to estimate required parameters. Thus, they eliminate all fund/month observations that are preceded by less than 60 months of history. This dramatically reduces sample size. For example, if I were to follow this procedure, 44% or

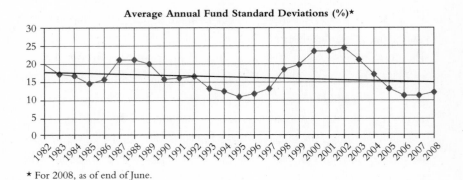

* For 2008, as of end of June.

Figure 13.3 Average Annual Fund Standard Deviations (%)

210,640 of my fund/month observations would be eliminated. Essentially, BSW have gutted their sample in order to feed the data voracious Carhart model.

- It turns out that funds with less than five years of history generate very attractive returns. In my sample, the fund/months with less than 60 months of history generate an average annual return 50bp higher than those with a longer history. By eliminating short history observations, BSW injects a downward bias into their results.

- In addition, there is a negative relationship between returns and fund history. That is, the longer the fund history, the lower the average return. This is a counterintuitive result in that most feel longer histories imply a better manager and thus higher returns. In fact, many in the industry demand long performance histories before a manager is even considered. But the evidence portrays the opposite, the shorter the history the better the performance. Thus any search for manager skill needs to include short history funds, which BSW does not.

- BSW compound their mistake by looking at life-of-fund alphas for evidence of managerial skill. This is consistent with the widely held belief that skilled managers perform consistently over time and skill cannot be detected without long performance histories. The data reveals a different reality. On average, superior manager skill exists early in the life of a fund, with declining performance thereafter. This means that it is easier to find a skilled manager among funds with short histories than among those with long histories. (Note that this is just the opposite of the approach used by most investors when looking for skilled managers). Any search for manager skill should consider these realties. BSW fail at this.

- The combination of shorter history funds performing better and deteriorating performance with lengthening fund history produces an undesirable end-of-sample bias in the BWS study. Over the last five years of their study (i.e., 2002–2006), no new funds are included and the funds that are included have ever-lengthening histories. Thus there was a growing downward bias in their results as the last sample year approaches. This may help explain why they observe a decline in manager skill at the end of their sample. Note that extending the sample will not remedy this bias. BSW must change their methodology in order to eliminate this bias.

204

- As a final comment, BSW cannot make the statement of having precise estimates of the number of lucky managers. This is because such estimates depend critically on the underlying statistical model being assumed. BSW assume three distributions, one each for unskilled, zero alpha, and skilled managers. This allows them to estimate precisely the number of lucky managers. But what if the truth is many distributions, one each for managers with slightly differing skills. Then it becomes impossible to estimate precisely the number of lucky managers. BSW overstate their level of precision.

Manager Skill Is Increasing

The number of skilled managers is a direct function of the overall average fund alpha. The higher the average alpha, the larger is the number of skilled managers. The results I have presented reveal an upward trend in fund alpha combined with a decline in fund volatility. These observations point to increasing managerial skill rather than decreasing skill as claimed by BSW. Today, the average active U.S. equity fund is delivering a solid value proposition to its investors.

My Synopsis of the Response to the Article This is the sort of debate that happens all of the time in the industry. Two finance professors conclude completely opposite things based on essentially similar data. Is it any wonder trustees and even financial advisers are confused?

Of course, from an objective perspective, one has to consider a few weaknesses in both of these papers. In the Wermers interview, the means by which funds were classified were based on broad subjective categories that potentially introduce some noise into the analysis, something acknowledged by the author. In Howard's response to Wermers that concluded the opposite, he uses the standard industry assumption that luck does not exist in his "research" and compares a bunch of funds to large-cap blend stocks that do not invest or even benchmark themselves to the large-cap blend, S&P 500 benchmark. Seeing this, I had to write a response based merely on the obvious weakness of Howard's assumptions. My response, also published in *Advisor Perspectives*, follows.

Article #3: When Will Objectivity Enter the Active versus Passive Debate?

David B. Loeper, CIMA®, CIMC®

In April 2003, I released a whitepaper entitled "Active vs. Passive: The Debate Continues" that highlighted exactly what has recently been happening in the saga of exchanges about skill versus luck in active management on *Advisor Perspectives*.

My original 2003 paper highlighted that there is a lot of marketing going on by BOTH "passive pundits" and "active advocates" instead of objective research. That paper demonstrated how it isn't objective science if the so-called "research" uses essentially the same data (as the Wermers and Howard pieces in *Advisor Perspectives*, 2008 did) yet comes to opposite conclusions. True objectivity and science are not that forgiving. Marketing, on the other hand, is explicitly designed to spin such data into a story that sounds compelling, or at least plausible, free of the bounds of scientific objectivity.

At the highest conceptual level, Wermers's work is stating something simple, rational and mathematically provable. Essentially, all Wermers is saying is that just because a fund outperformed (or underperformed) for some period of time, that doesn't mean it was necessarily skill (or the lack thereof), it may have just been luck. He didn't say skill doesn't exist. He didn't say he could tell which funds had skill. His FDR (False Discovery Rate) is in essence a statistical attempt to estimate how much luck exists in the universe of funds, back out that likely statistical luck from the universe, and thus estimate how much skill remains across that universe. He even acknowledges that there were data problems because of the weakness of fund objective consistency over the entire time period.

Wermers is saying that if 10,000 monkeys were picking stocks, that some monkeys would outperform and some would underperform. In the case of monkeys it would be all luck, but in the case of money managers only some of them would be luck. Wermers is saying that it is erroneous to assume 100% of all managers that outperform are skilled, and he is making a statistical attempt to identify how much luck is present in a universe of funds and separating that out to identify how much skill remains in the universe.

Enter Howard, who responds to Wermers's work but apparently thinks that all monkeys that outperform are "skilled" and completely discounts the notion that a lucky monkey could exist. All monkeys that outperform are skilled, according to Howard, at least according to his "research" methodology. There does not exist a lucky, unskilled manager in the Howard research. Surprisingly, in response to the *Advisor Perspectives* article about Wermers, even Ron Surz (whose PODS universes simulates all potential monkeys) chimed in as well with the standard industry bromides that are not measurable or provable (but are marketable) with "People, Process, and Philosophy" (a.k.a. the "Three Ps" of investment manager research).

In looking at the Wermers's work, as a skeptical scientist, I'm wondering if there is enough statistical significance to necessarily draw all of the conclusions he did, especially since the classification criteria is fairly arbitrary and would introduce a significant amount of error that he—to his credit—objectively acknowledges as a potential weakness (i.e., classification as Aggressive Growth Funds, Growth, Growth & Income, etc.).

But, in looking at Howard's response to Wermers, I do not find the same level of objectivity; I see marketing spin. Howard's first exhibit in his Wermers response showed a trend line of average negative alpha of 2%, "trending" upward to almost positive 2%. I wonder what Howard was saying back in the 1980s and early 1990s when his average alpha was negative? He must have been an indexer back then and now has become more enlightened with the upward trending slope that shows all managers combined can beat the entire market combined . . . hmmm . . . doesn't the market have to equal itself? (To be fair, Howard used average and not dollar weighted measurements. So, in theory, the market doesn't have to equal itself with his method.)

In reality, Howard's "alpha slope" is a slippery slope indeed. He is comparing all domestic equity funds (with very minor limitations) to the S&P 500. Forgetting that there is a large universe of small-cap, mid-cap, value and growth funds (many of which have index benchmarks that outperformed the S&P 500 over the last five years) in his domestic equity universe, he compounds the sleight of hand by attributing to all funds that outperformed the wrong benchmark a "growing alpha skill."

The way Howard built his statistics, by basing it on the average domestic "any" fund relative to a recently poor performing large-cap core benchmark, really shows nothing more than a large-cap blend was hard to beat before and has been easier to beat more recently. Shazaam! Money managers are getting smarter and the markets must be getting less efficient!

In our www.fundgrades.com data, if we go back over the last six years where this supposedly surging trend of alpha occurred, and look at the total number of funds that fit into one of our thirteen domestic equity categories (also using Thomson data) we find there were 5,745 funds that had at least 70% in equities, and an R-squared relative to at least one of our thirteen domestic equity benchmarks of at least 67.25% (a correlation coefficient of only .82). Only 618 (10.8%) of those funds fell into large blend as their best fits. Small, micro, mid and even total domestic equities would have all outperformed the S&P 500 over this recent period . . . IT MUST BE SKILL!!! Thus, based on a potentially very weak methodology, all Howard's "alpha trend line" really shows is the S&P 500 was a tough benchmark to beat in the 80s and 90s (back when his trend line said active managers were stupid and produced negative alpha) and recently became a benchmark just about any indexer of a sub class could beat (or the now brilliant managers that "have become more skilled at creating alpha").

All of this is caused by comparing his universe of domestic equity funds to a large blend benchmark, and is thus doing nothing other than attributing "alpha skill" to potentially 89.2% of the universe where most of the sub class indexes would have also outperformed his easy benchmark. (The data for just the first three of the six years ending June, 2008, shows a similar relationship with 5,882 funds fitting a domestic equity sub class criteria and only 557 of those fitting into large blend, thus 90.5% of the domestic funds were not large blend. Also, the second three-year period of the last six showed 87.0% of the 7,058 funds best fit was something other than large blend. Since we include expenses in our grading routine we do not group share classes of funds and grade each share class individually.)

OK, so Wermers is somewhat more objective than Howard; and Surz missed a marketing opportunity for the money manager monkeys Surz simulates in his objective PODS universes by reciting the active advocate mantra of the three Ps.

I cannot say that alpha doesn't exist. It is provable to exist with mere luck as Wermers's work and Surz PODS demonstrate. I cannot say that skill doesn't exist, and statistically one would think someone out there would have it. Intuitively therefore, I assume there is skill.

But, in my clients' interests I have to objectively assess whether the risk of attempting to identify that skill for potential outperformance is worth the risk of underperforming I have the choice to avoid. I also cannot just accept a marketing bromide that sounds good but is not provable. I need to be able to understand how the odds are stacked to know whether making the bet makes sense. Objectively, it is a bet with at least some of the odds being knowable.

For example, there is essentially zero chance that an index fund will even equal the index and, if it is well managed to minimize tracking error, it is nearly certain that it will underperform the benchmark by something close to the expenses. But with this nearly certain small underperformance of the index fund also comes nearly complete certainty that it will not materially underperform the benchmark. The certainty of the avoidance of the risk of material underperformance has value, despite what active advocates might claim. There is value to avoiding that risk.

As a skeptic worried about my clients' best interests, I need to understand whether the payoff for the bet of potential outperformance is worth the risk of potential underperformance, AND the odds of either occurring. Knowing the odds is the tough part. If you are objective and thus not either a passive pundit or active advocate, you must acknowledge the facts. Index funds are nearly certain to underperform by their expenses and have essentially no chance of either out-performing or materially underperforming their benchmark. This is fact, not marketing, so all of you active advocates should face it. Also, objectively, one would also have to acknowledge that any active bet introduces a risk of potentially materially underperforming, a risk that one can have nearly complete certainty of avoiding by indexing, yet the active bet also introduces a chance of potential outperformance that does not exist with the index fund. Passive pundits, face it!

This is not that complicated if you are objective and filter out the marketing noise and pseudo research of the passive pundits and active advocates. And Wermers's and Surz's works go along way toward measuring the luckiness that exists in the historical data; with both (sometimes) objectively acknowledging it isn't necessarily predictive.

But studies like Howard's that compare apples to oranges and assume that ANY outperformance is automatically skill, that lucky unskilled managers do not exist and that the money management industry was stupid but is now becoming smart do nothing for clients' interest. But it is good marketing.

While I put no weight on past relative performance, since I have yet to obtain a time machine that would make past performance useful, I couldn't help but test Howard's surging alpha "evidence" in our www.fundgrades.com database.

This is not proof of anything; it is just data. However, it is interesting to see how it contrasts with Howard's "research" on surging alpha skill and declining standard deviation.

We start with a universe of 12,039 funds and share classes that have six years of data ending June of 2008 to focus on Howard's recent alpha surge. Instead of arbitrary labeling of "domestic anything" funds relative to the S&P 500, we apply two criteria to benchmark the funds to help avoid some of the inherent misclassification and arbitrary mislabeling. One is the macro holdings: i.e., under our rules, an equity fund must have at least 70% in equities, a balanced fund must have at least 25% in both bonds and stocks, and a fixed income fund must have at least 70% in bonds, etc. Granted, this will eliminate alpha created by radical asset allocation skill AND luck, but Howard eliminates those, too. So give me a pass on that since I objectively admit this is nothing other than useless past data. Second, we benchmark the fund against its best fit of 31 subasset classes in an attempt, for example, to avoid giving false kudos to a mid-cap fund against the S&P500. This isn't rocket science, just rather basic common sense. It is benchmarking against the best fit style if the macro asset class holdings fit. The fundgrades web site lets you grade funds against any of the 31 subasset classes if you don't like how our screening criteria benchmarks the fund.

What do the six years of data show? Not surprisingly (unless you are fooled by Howard's easy bar to beat), 70% of the funds underperformed their best fit subasset class. So what. Keep in mind this is all funds against 31 subasset classes. Of the mere 618 funds and share classes whose best fit was the S&P500, 76.7% underperformed. Now there is some surging alpha!

Capturing the "newer fund" alpha supposedly identified by Howard's "research" of 12,039 funds in their first three years, 70.43% underperformed their best fit benchmark. And, the second three-year period of the entire six years clearly demonstrates Howard's surging "alpha skill trend" with a broader universe of 15,255 fund share classes having only 66.14% underperforming their best fit benchmark.

On the risk side, many funds have less risk than their benchmarks. This is to be expected since no benchmark includes cash and nearly every fund has some cash tempering at least a micronic amount of volatility with our precise measures. In fact, over the six-year period, 54% of all funds had less standard deviation than their benchmark (kudos go to the 59.2% of the large blend funds that had less standard deviation for holding a little cash to manage redemptions . . . What skill!). It is interesting that the average standard deviation was 100.25% of the benchmark standard deviation and the median was 99.32%. This is not statistically meaningful. But, as one would anticipate, all funds together, when classified appropriately against a broad universe of benchmarks, on average have about market risk.

Is there really anything surprising in these data? Not yet. Also not surprisingly, those funds that outperformed their benchmark had more risk relative to their benchmark, and those that underperformed had less risk. What a shocker here! Of the funds that outperformed their benchmark, they averaged 109% of the standard deviation of their benchmark and 59% of those funds had more standard deviation versus the 46% of all funds that had more risk. Those that underperformed averaged 96% of their benchmark's standard deviation with 60% of those underperformers having less risk. Those funds that did beat their benchmark had two and a half times more risk (26% versus 11%) of having a standard deviation greater than 115% of the benchmark standard deviation than the underperformers (our criteria for a relative risk grade of "F"). Still no surprise here.

You might have skill. Or, you might just think you do. There is a big difference. You might assume that all excess results are caused by skill. You might assume luck is a figment of every winning gambler's imagination. Winning gamblers also often falsely attribute their luck to skill, a betting system, or some other secret method, much like active advocates in money management.

I am fairly confident that skill exists, although I do not have very good evidence for it. For now, it remains an unprovable intuition. I suspect that such skill, should it exist, is somewhat rarer than the percentage of funds that happen to outperform because of luck, as I'm equally confident that luck also exists. The existence of luck is a lot easier to mathematically prove, but like Wermers's work, one cannot tell which funds were just lucky.

Beyond this, I have to think about the bet being made relative to odds that are knowable in my clients' interests. I don't know the odds of skill existing, how common it might be, or how much value can be obtained. To an objective scientist, the attempt to try to identify skill in historical data samples is not sufficiently provable when weighed against the odds that are knowable and how skilled one must be to make up for risks introduced of material underperformance in an attempt to outperform. Marketers won't sell this because real statistics are not marketable. However, your clients can benefit by keeping your level of skepticism high enough to avoid being fooled.

Reflecting on My Response The essence of my response focused on two basic critiques of Howard's "research." His conclusion of his alpha slope assumed no luck existed, assigning all outperformance as skill, and he was comparing apples and oranges—that is, the benchmark he chose to use concluded that large-cap blend stocks is an appropriate measure to determine whether fund universes that have funds that don't even benchmark themselves against a large blend index should be used to evaluate skill. The large-cap blend benchmark (the S&P 500) will sometimes outperform such a diverse universe of funds, and at other times will not. He obviously didn't like this criticism, and wrote a response that rescinded his previous "research" that assumed luck doesn't exist at all by concluding at the end that it indeed exists, but he doesn't adjust his research for this. He goes on to pontificate about a lot of things I actually agree with, but ignores the fundamental criticism of my questions. His response to my article was as follows.

Article #4: The New Ptolemains

C. Thomas Howard, Ph.D.
Professor, Reiman School of Finance
University of Denver

In the early 16th century, the world of astronomy was on the verge of dramatic change. The Ptolemaic theory of a geocentric world was in constant need of repair. The path of the Sun, moon, and stars through the sky behaved as predicted, but those seven closer stars (we now know them as planets) did not (think of them as the anomalies of their day). As telescopes grew more powerful and the paths of the planets were measured with greater precision, Ptolemains responded by adding ever more epicycles in order to produce acceptable predictions. When Copernicus introduced his heliocentric theory in 1543, it was the beginning of the end for the geocentric theory and its many epicycle patches.

In today's world of investing, the accepted theory is that markets are informationally efficient and as a result managers are unable to add value. The earliest version of this theory was that a manager could not beat the stock market as a whole. But when evidence began showing up that those who bought small stocks with low PE's consistently beat the market, the new Ptolemains began adding their version of epicycles. Now a manager had to not only beat the market, but beat a subset of the market defined by the anomaly. When more anomalies were uncovered, more subsets were created. As does Loeper, many of the new Ptolemains have taken this to the extreme, adding dozens of US equity manager subsets (Loeper has 31!). The epicycles did not disappear, they mutated into equity subsets!

Equity Market Subsets

Breaking the market into fund subsets, based on portfolio characteristics, makes little sense for creating performance benchmarks. To explain why, let's focus on the widely accepted manager characteristic based subsets of large-cap value, large-cap growth, small-cap value, and small-cap growth. The first question one might ask is, why these particular subsets? The reason is that research beginning in the 70's revealed that small capitalization stocks outperformed large stocks and low PE stocks outperformed high PE stocks even after adjusting for risk. This meant that a manager who bought small, low PE stocks could beat the market, or so it seemed at the time. In 1984 the first 2×2 manager "style grid" was introduced and the subset-ing of the manager market began. To understand what this means for performance evaluation, consider the 1982–2007 average annual returns for the S&P 500 and the four style indices shown below (Source: December 2007 Zephyr database).

	Value	Growth	Blend
Large-cap	14.93	13.18	**14.05**
Small-cap	15.33	10.25	**12.79**
	15.01	**12.59**	
	S&P 500	**14.19**	

A manager's performance is compared to one of the four style benchmarks, depending on how categorized, rather than to the market. Let's say a manager is categorized as a large-cap value manager (more about the problems associated with this process later). Then to be considered successful, a manager would have to earn a return greater than 14.93% rather than 14.19%. What happens to the 74bp difference between the style and market benchmarks? The manager does not get credit for it because the performance benchmark has been increased by this amount. From an investor standpoint, this only makes sense if the additional 74bp is a reward for risk or if the investor can easily capture the additional return on their own. Neither of these hold up in light of the evidence.

First, there is no agreement on whether the extra returns to size and PE are rewards for risk or simply a mispricing opportunity. So we really cannot say the 74bp is compensation for risk. Second, there are a number of problems with the investor picking up this return on their own. You will note in the table above that over this 26 year period large-cap outperformed small-cap stocks, just the opposite of what the initial research showed. So, is there a small firm or large firm effect? We need to know this to tilt the portfolio in order to earn this additional return. In terms of the so called value premium, a January 2007 study by Phalippou found that it disappears for those stocks largely held by institutions (93% of market capitalization). This means that the PE related value premium is unavailable to fund managers. So if there is no consistent size effect and no value premium, how can an investor or advisor go about picking up the 74bp through long term portfolio tilting? The answer is they can't.

How about placing short term style bets rather than executing a long term portfolio tilt? Here the evidence is not very encouraging. The general conclusion is that managers have stock picking skill but no style timing skill. If the fund managers cannot style time, then how likely is it that investors or their advisors can? Instead, why not allow managers an opportunity to capture, indirectly, this premium through their stock picking rather than taking it away by changing benchmarks. This is quite different from the current practice of saying, after the fact, the manager did well, not because the strategy was successfully pursued, but because the portfolio was tilted towards large-cap value stocks and they happen to do well. The moral is don't "Monday morning quarterback" the manager if you are unable to pick up the additional return yourself.

Problems with Categorizing Managers based on Portfolio Characteristics

So if the 74bp is not a reward for risk and the investor or the advisor cannot easily earn this additional return by tilting the portfolio or placing short term style bets, then why change the manager's benchmark from the S&P 500 to large-cap value? There is no good reason for such a decision. In fact, there are a number of residual problems that are created by categorizing managers based on portfolio characteristics.

Managers are categorized using portfolio holdings or style index returns. But what does this tell you about the strategy being pursued by a manager? The answer is little to nothing. Shouldn't a categorization system help you better understand the management process? But it is worse than this. Since many investment organizations use style designations for organizing and selling investment products, there is a strong motivation for the manager, once classified, to avoid drifting into another category. Thus is created the conflict between staying in a style box and consistently pursuing a strategy. Unfortunately, many managers choose the former to the detriment of performance. I and others, including Wermers, have documented the decline in performance resulting from a manager hugging an index or staying in a style box. This is the categorization system getting in the way of what a manager should be doing, relentlessly pursuing a well defined investment strategy.

Considering all of this, it begs the question why market cap and PE? There are hundreds of characteristics that could be used to categorize funds. For example, why not categorize funds based on their holdings' average ROE and earnings yield? The answer is there is no logic. It used to be argued that market cap and PE be used because they had a long term return advantage. But the recent evidence mentioned above throws this argument in doubt. But any portfolio characteristic will run into the same categorization problems as do market cap and PE. So it is time to look elsewhere for a way to think about managers.

Focus on Strategy Instead

Based on research conducted over the last five years, a better way to think about managers is the strategy they are pursuing. Once each manager has been strategy identified, it is possible to form meaningful peer groups. The advantage to this approach is that the manager self-declares a strategy and thus is free to pursue it without having to worry about fitting into a style box. Focusing on strategy avoids the conflict between doing what is right for your investors and doing what is right for selling your products. The manager can then be compared to a homogeneous peer group rather than to an arbitrary style box which always contains managers pursuing a variety of strategies and thus is a questionable basis for creating a benchmark. Focusing on strategy also provides insight into what the manager is doing, unlike the opaque style boxes.

Finding Successful Active Managers

I was a firm believer in indexing for the first 25 years of my academic and investment career based on the evidence that was available at the time. But my research over the last five years and the growing literature regarding the existence of manager skill and persistence has convinced me that indexing is now a second best alternative. It was only after the research began portraying a changing picture that Craig Callahan and I formed our company AthenaInvest in 2005. I am sure that Loeper feels just as strongly about the research underlying his firm.

One of the defenses put up by the new Ptolemains when evidence of manager skill pops up is to create additional subsets on which to build portfolio characteristic performance benchmarks. I have already described the problems with the best known of these benchmarks, those based on market cap and PE. So it makes you wonder if these subsets are introduced as a way to counter the manager skill evidence rather than as a way to better understand the investment process. It is possible to introduce enough subsets to wipe out evidence of manager skill even as little is added to our understanding of how to pick managers. Is this what Loeper has done?

So how do you find successful active managers? We believe that the starting point is first to identify the strategy being pursued by the fund. Then within that strategy peer group, identify the successful active managers using objective measures. Our resulting carefully researched, patent-pending system is called Strategy Based Investing. Based on our research and the research of others, we believe that it is possible to build better performing portfolios of successful active managers who are pursuing successful strategies.

Finally, past returns are a noisy signal for identifying skilled managers. *A manager who has produced good returns could just be lucky rather than skillful.* [emphasis added] That is why it is important to consider aspects other than long-term performance when building a portfolio of active managers. Those who bring other aspects beyond returns into the equation, such as Surz and Loeper, are moving in the right direction. We also go beyond returns when identifying successful active managers.

My Synopsis of the Article In reading this we see that Howard evaded the basic question of comparing apples to oranges and gives lip service to now acknowledging that luck exists, even though the "growing evidence of manager skill and persistence" in his own research of his alpha slope, which is supposedly part of this growing research has not been corrected for its assumption that all outperformance is skill and not luck. What would that research look like? He probably will not show it because it would contradict his beliefs.

As a fiduciary that takes full responsibility for all investment choices, I cannot rely on "beliefs." I must be a skeptic to protect trustees and participants. I have to question things from a completely rational, objective, and scientific perspective. I cannot rely on subjective things that I emotionally might hope for and call doing so acting with the care and diligence of one familiar with such matters. There is not yet a resolution to the luck versus skill debate. There is academic research on both sides, and some of it is more objective than others.

But as a fiduciary, I have to address criticisms of my questions directly instead of evade them. I have to acknowledge both sides of a debate, and acknowledge the possibility of things that are not provable one way or the other. I have to acknowledge uncertainties that may be present in my research as well as others and freely admit and disclose them. If you read through these articles, you will hopefully perceive the difference between objectivity and an agenda.

How hard would it have been for Howard to acknowledge that his original alpha slope "research" completely evaded the existence of luck? Why didn't he acknowledge it? Who knows, I certainly don't. It could be that he doesn't understand how to calculate the effect of luck in the universe, which may be why he criticized the Wermers' article in the first place. It could be that he has a story to sell and he wants to misdirect readers toward his beliefs. It could be that he does understand, as he later acknowledged, that luck indeed exists, and incorporating that understanding into his growing alpha slope research may have contradicted his original research.

But true science is objective and doesn't evade directly answering questions in review by "peers" (pun intended). True science acknowledges weaknesses and potential pitfalls of conclusions instead of defending them.

My last response to Howard's piece follows. See if you can tell the objectivity and depth of attempting to get some basic questions answered and the evidence that is equally valid (or potentially more so).

Article #5: Howard Is Right . . . The World Is Flat!

David B. Loeper, CIMA®, CIMC®

I have to admit, C. Thomas Howard is right. In response to my *Advisor Perspectives* article *(When Will Objectivity Enter the Active v. Passive Debate?)* he introduces many rational critiques of my article that anyone who is objective would have to acknowledge. Like me, he questions "why market cap and PE" (although I think most of the academic work is based on book to market, not PE) should, or should not be used to categorize funds.

He is also right that defenders of geocentric theory (the earth being the center of the universe) invented convoluted calculations in attempts to defend their treasured theory in the face of the mounting evidence Copernicus had that proved otherwise.

I share with Howard (and have written in many of my papers) the notion that all of this slicing and dicing of the markets into style and market cap boxes is not really creating new asset classes and is just manufacturing non-diversified pieces of markets and thus it is worthy of skepticism. Forcing managers to stick to a style box wasn't something of my creation, yet there are many, many funds that self select themselves into one of those style boxes by choice, often to get a better "peer" ranking. That is why in www.fundgrades.com, we permit the user to grade their funds against any of 31 subasset classes (including 13 domestic equity classes, not 31—Howard's minor error).

Howard is right about one more point. If I take all 5,745 of the domestic equity funds from my original response to Howard's criticism of Wermers (those funds that had some semblance of matching any one of THIRTEEN domestic equity classes and sub classes) 60.15% of them BEAT THE S&P 500 in the first three years of the six-year period, and 58.91% beat the S&P 500 over the entire six-year period. Howard is right! Most domestic equity funds beat the S&P 500! Therefore, skill is the cause and managers are getting more skillful as Howard's original response to Wermers' stated. I thank Howard for helping me see the errors of my ways.

How's that for objective?

Of course, in looking at this one would have to question why we are comparing all of the different flavors of these various types of domestic equity funds to the S&P 500 when most of them don't own it. Why not compare them to bonds or real estate, gold or oil? That would obviously be nuts, comparing **apples to oranges** as I (and many other readers commenting on Howard's first "research" response to Wermers) pointed out, but he evaded in his response shifting to subjective peer groups for which he provided no evidence of skill. Howard failed to respond to my basic criticisms of his choice of a large-cap blend benchmark to grade all domestic equity funds. At the end of his article, he acknowledged that luck indeed exists, but ignored responding that the premise of his "research" showing an increasing "alpha slope" assumed that luck cannot exist and all outperformance was therefore skill. Instead, like many sailors before Columbus who thought the world was flat based on their limited visual horizon benchmark, Howard criticizes objective attempts to measure how much skill and luck exist as if it were data mining.

Howard is right, not all funds are, nor should be, compared to style boxes. His answer is "Focus on Strategy," even though the evidence in his supposed research didn't measure it that way and instead benchmarked it against the S&P 500. This is a very interesting logical quandary. Howard states that skill is increasing *because* more and more funds have been beating the S&P 500, or have been doing so to a greater extent. Then, he argues that we shouldn't benchmark them against an index at all, but instead base it on something completely subjective, "Strategy Peer Groups." He offers no measurements here to prove the increase in skill, and I think that I might know why.

Let's lose the style boxes, as Howard argues we should, and let's make the assumption that managers will demonstrate skill by security selection, style shifts, and market cap movements, freely among all reasonably tradable domestic equity securities. There is a large mish mosh of strategies being deployed amongst these managers. Presumably, Dr. Howard would accept these assumptions. Let's also assume that skill doesn't necessarily evidence itself as higher returns and might also be represented by lower risk. Then, let's take all those 5,745 funds of various domestic equity flavors from my initial response to Howard and compare them to a benchmark that is more similar to the securities they can choose from for their portfolios, like the Russell 3000, which represents 98% of the investable domestic equity market.

Why didn't Howard use the Russell 3000 or Wilshire 5000 as his benchmark for his "alpha slope research" instead of the S&P 500, which is only 75% of domestic equities by market capitalization? The only answer I could come up with is it didn't show that the earth was flat. Looking beyond his large-cap horizon and taking all domestic equity funds versus a benchmark of basically all domestic equities comes up with a different answer. That answer, of the 5,745 domestic "any" funds, only 47.33% had higher return and only 27.46% had less risk over the entire six years. In the first three years, 48.38% had higher returns and 36% had less risk. An increasing alpha slope indeed!

Howard's lack of attention to his critics' fundamental questions impugns his credibility. I, along with others, identified that his regression alpha slope trend line demonstrated nothing other than large cap blend stocks are something that is easy or hard to beat at different times. He did not really materially respond to this assertion.

Like Howard, I could acknowledge that many domestic equity funds do not stick strictly to style boxes and may even have some foreign exposure. But, isn't choosing some foreign stocks part of the skill managers might have? After all, aren't stocks, stocks? Is where a company locates its headquarters really moving it between asset classes? Chrysler has moved back and forth from foreign and domestic several times over recent years. It is still a company trying to make profits and has since moved to another invented asset class, "private equity." There are foreign stocks in many domestic equity funds, so maybe we should benchmark all equity funds, of all types, against a World Equity benchmark? Why choose an easy benchmark that is just one box in the style box matrix Howard and I both hate so much?

Of course, based on the random noise of Howard's alpha analysis relative to the S&P 500 in his "alpha slope," he would not like the results of such a comparison to World Equities. (Incidentally, I do not see where Howard calculated the r-squared of his randomly bouncing alpha dots to see if his trend line was statistically significant.) Howard would likely complain that World Equities is a bad benchmark for domestic equity funds, yet he would still automatically credit all domestic funds that had some foreign exposure as being "skilled." Likewise, small-cap funds are skilled for beating the S&P 500, which somehow is a good benchmark for them.

Expanding the universe to be all equity funds of any flavor against global equities we find only 27.27% beat the index for return and only 29.59% have less risk. Now, as an objectivist, I'm not going to state this means anything other than over the measurement period observed, foreign stocks generally did better than domestic and the universe was statistically overpopulated with a lot of funds that had little to no foreign stocks relative to the World Equities benchmark. Like Howard's "increasing alpha slope research," it does not mean anything of any value. This is no different than Howard's universe that had the vast majority of the funds populating the universe that were something other than large blend. The only difference is Howard's mismatched benchmark made alpha look easy and my mismatched benchmark is an idiotic example that made it look hard. Both are still idiotic. Neither are good measures of anything other than noise. Shouldn't we acknowledge that it is equally misleading to compare a bunch of funds that are not large cap blend funds to an easy to beat large cap blend benchmark? C'mon . . . toss your critics a bone here and admit it.

And where did all of this series of debates begin? *Advisor Perspectives* started the debate by publishing an article about Wermers's research that attempted to statistically measure how much skill **and** how much luck existed in a universe. Howard followed with an article that criticized Wermers' objective piece supposedly showing growing skill based on past performance of funds relative to a recently easy to beat (and mismatched benchmark), the premise thereof **assumed luck does not exist.** I, among several other letters to the editor, exposed the slippery slope of comparing apples to oranges and the assumption in Howard's analysis that ALL outperformance was skill, and luck cannot exist at all. Howard's response completely evaded the benchmark mismatch (maybe he has some rationale for using one box in the style box matrix he hates?) and merely commented that luck exists while his alpha slope assumed luck does not exist. He uses this alpha slope as "evidence" skill is increasing despite acknowledging that luck exists in his response to my letter.

Neither Wermers nor I said skill does not exist. In fact, both of us said it probably does. Neither of us stated there is a small or value premium, as Howard pontificated as the basis of the style boxes I used in my initial response to him, yet ignored that many managers themselves self select as benchmarks for their funds. The bottom line concept is that all we said is luck exists, analysis attempting to identify skill should include this fact too instead of ignoring it. So, Howard does not have to worry about sailing off the end of the earth. It might look flat when compared to the S&P 500 horizon, but the convoluted math that proves it is round is real science.

The Fiduciary Summary of This Debate

So what does all of this debate mean to fiduciaries? If you go back over prior chapters you may remember that there are requirements in ERISA that hold you to very high standards and require that bets against diversification be "clearly prudent" from the standard of an expert that is familiar with these matters.

As a fiduciary, you have to put aside your unprovable beliefs and deal with that which is knowable. *No one* knows for a fact how much skill exists, or whether it is worth the price for what it costs. There are many believers in this, but it is not proven that the risk of underperforming is worth the hope of outperforming. There are some academic (and a lot of not so academic) research (and sales pitches) on either side of this unprovable debate.

Dr. Edesess said it is not whether skill exists or not, but whether we can identify it in advance, and if we can, would it not be arbitraged away? This is a valid question, the answer to which so far is unknown. I also introduced this question: Even if we are right in our ability to identify skill in advance, what benefit do you as an adviser fiduciary or a fiduciary trustee obtain from it?

Charlie Ellis wrote a great and very popular book, much of which was based on the core premises of ERISA called *How to Win the Loser's Game*. It should be required reading for all fiduciaries. Making bets against your investment policy benchmarks is a loser's game. If you are right, you really do not win as a fiduciary, yet you may feel good about it. As we showed, though, when it comes to participant-directed plans, you need to be not only right in the long term but right every time, for every potential participant, because when superior results occur they can still create unfortunate impairment of any one participant's assets. Why take this risk? If you are wrong, you might lose, and you could personally be on the hook for it. It is something you have the choice to avoid, with near certainty. If that doesn't sound like a loser's game, I do not know what does.

Summary

If you are an employer, adviser, plan sponsor, or trustee of a participant-directed retirement plan, the future liability you face has dramatically changed. Advisers outside of ERISA's purview are also at risk if they do not adapt their services to the new standards of fiduciary care that will evolve from the antiquated processes of the past.

Many of the premises outlined in this book were justifiable perspectives for legitimate suits under ERISA prior to the February 2008 Supreme Court ruling. The actual case, while not specific for the breaches outlined here, nonetheless ended with a ruling that any breach of ERISA's fiduciary duties that negatively impairs a participant's individual plan balance is now fair game for scrutiny and lawsuits.

Whether you are a trustee who wants to protect yourself from needless liability, or an ethical financial adviser who wants to deliver valuable, objective, and fiduciary care to your wealth management clients, the tide is turning, and if you do not adapt, the wave will roll over you like a tsunami.

The question really boils down to one of ethics and integrity. It is difficult to regulate integrity, as we have so often seen. Those who lack integrity find loopholes, deliver the minimum necessary to position a possible defense for potential cases, or hire armies of lawyers to craft agreements that evade real fiduciary responsibility. Earlier, I mentioned that the macro purpose of ERISA was an attempt to regulate ethics. To date, it has had only a marginal impact of preventing abuse or obtaining recovery for only the most egregious violations. If the vendors acted ethically, with integrity of comprehending the weight of the real responsibility they have of impacting people's lives and decades of compromises each individual made with their lifelong retirement savings, we wouldn't have a need for the regulations. Unfortunately, instead many vendors see how much they can get away with, yet still avoid tipping the liability scale too much against them.

As my company celebrates its tenth anniversary, our mission of being ethical, objective, honest, and acting with moral integrity has not changed. Each of my associates acts with that integrity every day. No one continues to work with us without meeting this fundamental standard—it is one area where zero tolerance must apply. You cannot be half ethical, any more than you can be half pregnant.

I have a tradition of giving a personalized gift to each of my associates over the holiday season. This year, though, I gave something that was not personalized with their name. Instead, it was the simple message of what we stand for, what we care about, and how we perform our duties. It was a crystal plaque with the following engraving:

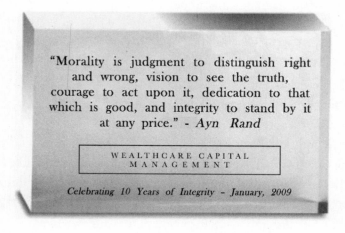

"Morality is judgment to distinguish right and wrong, vision to see the truth, courage to act upon it, dedication to that which is good, and integrity to stand by it at any price." - *Ayn Rand*

WEALTHCARE CAPITAL MANAGEMENT

Celebrating 10 Years of Integrity - January, 2009

Summary

Although not explicitly part of our obligations as fiduciaries under ERISA, Ayn Rand's quote still captures the true essence of what where our responsibilities lie.

Many trustees have been victimized by some of the largest vendors in this marketplace, based on the "brand" reputation of the vendor, with contracts that creatively avoid any responsibility for the suits that will come from their actions, leaving the trustees hanging in the noose the vendor created with their "advice" (or lack thereof).

Take the recent Walmart class-action suit as an example. In *Braden vs. Wal-mart,*[1] the plaintiff alleges that this multibillion-dollar plan affecting nearly a million participants used retail-share classes of funds that provided compensation to the fiduciary (the vendor of the investment products used), even though lower-cost institutional share classes were available. The claim is $60 million for this breach. This is a big plan with a big "reputable" product vendor. Nevertheless, the vendor's conflict of interest in receiving revenue sharing that was not disclosed to participants, and the fact that the vendor was aware of lower-cost alternatives yet did not advise or utilize them for the benefit of participants as they are required to do as a fiduciary under ERISA, makes this a very legitimate case. The basic defense of the product vendor is, of course, they weren't a fiduciary from this perspective because of their specific contract language that relieved them from it.

Regardless of what the courts decide on this, when you have armies of attorneys from massive financial firms with cleverly drafted contracts that attempt to skirt their fiduciary responsibility, the court case outcome is uncertain from a purely legal perspective. But is a legal perspective the only thing that matters? Is responsibility here really unclear from an ethics or integrity perspective? Should a firm be able to skim $60 million ($20 million a year) from a million workers' retirement savings when *they know* there are lower-cost options available? When these large firms act as product sellers yet promote themselves as caring about their clients, promoting the depth of their advisory resources, when they advertise their integrity and the trust you can place with them, doesn't this just seem to be one big lie? I don't really care about the outcome of the lawsuit; the question to me is much bigger than that. It is the fact that a firm with as much experience and knowledge of any of the firms in the market *knew* that the participants were paying higher prices than needed, and they profited from it while representing that they were large, trustworthy, and had integrity.

I recently spoke with one of the attorneys for the plaintiff on this case. I can assure you that there are more of these cases coming. The courts will be the final arbiters of whether legal fiduciary breaches occurred, and whether the trustees or the product vendors will be held accountable or had creatively covered their tracks in agreements and disclosures to evade real fiduciary responsibility. Perhaps the courts will rule in favor of the victims and hold those parties accountable that shamelessly profit with misleading marketing materials under false pretenses of trust, and do so at the expense of people's lives. It shouldn't take a court action to get paid fiduciaries to act like fiduciaries.

Yet, the mountain of cases coming will probably be what it takes to get fiduciaries to really put the beneficiary's interests above their own. Only time will tell how long this shift takes, or if it even will occur.

Fiduciaries that have honor, ethics, and integrity will not wait for the cases to occur. They are not profiting by sacrificing participants on the product vendor's altar and do not need the threat of a lawsuit to act in the fiduciary role they accept. They may need education or help sifting through sales propaganda and impressive glossy brochures. They might have a need for assistance in ferreting through the treasure map of disclosures (or use our free "Fee Compliance Kit" that provides competitive custom-pricing quotes and request kit for the current vendor to be submitted in DOL-suggested disclosure formats, available at www.401kripoff.com/plansponsors.htm) to know who is responsible for what and who is getting paid how much for that "what" they are providing, and where conflicts of interest exist.

Also, some providers might take the high road and change their practices, knowing that the short-term cost of compromising current unethical practices has a long-term benefit of actually delivering the trust they merely currently advertise.

Summary

In the end, it is about the participant. Each of the 100 million people that elect to defer a portion of their income each paycheck expect that their employer is looking out for their interests, with the care, skill, and prudence of an expert familiar with such matters. They expect that the vendors providing 404(c) education are really doing so, and not just providing sales spin that skims their hard-earned lifetime savings. It is possible to deliver on the legitimate expectations that participants have for you as a trustee or adviser. The question now is merely, are you going to wait until a lawsuit occurs, like many trustees or advisers will, to protect the current gravy train? Or, will you act ethically with integrity and change your practices to fulfill your obligations of the four pillars of retirement plans?

The choice is yours, but I urge you to choose wisely.

Notes

Introduction

1. Private Pension Plan Bulletin. Abstract of 2005 Form 5500 Annual Reports www.dol.gov/ebsa/PDF/2005pensionplanbulletin.PDF.

2. A few examples: *Hughes Aircraft Co. v. Jacobson,* 525 U.S. 432, 439–40 (1999), *Roth v. Sawyer-Cleator Lumber Co.,* 16 F.3d 915, 917 (8th Cir. 1994), and *Carol Harley et al. v. Minnesota Mining and Manufacturing Company* (No. 01-1213 available at: www.ca8.uscourts.gov/opndir/02/03/002214P.pdf).

Chapter 1: The Four Pillars of Fiduciary Conduct

1. Excerpt from ERISA section 404(a)(1)(B).

2. Excerpt from ERISA section 404(a)(1)(C).

3. United States Court of Appeals for the 8th Circuit. No. 00-2214. www.ca8 .uscourts.gov/opndir/02/03/002214P.pdf.

4. For a sampling of media coverage, review the web site www.retirementripoff .com/in_the_news.html.

5. See H.R. 3185 Rep. George Miller (D-CA), H.R. 3765 Rep. Richard Neal (D-MA), and Defined Contribution Fee Disclosure Act of 2007—Senator Tom Harkin (D-IA) and Senator Herbert Kohl (D-WI).

6. www.gao.gov/new.items/d0721.pdf and http://assets.aarp.org/rgcenter/econ/401k_fees.pdf.

7. Alicia H. Munneli, "Investment Returns: Defined Benefit vs. 401(k) Plans," Brief 52, Center for Retirement Research, Boston College (September 2006).

8. ". . . anyone with discretionary authority or responsibility for the administration of a plan, or *anyone who provides investment advice to a plan for compensation*" available at: www.dol.gov/dol/topic/retirement/fiduciaryresp.htm.

9. Fin. Planning Ass'n v. SEC, No. 04-1242, Consolidated with No. 05-1145, UNITED STATES COURT OF APPEALS FOR THE DISTRICT OF COLUMBIA CIRCUIT, March 30, 2007, Decided from www.lexisone.com: Overview: The SEC's new final rule in 17 C.F.R. § 275.202(a) (11)-1 (2005) was inconsistent with the Investment Advisers Act because it failed to meet either of the requirements for an exemption under 15 U.S.C.S. § 80b-2(a) (11) (F) (now § 80b-2(a) (11) (G)); the financial planning professionals' association's petition was granted and the rule was vacated.

Chapter 2: Pillar #1: Assets Are Invested for the Sole Benefit of Participants

1. Speech by SEC Commissioner: Remarks before the Financial Services Institute 3rd Annual Public Policy Day. Commissioner Annette L. Nazareth. September 13, 2006. www.sec.gov/news/speech/2006/spch091306aln.htm.

2. Kimberly Lankford, "The Great Annuity Rip-Off," *Kiplinger's Personal Finance magazine,* January 2007. www.kiplinger.com/magazine/archives/2007/01/annuities.html.

3. ABC PLAN: 401(k) PLAN FEE DISCLOSURE FORM For Services Provided by XYZ Company. www.dol.gov/ebsa/pdf/401kfefm.pdf.

4. If trustees wish to avoid researching other vendors and dealing with sales pitches from them, the web site for this book offers a free "fee compliance kit" that includes a custom competitive quote in DOL-suggested format, a blank DOL fee disclosure form for your existing vendor, and a form letter to your existing vendor requesting completion of the DOL fee disclosure form. See www.retirementripoff.com/plan_sponsors.aspx.

Chapter 4: Pillar #3: Costs Are Reasonable for the Services Being Provided

1. U.S. Government Accountability Office, "Private Pensions: Changes Needed to Provide 401(k) Plan Participants and the Department of Labor Better Information of Fees," GAO-07-2 (November 2006), 21.

2. Alicia H. Munneli, "Investment Returns: Defined Benefit vs. 401(k) Plans," Brief 52, Center for Retirement Research, Boston College (September 2006).

3. "The Economics of Providing 401(k) Plans: Services, Fees, and Expenses," *ICI* (November 2006).

Chapter 5: Pillar #4: Diversification Is Applied to Participant Direction

1. Lawrence Fisher and James H. Lorie, "Some Studies of Variability of Returns on Investments in Common Stocks," *Journal of Business* 43 (2) (April 1970).
2. The Truth about Diversification by the Numbers, http://ppca-inc.com/pdf/ DiversByNumbers.pdf.
3. Material risk on fundgrades.com is based on a grade of C– or worse, which requires the standard deviation of the fund to be at least 103% of the benchmark's standard deviation.

Chapter 6: Exposing the Wealth Management Contradiction

1. "Champagne of Beers" is a registered trademark of Miller Brewing Company, Milwaukee, Wisconsin.

Chapter 7: Comparing Approaches—Managing Wealth versus Managing Return

1. Immunization of liabilities by pension trusts is effectively the same as reducing portfolio risk by either purchasing annuities for specific liabilities, thus moving liability risk to an insurance company, or by purchasing zero coupon bonds that are tied to a specific set of future liabilities. In either case, these actions effectively get the liabilities "off the balance sheet." Regardless of the approach, the net overall portfolio allocation is effectively reducing the equity market risks because taking that needless risk when there is excess funding is imprudent for the plan, given the liabilities of the plan.
2. www.financeware.com/ruminations/WP_EfficiencyDeficiency.pdf.
3. For purposes of the demonstration of the mathematics behind tying allocation choices to the funded status for a *particular set* of wealth goals, we use our software's six default portfolio allocations, which are 30, 45, 60, 80, 90, and 100 percent equities. *Overfunding* is defined as more than 90 percent confidence and *underfunding* is defined as less than 75 percent confidence using a Monte Carlo simulation and our capital market assumptions. This **should not** be construed to imply a track record, but instead should be viewed merely as a means of conveying the mathematical dollar effect of adjusting equity risk exposure for *a particular liability stream*, following these simple rules. It is important to note that the shifts to various portfolio allocations are completely dependent on the market's impact on a unique set of investor circumstances and that extreme market environments will cause the confidence level to fall

outside the targeted range, and that range cannot be met in all years merely by adjusting the allocation. In such cases, the allocation used is the one that brings us closest to our targeted confidence level. This is why real wealth management would consider adjustments to contributions, withdrawals, timing of either of these, or terminal value in addition to the allocation choice.

Chapter 8: Market Misbehavior: Over- or Underfunding Investor Goals

1. David Loeper, "Understanding Monte Carlo Simulation," www.financeware .com/ruminations/WP_understandingmontecarlo.pdf.

2. Shawn Brayman, "Beyond Monte Carlo Analysis," *Journal of Financial Planning* (December 2007).

Chapter 11: Safe Harbors that Are Unsafe (Particularly Section 404(c))

1. U.S. Government Accountability Office, "Private Pensions: Changes Needed to Provide 401(k) Plan Participants and the Department of Labor Better Information of Fees," GAO–07–2 (November 2006), www.gao.gov/new .items/d0721.pdf and http://assets.aarp.org/rgcenter/econ/401k_fees.pdf.

2. Any investment manager is by definition a named, paid fiduciary. However, most product sellers and investment managers only accept fiduciary responsibility for each individual investment portfolio they manage, *not* the plan overall which in essence minimizes any real liability they have and explicitly and contractually leaves the ultimate responsibility with the plan trustees.

Summary

1. Gordon Gibb, "Mutual Fund ERISA: *Braden vs. Wal-Mart*," April 17, 2008. www.lawyersandsettlements.com/articles/10446/mutual-fund-erisawal-mart .html?ref=rss.

About the Author

David B. Loeper is a Certified Investment Management Analyst®, a Certified Investment Management Consultant® and the CEO of Financeware, Inc. An SEC Registered Investment Adviser with more than 23 years experience, Loeper has appeared on CNBC and has been a featured contributor on Yahoo Financevision and Bloomberg TV.

Born in Milwaukee, Wisconsin, Loeper began his career in finance as an investment representative with Century Companies of America in 1984. In 1986 he joined Richard Schilffarth & Associates as an investment consultant and also served as an officer of its broker/dealer, Investment Account Services Corp.

Loeper joined Wheat First Securities as vice president of investment consulting in 1988, where he served for 10 years. He was promoted to managing director of investment consulting, and then eventually to managing director of strategic planning for the retail brokerage division. He left his position at Wheat First Securities in 1999 and founded his current company, Financeware, Inc., which operates as Wealthcare Capital Management.

Active in industry associations throughout his career, Loeper has been a member of the Investment Management Consultants Association (IMCA) for nearly 20 years, serving on the advisory council for more than 5 years, most recently as chairman. He also served as a founding member of the Asset Consulting Roundtable, an independent group composed of the heads of investment consulting groups from numerous brokerage firms. Loeper has also served on the Investment Advisory Committee of the nearly $30 billion Virginia Retirement System. He received his CIMA® designation in 1990 by completing a program offered through Wharton Business School, in conjunction with IMCA.

Drawing on years of experience in financial services including serving as a fiduciary for all types of ERISA plans, Loeper's new book, *The Four Pillars of Retirement Plans: A Fiduciary Guide to Participant Directed Retirement Plans* (John Wiley & Sons, 2009), serves as a guide to plan sponsors, advisors and other fiduciaries to prevent liability from what he forecasts will be a groundswell of new fiduciary liability suits based on the 2008 Supreme Court ruling of LaRue v. DeWolff. He is also the author of *Stop the Retirement Rip-off* and *Stop the Investing Rip-off* both of which were published by John Wiley & Sons in spring of 2009.

Index

Index

5